grzimek's
Student Animal Life Resource

• • • •

grzimek's
Student Animal Life Resource

• • • •

Mammals
volume 5

Pangolins to Sengis

THOMSON

GALE

Detroit • New York • San Francisco • San Diego • New Haven, Conn. • Waterville, Maine • London • Munich

THOMSON
GALE
™

Grzimek's Student Animal Life Resource
Mammals

Project Editor
Melissa C. McDade

Editorial
Julie L. Carnagie, Madeline Harris, Elizabeth Manar, Heather Price

Indexing Services
Synapse, the Knowledge Link Corporation

Rights and Acquisitions
Sheila Spencer, Mari Masalin-Cooper

Imaging and Multimedia
Randy Bassett, Michael Logusz, Dan Newell, Chris O'Bryan, Robyn Young

Product Design
Tracey Rowens, Jennifer Wahi

Composition
Evi Seoud, Mary Beth Trimper

Manufacturing
Wendy Blurton, Dorothy Maki

LIBRARY OF CONGRESS CATALOGING-IN-PUBLICATION DATA

Grzimek's student animal life resource. Mammals / Melissa C. McDade, project editor.
    p. cm.
    Includes bibliographical references and index.
    ISBN 0-7876-9183-6 (set hardcover : alk. paper) — ISBN 0-7876-9184-4 (volume 1) — ISBN 0-7876-9185-2 (volume 2) — ISBN 0-7876-9187-9 (volume 3) — ISBN 0-7876-9188-7 (volume 4) — ISBN 0-7876-9234-4 (volume 5)
    1. Mammals—Juvenile literature. I. Grzimek, Bernhard. II. McDade, Melissa C.
QL703.G79 2005
599—dc22
                                             2004015604

ISBN 0-7876-9402-9 (21-vol set), ISBN 0-7876-9183-6 (Mammals set),
ISBN 0-7876-9184-4 (v.1), ISBN 0-7876-9185-2 (v.2), ISBN 0-7876-9187-9 (v.3),
ISBN 0-7876-9188-7 (v.4), ISBN 0-7876-9234-4 (v.5)

This title is also available as an e-book
Contact your Thomson Gale sales representative for ordering information.

Printed in Canada
10 9 8 7 6 5 4 3 2 1

Contents

MAMMALS: VOLUME 3

Reader's Guide

Grzimek's Student Animal Life Resource: Mammals offers readers comprehensive and easy-to-use information on Earth's mammals. Entries are arranged by taxonomy, the science through which living things are classified into related groups. Order entries provide an overview of a group of families, and family entries provide an overview of a particular family. Each entry includes sections on physical characteristics; geographic range; habitat; diet; behavior and reproduction; animals and people; and conservation status. Family entries are followed by one or more species accounts with the same information as well as a range map and photo or illustration for each species. Entries conclude with a list of books, periodicals, and Web sites that may be used for further research.

ADDITIONAL FEATURES

Each volume of *Grzimek's Student Animal Life Resource: Mammals* includes a pronunciation guide for scientific names, a glossary, an overview of Mammals, a list of species in the set by biome, a list of species by geographic location, and an index. The set has 540 full-color maps, photos, and illustrations to enliven the text, and sidebars provide additional facts and related information.

NOTES

The classification of animals into orders, families, and even species is not a completed exercise. As researchers learn more about animals and their relationships, classifications may change. In some cases, researchers do not agree on how or whether to make a change. For this reason, the heading "Number of species" in the introduction of an entry may read "About 36 species" or "34 to 37 species." It is not a question of whether some animals exist or not, but a question of how they are classified. Some researchers are more likely to "lump" animals into the same species classification, while others may "split" animals into separate species.

Grzimek's Student Animal Life Resource: Mammals has standardized information in the Conservation Status section. The IUCN Red List provides the world's most comprehensive inventory of the global conservation status of plants and animals. Using a set of criteria to evaluate extinction risk, the IUCN recognizes the following categories: Extinct, Extinct in the Wild, Critically Endangered, Endangered, Vulnerable, Conservation Dependent, Near Threatened, Least Concern, and Data Deficient. These terms are defined where they are used in the text, but for a complete explanation of each category, visit the IUCN web page at http://www.iucn.org/themes/ssc/redlists/RLcats2001booklet.html.

ACKNOWLEDGEMENTS

Special thanks are due for the invaluable comments and suggestions provided by the *Grzimek's Student Animal Life Resource: Mammals* advisors:

- Mary Alice Anderson, Media Specialist, Winona Middle School, Winona, Minnesota
- Thane Johnson, Librarian, Oklahoma City Zoo, Oklahoma City, Oklahoma
- Debra Kachel, Media Specialist, Ephrata Senior High School, Ephrata, Pennsylvania
- Nina Levine, Media Specialist, Blue Mountain Middle School, Courtlandt Manor, New York
- Ruth Mormon, Media Specialist, The Meadows School, Las Vegas, Nevada

COMMENTS AND SUGGESTIONS

We welcome your comments on *Grzimek's Student Animal Life Resource: Mammals* and suggestions for future editions of this work. Please write: Editors, *Grzimek's Student Animal Life Resource: Mammals*, U•X•L, 27500 Drake Rd., Farmington Hills, Michigan 48331-3535; call toll free: 1-800-877-4253; fax: 248-699-8097; or send e-mail via www.gale.com.

Pronunciation Guide for
Scientific Names

Abrocoma cinerea AB-ruh-KOH-muh sin-EAR-ee-uh

Abrocomidae ab-ruh-KOH-muh-dee

Acomys cahirinus ak-OH-meez kay-hih-RYE-nuhs

Acrobates pygmaeus ak-CROW-bah-teez pig-MEE-uhs

Acrobatidae ak-crow-BAH-tuh-dee

Agouti paca ah-GOO-tee PAY-cuh

Agoutidae ah-GOO-tuh-dee

Ailuropoda melanoleuca AYE-lur-uh-POD-uh MEL-uh-noh-
LYOO-kuh

Ailurus fulgens AYE-lur-uhs FULL-jens

Alces alces AL-ceez AL-ceez

Alouatta seniculus ah-loo-AH-tuh se-NIH-kul-uhs

Anomaluridae ah-nuh-mah-LOOR-uh-dee

Anomalurus derbianus ah-nuh-MAH-loor-uhs der-BEE-an-uhs

Antilocapra americana AN-til-uh-KAP-ruh uh-mer-uh-KAN-uh

Antilocapridae an-til-uh-KAP-ruh-dee

Antrozous pallidus an-tro-ZOH-uhs PAL-uh-duhs

Aotidae ay-OH-tuh-dee

Aotus trivirgatus ay-OH-tuhs try-VER-gah-tuhs

Aplodontia rufa ap-loh-DON-shuh ROO-fah

Aplodontidae ap-loh-DON-tuh-dee

Arctocephalus gazella ARK-tuh-SEFF-uh-luhs guh-ZELL-uh

Artiodactyla AR-tee-uh-DAK-til-uh

Asellia tridens ah-SELL-ee-uh TRY-denz

Ateles geoffroyi ah-TELL-eez JEFF-roy-eye

Atelidae ah-TELL-uh-dee

Babyrousa babyrussa   bah-bee-ROO-suh bah-bee-ROO-suh

Balaena mysticetus   bah-LEE-nuh mis-tuh-SEE-tuhs

Balaenidae   bah-LEE-nuh-dee

Balaenoptera acutorostrata   bah-lee-NOP-teh-ruh uh-KYOOT-uh-ROS-trah-tuh

Balaenoptera musculus   bah-lee-NOP-teh-ruh muhs-KU-luhs

Balaenopteridae   bah-lee-nop-TEH-ruh-dee

Barbastella barbastellus   bar-buh-STELL-uh bar-buh-STELL-uhs

Bathyergidae   bath-ih-ER-juh-dee

Bettongia tropica   bee-ton-JEE-uh TROP-ik-uh

Bison bison   BI-sun BI-sun

Bovidae   BOH-vuh-dee

Bradypodidae   brad-ih-POD-uh-dee

Bradypus variegatus   BRAD-ih-puhs vair-ee-uh-GAH-tuhs

Bubalus bubalis   BYOO-bal-uhs BYOO-bal-is

Burramyidae   bur-ruh-MY-uh-dee

Cacajao calvus   KA-ka-jah-oh KAL-vuhs

Caenolestes fuliginosus   kee-NOH-less-teez fyoo-li-JEH-noh-suhs

Caenolestidae   kee-noh-LESS-tuh-dee

Callicebus personatus   kal-luh-SEE-buhs per-SON-ah-tuhs

Callimico goeldii   kal-luh-MEE-koh geel-DEE-eye

Callitrichidae   kal-luh-TRIK-uh-dee

Camelidae   kam-EL-uh-dee

Camelus dromedarius   KAM-el-uhs drom-uh-DARE-ee-uhs

Canidae   KAN-uh-dee

Canis lupus   KAN-is LYOO-puhs

Caperea marginata   kay-per-EE-uh mar-JIN-ah-tuh

Capricornis sumatraensis   kap-rih-KOR-nis soo-mah-TREN-sis

Capromyidae   kap-roh-MY-uh-dee

Capromys pilorides   KAP-roh-meez pi-LOH-ruh-deez

Carnivora   kar-NIH-voh-ruh

Castor canadensis   KAS-tor kan-uh-DEN-sis

Castoridae   kas-TOR-uh-dee

Caviidae   kave-EYE-uh-dee

Cebidae   SEE-buh-dee

Cebuella pygmaea   see-boo-ELL-uh pig-MEE-uh

Cebus capucinus   SEE-buhs kap-oo-CHIN-uhs

Cebus olivaceus   SEE-buhs ah-luh-VAY-see-uhs

Ceratotherium simum   suh-rah-tuh-THER-ee-um SIM-um

Cercartetus nanus   ser-kar-TEE-tuhs NAN-uhs

Cercopithecidae ser-koh-pith-EEK-uh-dee

Cervidae SER-vuh-dee

Cervus elaphus SER-vuhs EL-laff-uhs

Cetacea sih-TAY-she-uh

Cheirogaleidae KY-roh-GAL-uh-dee

Cheiromeles torquatus ky-ROH-mel-eez TOR-kwah-tuhs

Chinchilla lanigera chin-CHILL-uh la-NIJ-er-uh

Chinchillidae chin-CHILL-uh-dee

Chironectes minimus ky-roh-NECK-teez MIN-ih-muhs

Chiroptera ky-ROP-ter-uh

Chlamyphorus truncatus klam-EE-for-uhs TRUN-kah-tuhs

Choloepus hoffmanni koh-LEE-puhs HOFF-man-eye

Chrysochloridae krih-soh-KLOR-uh-dee

Chrysocyon brachyurus krih-SOH-sigh-on bra-kee-YOOR-uhs

Civettictis civetta sih-VET-tick-tis SIH-vet-uh

Coendou prehensilis SEEN-doo prih-HEN-sil-is

Condylura cristata KON-dih-LUR-uh KRIS-tah-tuh

Connochaetes gnou koh-nuh-KEE-teez NEW

Craseonycteridae kras-ee-oh-nick-TER-uh-dee

Craseonycteris thonglongyai kras-ee-oh-NICK-ter-is thong-
LONG-ee-aye

Cricetomys gambianus kry-see-TOH-meez GAM-bee-an-uhs

Cricetus cricetus kry-SEE-tuhs kry-SEE-tuhs

Crocuta crocuta kroh-CUE-tuh kroh-CUE-tuh

Cryptomys damarensis krip-TOH-meez DAM-are-en-sis

Cryptoprocta ferox krip-TOH-prok-tuh FAIR-oks

Cryptotis parva krip-TOH-tis PAR-vuh

Ctenodactylidae ten-oh-dak-TIL-uh-dee

Ctenomyidae ten-oh-MY-uh-dee

Ctenomys pearsoni TEN-oh-meez PEAR-son-eye

Cyclopes didactylus SIGH-kluh-peez die-DAK-til-uhs

Cynocephalidae sigh-nuh-seff-UH-luh-dee

Cynocephalus variegatus sigh-nuh-SEFF-uh-luhs VAIR-ee-
uh-GAH-tus

Cynomys ludovicianus SIGH-no-mees LOO-doh-vih-SHE-an-
uhs

Dasypodidae das-ih-POD-uh-dee

Dasyprocta punctata das-IH-prok-tuh PUNK-tah-tuh

Dasyproctidae das-ih-PROK-tuh-dee

Dasypus novemcinctus DAS-ih-puhs noh-VEM-sink-tuhs

Dasyuridae das-ih-YOOR-uh-dee

Dasyuromorphia das-ih-yoor-oh-MOR-fee-uh

Daubentoniidae daw-ben-tone-EYE-uh-dee

Daubentonia madagascariensis daw-ben-TONE-ee-uh mad-uh-GAS-kar-EE-en-sis

Delphinapterus leucas del-fin-AP-ter-uhs LYOO-kuhs

Delphinidae del-FIN-uh-dee

Dendrohyrax arboreus den-droh-HI-raks are-BOHR-ee-uhs

Dendrolagus bennettianus den-droh-LAG-uhs BEN-net-EE-an-uhs

Dermoptera der-MOP-ter-uh

Desmodus rotundus dez-MOH-duhs ROH-tun-duhs

Dicerorhinus sumatrensis die-ser-uh-RHY-nuhs soo-mah-TREN-sis

Didelphidae die-DELF-uh-dee

Didelphimorphia die-delf-uh-MOR-fee-uh

Didelphis virginiana DIE-delf-is ver-JIN-ee-an-uh

Dinomyidae die-noh-MY-uh-dee

Dinomys branickii DIE-noh-meez BRAN-ick-ee-eye

Dipodidae dih-POD-uh-dee

Dipodomys ingens dih-puh-DOH-meez IN-jenz

Diprotodontia dih-pro-toh-DON-she-uh

Dipus sagitta DIH-puhs SAJ-it-tuh

Dolichotis patagonum doll-ih-KOH-tis pat-uh-GOH-num

Dromiciops gliroides droh-MISS-ee-ops gli-ROY-deez

Dugong dugon DOO-gong DOO-gon

Dugongidae doo-GONG-uh-dee

Echimyidae ek-ih-MY-uh-dee

Echinosorex gymnura EH-ky-noh-SORE-eks JIM-nyoor-uh

Echymipera rufescens ek-ee-MIH-per-uh ROO-fehs-sens

Ectophylla alba ek-toh-FILE-luh AHL-buh

Elephantidae el-uh-FAN-tuh-dee

Elephas maximus EL-uh-fuhs MAX-im-uhs

Emballonuridae em-bal-lun-YOOR-uh-dee

Equidae EK-wuh-dee

Equus caballus przewalskii EK-wuhs CAB-uh-luhs prez-VAL-skee-eye

Equus grevyi EK-wuhs GREH-vee-eye

Equus kiang EK-wuhs KY-an

Eremitalpa granti er-uh-MIT-ahl-puh GRAN-tie

Erethizon dorsatum er-uh-THY-zun DOR-sah-tum

Erethizontidae er-uh-thy-ZUN-tuh-dee

Erinaceidae er-ih-nay-SIGH-dee

Erinaceus europaeus er-ih-NAY-shuhs yoor-uh-PEE-uhs

Eschrichtiidae ess-rick-TIE-uh-dee

Eschrichtius robustus ess-RICK-shuhs roh-BUHS-tuhs

Eubalaena glacialis yoo-bah-LEE-nuh glay-SHE-al-is

Felidae FEE-luh-dee

Furipteridae fur-ip-TER-uh-dee

Galagidae gal-AG-uh-dee

Galago senegalensis GAL-ag-oh sen-ih-GAHL-en-sis

Galidia elegans ga-LID-ee-uh EL-uh-ganz

Gazella thomsonii guh-ZELL-uh TOM-son-ee-eye

Genetta genetta JIN-eh-tuh JIN-eh-tuh

Geomyidae gee-oh-MY-uh-dee

Giraffa camelopardalis JIH-raf-uh KAM-el-uh-PAR-dal-is

Giraffidae jih-RAF-uh-dee

Glaucomys volans glo-KOH-meez VOH-lans

Glossophaga soricina glos-SUH-fag-uh sore-ih-SEE-nuh

Gorilla gorilla guh-RILL-uh guh-RILL-uh

Hemicentetes semispinosus hemi-sen-TEE-teez semi-PINE-oh-
  suhs

Herpestidae her-PES-tuh-dee

Heterocephalus glaber HEH-tuh-roh-SEFF-uh-luhs GLAH-ber

Heteromyidae HEH-tuh-roh-MY-uh-dee

Hexaprotodon liberiensis hek-suh-PRO-tuh-don lye-BEER-ee-
  en-sis

Hippopotamidae HIP-poh-pot-UH-muh-dee

Hippopotamus amphibius HIP-poh-POT-uh-muhs am-FIB-ee-
  uhs

Hipposideridae HIP-poh-si-DER-uh-dee

Hominidae hom-IN-uh-dee

Homo sapiens HOH-moh SAY-pee-enz

Hyaenidae hi-EE-nuh-dee

Hydrochaeridae hi-droh-KEE-ruh-dee

Hydrochaeris hydrochaeris hi-droh-KEE-ris hi-droh-KEE-ris

Hydrodamalis gigas hi-droh-DAM-uhl-is JEE-guhs

Hylobates lar hi-loh-BAY-teez lahr

Hylobates pileatus hi-loh-BAY-teez pie-LEE-ah-tuhs

Hylobatidae hi-loh-BAY-tuh-dee

Hylochoerus meinertzhageni   hi-loh-KEE-ruhs MINE-ertz-hah-gen-eye

Hyperoodon ampullatus   hi-per-OH-uh-don am-PUH-lah-tuhs

Hypsiprymnodontidae   HIP-see-PRIM-nuh-DON-shuh-dee

Hypsiprymnodon moschatus   hip-see-PRIM-nuh-don MOS-kah-tuhs

Hyracoidea   HI-rah-koy-DEE-uh

Hystricidae   hiss-TRIK-uh-dee

Hystrix africaeaustralis   HISS-triks AF-rik-ee-au-STRA-lis

Hystrix indica   HISS-triks IN-dik-uh

Indri indri   IN-dri IN-dri

Indriidae   in-DRY-uh-dee

Inia geoffrensis   in-EE-uh JEFF-ren-sis

Iniidae   in-EYE-uh-dee

Insectivora   IN-sek-TIV-uh-ruh

Kerodon rupestris   KER-uh-don ROO-pes-tris

Kogia breviceps   koh-JEE-uh BREV-ih-seps

Lagomorpha   LAG-uh-MOR-fuh

Lagothrix lugens   LAG-uh-thriks LU-jens

Lama glama   LAH-muh GLAH-muh

Lama pacos   LAH-muh PAY-kuhs

Lemmus lemmus   LEM-muhs LEM-muhs

Lemur catta   LEE-mer KAT-tuh

Lemur coronatus   LEE-mer KOR-roh-nah-tuhs

Lemuridae   lee-MYOOR-uh-dee

Lepilemur leucopus   lep-uh-LEE-mer LYOO-koh-puhs

Lepilemur ruficaudatus   lep-uh-LEE-mer ROO-fee-KAW-dah-tuhs

Lepilemuridae   LEP-uh-lee-MOOR-uh-dee

Leporidae   lep-OR-uh-dee

Lepus americanus   LEP-uhs uh-mer-uh-KAN-uhs

Lepus timidus   LEP-uhs TIM-id-uhs

Lipotes vexillifer   lip-OH-teez veks-ILL-uh-fer

Lipotidae   lip-OH-tuh-dee

Lorisidae   lor-IS-uh-dee

Loxodonta africana   LOK-suh-DON-tuh AF-rih-kan-uh

Loxodonta cyclotis   LOK-suh-DON-tuh SIGH-klo-tis

Lutra lutra   LOO-truh LOO-truh

Lynx rufus   LINKS ROO-fuhs

Macaca mulatta   muh-KAY-kuh MYOO-lah-tuh

Macroderma gigas ma-CROW-der-muh JEE-guhs

Macropodidae ma-crow-POD-uh-dee

Macropus giganteus ma-CROW-puhs jy-GAN-tee-uhs

Macropus rufus ma-CROW-puhs ROO-fuhs

Macroscelidea MA-crow-sel-uh-DEE-uh

Macroscelididae MA-crow-sel-UH-duh-dee

Macrotis lagotis ma-CROW-tis la-GO-tis

Macrotus californicus ma-CROW-tuhs kal-uh-FORN-uh-kuhs

Madoqua kirkii ma-DOH-kwah KIRK-ee-eye

Mandrillus sphinx man-DRILL-uhs SFINKS

Manidae MAN-uh-dee

Manis temminckii MAN-is TEM-ink-ee-eye

Marmota marmota MAR-mah-tuh MAR-mah-tuh

Massoutiera mzabi mas-soo-TEE-er-uh ZA-bye

Megadermatidae meg-uh-der-MUH-tuh-dee

Megalonychidae meg-uh-loh-NICK-uh-dee

Megaptera novaeangliae meg-uh-TER-uh NOH-vee-ANG-lee-dee

Meles meles MEL-eez MEL-eez

Mephitis mephitis MEF-it-is MEF-it-is

Microbiotheria my-crow-bio-THER-ee-uh

Microbiotheriidae my-crow-bio-ther-EYE-uh-dee

Microcebus rufus my-crow-SEE-buhs ROO-fuhs

Micropteropus pusillus my-crop-TER-oh-puhs pyoo-SILL-uhs

Miniopterus schreibersi min-ee-OP-ter-uhs shry-BER-seye

Mirounga angustirostris MIR-oon-guh an-GUHS-tih-ROS-tris

Molossidae mol-OS-suh-dee

Monachus schauinslandi MON-ak-uhs SHOU-inz-land-eye

Monodon monoceros MON-uh-don mon-UH-ser-uhs

Monodontidae mon-uh-DON-shuh-dee

Monotremata mon-uh-TREEM-ah-tuh

Mormoopidae mor-moh-UP-uh-dee

Moschus moschiferus MOS-kuhs mos-KIF-er-uhs

Muntiacus muntjak mun-SHE-uh-kuhs MUNT-jak

Muridae MUR-uh-dee

Mustela erminea MUS-tuh-luh er-MIN-ee-uh

Mustelidae mus-TUH-luh-dee

Myocastor coypus MY-oh-KAS-tor COI-puhs

Myocastoridae MY-oh-kas-TOR-uh-dee

Myotis lucifugus my-OH-tis loo-SIFF-ah-guhs

Myoxidae my-OKS-uh-dee

Myoxus glis MY-oks-uhs GLIS

Myrmecobiidae mur-mih-koh-BYE-uh-dee

Myrmecobius fasciatus mur-mih-KOH-bee-uhs fah-SHE-ah-tuhs

Myrmecophaga tridactyla mur-mih-KOH-fag-uh try-DAK-til-uh

Myrmecophagidae mur-mih-koh-FAJ-uh-dee

Mystacina tuberculata miss-tih-SEE-nuh too-ber-KYOO-lah-tuh

Mystacinidae miss-tih-SEE-nuh-dee

Myzopoda aurita my-zoh-POD-uh OR-it-uh

Myzopodidae my-zoh-POD-uh-dee

Nasalis larvatus NAY-zal-is LAR-vah-tuhs

Natalidae nay-TAL-uh-dee

Natalus stramineus NAY-tal-uhs struh-MIN-ee-uhs

Neobalaenidae nee-oh-bah-LEE-nuh-dee

Noctilio leporinus nok-TIHL-ee-oh leh-por-RYE-nuhs

Noctilionidae nok-tihl-ee-ON-uh-dee

Notomys alexis noh-TOH-meez ah-LEK-sis

Notoryctemorphia noh-toh-rik-teh-MOR-fee-uh

Notoryctes typhlops noh-TOH-rik-teez TIE-flopz

Notoryctidae noh-toh-RIK-tuh-dee

Nycteridae nik-TER-uh-dee

Nycteris thebaica NIK-ter-is the-BAH-ik-uh

Nycticebus pygmaeus nik-tih-SEE-buhs pig-MEE-uhs

Nyctimene robinsoni nik-TIM-en-ee ROB-in-son-eye

Ochotona hyperborea oh-koh-TOH-nuh hi-per-BOHR-ee-uh

Ochotona princeps oh-koh-TOH-nuh PRIN-seps

Ochotonidae oh-koh-TOH-nuh-dee

Octodon degus OK-tuh-don DAY-gooz

Octodontidae ok-tuh-DON-tuh-dee

Odobenidae oh-duh-BEN-uh-dee

Odobenus rosmarus oh-DUH-ben-uhs ROS-mahr-uhs

Odocoileus virginianus oh-duh-KOI-lee-uhs ver-JIN-ee-an-nuhs

Okapia johnstoni oh-KAH-pee-uh JOHNS-ton-eye

Ondatra zibethicus ON-dat-ruh ZIB-eth-ih-kuhs

Onychogalea fraenata oh-nik-uh-GAL-ee-uh FREE-nah-tuh

Orcinus orca OR-sigh-nuhs OR-kuh

Ornithorhynchidae OR-nith-oh-RIN-kuh-dee

Ornithorynchus anatinus OR-nith-oh-RIN-kuhs an-AH-tin-uhs

Orycteropodidae or-ik-ter-uh-POD-uh-dee

Orycteropus afer or-ik-TER-uh-puhs AF-er

Otariidae oh-tar-EYE-uh-dee

Otolemur garnettii oh-tuh-LEE-mer GAR-net-ee-eye

Ovis canadensis OH-vis kan-uh-DEN-sis

Pagophilus groenlandicus pa-GO-fil-luhs GREEN-land-ih-cuhs

Pan troglodytes PAN trog-luh-DIE-teez

Panthera leo PAN-ther-uh LEE-oh

Panthera tigris PAN-ther-uh TIE-gris

Paucituberculata paw-see-too-ber-KYOO-lah-tuh

Pedetidae ped-ET-uh-dee

Peramelemorphia per-uh-mel-eh-MOR-fee-uh

Peramelidae per-uh-MEL-uh-dee

Perameles gunnii PER-uh-MEL-eez GUN-ee-eye

Perissodactyla peh-RISS-uh-DAK-til-uh

Perodicticus potto per-uh-DIK-tuh-kuhs POT-toh

Perognathus inornatus PER-ug-NAH-thuhs in-AWR-nah-tuhs

Peropteryx kappleri per-OP-ter-iks KAP-ler-eye

Peroryctidae per-uh-RIK-tuh-dee

Petauridae pet-OR-uh-dee

Petauroides volans pet-or-OY-deez VOH-lanz

Petaurus breviceps PET-or-uhs BREV-ih-seps

Petrogale penicillata pet-ROH-gah-lee pen-ih-SIL-lah-tuh

Petromuridae pet-roh-MUR-uh-dee

Petromus typicus PET-roh-muhs TIP-ih-kuhs

Phalanger gymnotis FAH-lan-jer jim-NOH-tis

Phalangeridae fah-lan-JER-uh-dee

Phascogale tapoatafa fas-KOH-gah-lee TAP-oh-uh-TAH-fuh

Phascolarctidae fas-koh-LARK-tuh-dee

Phascolarctos cinereus fas-KOH-lark-tuhs sin-EAR-ee-uhs

Phocidae FOE-suh-dee

Phocoena phocoena FOE-see-nuh FOE-see-nuh

Phocoena spinipinnis FOE-see-nuh SPY-nih-PIN-is

Phocoenidae foe-SEE-nuh-dee

Pholidota foe-lih-DOH-tuh

Phyllostomidae fill-uh-STOH-muh-dee

Physeter macrocephalus FY-se-ter ma-crow-SEFF-uh-luhs

Physeteridae fy-se-TER-uh-dee

Piliocolobus badius fill-ee-oh-KOH-loh-buhs BAD-ee-uhs

Pithecia pithecia pith-EEK-ee-uh pith-EEK-ee-uh

Pitheciidae pith-eek-EYE-uh-dee

Plantanista gangetica plan-TAN-is-tuh gan-JET-ik-uh

Platanistidae plan-tan-IS-tuh-dee

Pongo pygmaeus PON-goh pig-MEE-uhs

Pontoporia blainvillei pon-toh-POR-ee-uh BLAIN-vill-ee-eye

Pontoporiidae PON-toh-por-EYE-uh-dee

Potoroidae pot-uh-ROY-dee

Primates PRY-maytes

Proboscidea proh-BOS-see-uh

Procavia capensis proh-CAVE-ee-uh KAP-en-sis

Procaviidae proh-kave-EYE-uh-dee

Procyon lotor proh-SIGH-on LOH-tor

Procyonidae proh-sigh-ON-uh-dee

Proechimys semispinosus proh-EK-ih-meez sem-ih-SPY-noh-suhs

Propithecus edwardsi proh-PITH-eek-uhs ED-werds-eye

Proteles cristatus PROH-tell-eez KRIS-tah-tuhs

Pseudocheiridae soo-doh-KY-ruh-dee

Pseudocheirus peregrinus soo-doh-KY-ruhs PEHR-eh-GRIN-uhs

Pteronotus parnellii ter-uh-NOH-tuhs PAR-nell-ee-eye

Pteropodidae ter-uh-POD-uh-dee

Pteropus giganteus ter-OH-puhs jy-GAN-tee-uhs

Pteropus mariannus ter-OH-puhs MARE-ih-an-uhs

Pudu pudu POO-doo POO-doo

Puma concolor PYOO-muh CON-kuh-luhr

Puripterus horrens PYOOR-ip-TER-uhs HOR-renz

Pygathrix nemaeus PIG-uh-thriks neh-MEE-uhs

Rangifer tarandus RAN-jih-fer TAR-an-duhs

Rhinoceros unicornis rye-NOS-er-uhs YOO-nih-KORN-is

Rhinocerotidae rye-NOS-er-UH-tuh-dee

Rhinolophidae rye-noh-LOH-fuh-dee

Rhinolophus capensis rye-noh-LOH-fuhs KAP-en-sis

Rhinolophus ferrumequinum rye-noh-LOH-fuhs FEHR-rum-EK-wy-num

Rhinopoma hardwickei rye-noh-POH-muh HARD-wik-eye

Rhinopomatidae rye-noh-poh-MAT-uh-dee

Rhynchocyon cirnei rin-koh-SIGH-on SIR-neye

Rodentia roh-DEN-she-uh

Rousettus aegyptiacus ROO-set-tuhs ee-JIP-tih-kuhs

Saccopteryx bilineata sak-OP -ter-iks BY-lin-EE-ah-tuh

Saguinus oedipus SAG-win-uhs ED-uh-puhs

Saimiri sciureus SAY-meer-eye sigh-OOR-ee-uhs

Sarcophilus laniarius SAR-kuh-FIL-uhs lan-ee-AIR-ee-uhs

Scalopus aquaticus SKA-loh-puhs uh-KWAT-ik-uhs

Scandentia skan-DEN-she-uh

Sciuridae sigh-OOR-uh-dee

Sciurus carolinensis SIGH-oor-uhs kar-uh-LINE-en-sis

Sigmodon hispidus SIG-muh-don HISS-pid-uhs

Sirenia sy-REEN-ee-uh

Solenodon paradoxus so-LEN-uh-don PAR-uh-DOCKS-uhs

Solenodontidae so-len-uh-DON-shuh-dee

Sorex palustris SOR-eks PAL-us-tris

Soricidae sor-IS-uh-dee

Stenella longirostris steh-NELL-uh LAWN-juh-ROS-tris

Suidae SOO-uh-dee

Sus scrofa SOOS SKRO-fuh

Sylvilagus audubonii SILL-vih-LAG-uhs AW-duh-BON-ee-eye

Symphalangus syndactylus SIM-fuh-LAN-guhs sin-DAK-til-uhs

Tachyglossidae TAK-ih-GLOS-suh-dee

Tachyglossus aculeatus TAK-ih-GLOS-suhs ak-YOOL-ee-ah-tuhs

Tadarida brasiliensis ta-DARE-ih-dah bra-ZILL-ee-en-sis

Talpidae TAL-puh-dee

Tamias striatus TAM-ee-uhs stry-AH-tuhs

Tapiridae tay-PUR-uh-dee

Tapirus indicus TAY-pur-uhs IN-dih-kuhs

Tapirus terrestris TAY-pur-uhs TER-rehs-tris

Tarsiidae tar-SIGH-uh-dee

Tarsipedidae tar-sih-PED-uh-dee

Tarsipes rostratus TAR-si-peez ROS-trah-tuhs

Tarsius bancanus TAR-see-uhs BAN-kan-uhs

Tarsius syrichta TAR-see-uhs STRIK-tuh

Tasmacetus shepherdi taz-muh-SEE-tuhs SHEP-erd-eye

Tayassu tajacu TAY-yuh-soo TAY-jah-soo

Tayassuidae tay-yuh-SOO-uh-dee

Tenrec ecaudatus TEN-rek ee-KAW-dah-tuhs

Tenrecidae ten-REK-uh-dee

Thomomys bottae TOM-oh-meez BOTT-ee

Thryonomyidae thry-oh-noh-MY-uh-dee

Thryonomys swinderianus THRY-oh-NOH-meez SWIN-der-EE-an-uhs

Thylacinidae thy-luh-SEEN-uh-dee

Thylacinus cynocephalus THY-luh-SEEN-uhs sigh-nuh-SEFF-uh-luhs

Thyroptera tricolor thy-ROP-ter-uh TRY-kuh-luhr
Thyropteridae thy-rop-TER-uh-dee
Tragulidae tray-GOO-luh-dee
Tragulus javanicus TRAY-goo-luhs jah-VAHN-ih-kuhs
Trichechidae trik-EK-uh-dee
Trichechus manatus TRIK-ek-uhs MAN-uh-tuhs
Trichosurus vulpecula TRIK-uh-SOOR-uhs vul-PEK-yoo-luh
Tubulidentata toob-yool-ih-DEN-tah-tuh
Tupaia glis too-PUH-ee-uh GLIS
Tupaiidae too-puh-EYE-uh-dee
Tursiops truncatus tur-SEE-ops TRUN-kah-tuhs
Uncia uncia UN-see-uh UN-see-uh
Ursidae UR-suh-dee
Ursus americanus UR-suhs uh-mer-uh-KAN-uhs
Ursus maritimus UR-suhs mar-ih-TIME-uhs
Vespertilionidae ves-puhr-TEEL-ee-UHN-uh-dee
Viverridae vy-VER-ruh-dee
Vombatidae vom-BAT-uh-dee
Vombatus ursinus VOM-bat-uhs ur-SIGH-nuhs
Vulpes vulpes VUHL-peez VUHL-peez
Xenarthra ZEN-areth-ruh
Yerbua capensis YER-byoo-uh KAP-en-sis
Zalophus californianus ZA-loh-fuhs kal-uh-FORN-uh-kuhs
Zalophus wollebaeki ZA-loh-fuhs VOLL-back-eye
Ziphiidae ziff-EYE-uh-dee

Words to Know

A

Aborigine: Earliest-known inhabitant of an area; often referring to a native person of Australia.

Adaptation: Any structural, physiological, or behavioral trait that aids an organism's survival and ability to reproduce in its existing environment.

Algae: Tiny plants or plantlike organisms that grow in water and in damp places.

Anaconda: A large snake of South America; one of the largest snakes in the world.

Aphrodisiac: Anything that intensifies or arouses sexual desires.

Aquatic: Living in the water.

Arboreal: Living primarily or entirely in trees and bushes.

Arid: Extremely dry climate, with less than 10 inches (25 centimeters) of rain each year.

Arthropod: A member of the largest single animal phylum, consisting of organisms with segmented bodies, jointed legs or wings, and exoskeletons.

B

Baleen: A flexible, horny substance making up two rows of plates that hang from the upper jaws of baleen whales.

Biogeography: The study of the distribution and dispersal of plants and animals throughout the world.

Bipedal: Walking on two feet.

Blowhole: The nostril on a whale, dolphin, or porpoise.

Blubber: A layer of fat under the skin of sea mammals that protects them from heat loss and stores energy.

Brachiation: A type of locomotion in which an animal travels through the forest by swinging below branches using its arms.

Brackish water: Water that is a mix of freshwater and saltwater.

Burrow: Tunnel or hole that an animal digs in the ground to use as a home.

C

Cache: A hidden supply area.

Camouflage: Device used by an animal, such as coloration, allowing it to blend in with the surroundings to avoid being seen by prey and predators.

Canine teeth: The four pointed teeth (two in each jaw) between the incisors and bicuspids in mammals; designed for stabbing and holding prey.

Canopy: The uppermost layer of a forest formed naturally by the leaves and branches of trees and plants.

Carnivore: Meat-eating organism.

Carrion: Dead and decaying animal flesh.

Cecum: A specialized part of the large intestine that acts as a fermentation chamber to aid in digestion of grasses.

Cervical vertebrae: The seven neck bones that make up the top of the spinal column.

Clan: A group of animals of the same species that live together, such as badgers or hyenas.

Cloud forest: A tropical forest where clouds are overhead most of the year.

Colony: A group of animals of the same type living together.

Coniferous: Refers to evergreen trees, such as pines and firs, that bear cones and have needle-like leaves that are not shed all at once.

Coniferous forest: An evergreen forest where plants stay green all year.

Continental shelf: A gently sloping ledge of a continent that is submerged in the ocean.

Convergence: In adaptive evolution, a process by which unrelated or only distantly related living things come to resemble one another in adapting to similar environments.

Coprophagous: Eating dung. Some animals do this to extract nutrients that have passed through their system.

Crepuscular: Most active at dawn and dusk.

Critically Endangered: A term used by the IUCN in reference to a species that is at an extremely high risk of extinction in the wild.

D

Data Deficient: An IUCN category referring to a species that is not assigned another category because there is not enough information about the species' population.

Deciduous: Shedding leaves at the end of the growing season.

Deciduous forest: A forest with four seasons in which trees drop their leaves in the fall.

Deforestation: Those practices or processes that result in the change of forested lands to non-forest uses, such as human settlement or farming. This is often cited as one of the major causes of the enhanced greenhouse effect.

Delayed implantation: A process by which the fertilized egg formed after mating develops for a short time, then remains inactive until later when it attaches to the uterus for further development, so that birth coincides with a better food supply or environmental conditions.

Den: The shelter of an animal, such as an underground hole or a hollow log.

Dentin: A calcareous material harder than bone found in teeth.

Desert: A land area so dry that little or no plant or animal life can survive.

Digit: Division where limbs terminate; in humans this refers to a finger or toe.

Digitigrade: A manner of walking on the toes, as cats and dogs do, as opposed to walking on the ball of the feet, as humans do.

Dingo: A wild Australian dog.

Diurnal: Refers to animals that are active during the day.

Domesticated: Tamed.

Dominant: The top male or female of a social group, sometimes called the alpha male or alpha female.

Dorsal: Located in the back.

Dung: Feces, or solid waste from an animal.

E

Echolocation: A method of detecting objects by using sound waves.

Ecotourist: A person who visits a place in order to observe the plants and animals in the area while making minimal human impact on the natural environment.

Electroreception: The sensory detection of small amounts of natural electricity by an animal (usually underwater), by means of specialized nerve endings.

Elevation: The height of land when measured from sea level.

Endangered: A term used by the U. S. Endangered Species Act of 1973 and by the IUCN in reference to a species that is facing a very high risk of extinction from all or a significant portion of its natural home.

Endangered Species Act: A U. S. law that grants legal protection to listed endangered and threatened species.

Endemic: Native to or occurring only in a particular place.

Erupt: In teeth, to break through the skin and become visible.

Estivation: State of inactivity during the hot, dry months of summer.

Estuary: Lower end of a river where ocean tides meet the river's current.

Eutherian mammal: Mammals that have a well-developed placenta and give birth to fully formed live young.

Evergreen: In botany, bearing green leaves through the winter and/or a plant having foliage that persists throughout the year.

Evolve: To change slowly over time.

Extinct: A species without living members.

Extinction: The total disappearance of a species or the disappearance of a species from a given area.

F

Family: A grouping of genera that share certain characteristics and appear to have evolved from the same ancestors.

Feces: Solid body waste.

Fermentation: Chemical reaction in which enzymes break down complex organic compounds into simpler ones. This can make digestion easier.

Forage: To search for food.

Forb: Any broad-leaved herbaceous plant that is not a grass; one that grows in a prairie or meadow, such as sunflower, goldenrod, or clover.

Fragment: To divide or separate individuals of the same species into small groups that are unable to mingle with each other.

Frugivore: Animal that primarily eats fruit. Many bats and birds are frugivores.

Fuse: To become joined together as one unit.

G

Genera: Plural of genus.

Genus (pl. genera): A category of classification made up of species sharing similar characteristics.

Gestation: The period of carrying young in the uterus before birth.

Gland: A specialized body part that produces, holds, and releases one or more substances (such as scent or sweat) for use by the body.

Gleaning: Gathering food from surfaces.

Grassland: Region in which the climate is dry for long periods of the summer, and freezes in the winter. Grasslands are characterized by grasses and other erect herbs, usually without trees or shrubs, and occur in the dry temperate interiors of continents.

Grooming: An activity during which primates look through each other's fur to remove parasites and dirt.

Guano: The droppings of birds or bats, sometimes used as fertilizer.

Guard hairs: Long, stiff, waterproof hairs that form the outer fur and protect the underfur of certain mammals.

Gum: A substance found in some plants that oozes out in response to a puncture, as plant sap, and generally hardens after exposure to air.

H

Habitat: The area or region where a particular type of plant or animal lives and grows.

Habitat degradation: The diminishment of the quality of a habitat and its ability to support animal and plant communities.

Hallux: The big toe, or first digit, on the part of the foot facing inwards.

Harem: A group of two or more adult females, plus their young, with only one adult male present.

Haul out: To pull one's body out of the water onto land, as when seals come out of the water to go ashore.

Herbivore: Plant-eating organism.

Hibernation: State of rest or inactivity during the cold winter months.

Hierarchy: A structured order of rank or social superiority.

Home range: A specific area that an animal roams while performing its activities.

I

Ice floe: A large sheet of floating ice.

Incisor: One of the chisel-shaped teeth at the front of the mouth (between the canines), used for cutting and tearing food.

Indigenous: Originating in a region or country.

Insectivore: An animal that eats primarily insects.

Insulate: To prevent the escape of heat by surrounding with something; in an animal, a substance such as fur or body fat serves to retain heat in its body.

Invertebrate: Animal lacking a spinal column (backbone).

IUCN: Abbreviation for the International Union for Conservation of Nature and Natural Resources, now the World Conservation Union. A conservation organization of government agencies and nongovernmental organizations best known for its Red Lists of threatened and endangered species.

K

Keratin: Protein found in hair, nails, and skin.

Krill: Tiny shrimp-like animals that are the main food of baleen whales and are also eaten by seals and other marine mammals.

L

Lactate: To produce milk in the female body, an activity associated with mammals.

Larva (pl. larvae): Immature form (wormlike in insects; fishlike in amphibians) of an organism capable of surviving on its own. A larva does not resemble the parent and must go through metamorphosis, or change, to reach its adult stage.

Leprosy: A disease of the skin and flesh characterized by scaly scabs and open sores.

Lichen: A complex of algae and fungi found growing on trees, rocks, or other solid surfaces.

Litter: A group of young animals, such as pigs or kittens, born at the same time from the same mother. Or, a layer of dead vegetation and other material covering the ground.

M

Malaria: A serious disease common in tropical countries, spread by the bites of female mosquitoes, that causes complications affecting the brain, blood, liver, and kidneys and can cause death.

Mammae: Milk-secreting organs of female mammals used to nurse young.

Mammals: Animals that feed their young on breast milk, are warm-blooded, and breathe air through their lungs.

Mangrove: Tropical coastal trees or shrubs that produce many supporting roots and that provide dense vegetation.

Marsupial: A type of mammal that does not have a well-developed placenta and gives birth to immature and under-developed young after a short gestation period. It continues to nurture the young, often in a pouch, until they are able to fend for themselves.

Matriarchal: Headed by a dominant female or females; said of animal societies.

Mechanoreceptor: Sensory nerve receptor modified to detect physical changes in the immediate environment, often having to do with touch and change of pressure or turbulence in water or air. In the platypus, mechanoreceptors in its bill may detect prey and obstacles.

Megachiroptera: One of the two groups of bats; these bats are usually larger than the microchiroptera.

Melon: The fatty forehead of a whale or dolphin.

Membrane: A thin, flexible layer of plant or animal tissue that covers, lines, separates or holds together, or connects parts of an organism.

Microchiroptera: One of two categories of bats; these make up most of the bats in the world and are generally smaller than the megachiroptera.

Migrate: To move from one area or climate to another as the seasons change, usually to find food or to mate.

Migratory pattern: The direction or path taken while moving seasonally from one region to another.

Molar: A broad tooth located near the back of the jaw with a flat, rough surface for grinding.

Mollusk: A group of animals without backbones that includes snails, clams, oysters, and similar hard-shelled animals.

Molt: The process by which an organism sheds its outermost layer of feathers, fur, skin, or exoskeleton.

Monogamous: Refers to a breeding system in which a male and a female mate only with each other during a breeding season or lifetime.

Muzzle: The projecting part of the head that includes jaws, chin, mouth, and nose.

Myxomatosis: A highly infectious disease of rabbits caused by a pox virus.

N

Near Threatened: A category defined by the IUCN suggesting that a species could become threatened with extinction in the future.

Nectar: Sweet liquid secreted by the flowers of various plants to attract pollinators (animals that pollinate, or fertilize, the flowers).

Neotropical: Relating to a geographic area of plant and animal life east, south, and west of Mexico's central plateau that includes Central and South America and the West Indies.

New World: Made up of North America, Central America, and South America; the western half of the world.

Nocturnal: Occurring or active at night.

Non-prehensile: Incapable of grasping; used to describe an animal's tail that cannot wrap around tree branches.

Noseleaf: Horseshoe-shaped flap of skin around the nose.

Nurse: To feed on mother's milk.

O

Old World: Australia, Africa, Asia, and Europe; in the eastern half of the world.

Omnivore: Plant- and meat-eating animal.

Opportunistic feeder: An animal that eats whatever food is available, either prey they have killed, other animals' kills, plants, or human food and garbage.

P

Pack ice: Large pieces of ice frozen together.

Patagium: The flap of skin that extends between the front and hind limbs. In bats, it stretches between the hind legs and helps the animal in flight; in colugos this stretches from the side of the neck to the tips of its fingers, toes, and tail.

Phylogenetics: Field of biology that deals with the relationships between organisms. It includes the discovery of these relationships, and the study of the causes behind this pattern.

Pinnipeds: Marine mammals, including three families of the order Carnivora, namely Otariidae (sea lions and fur seals), Phocidae (true seals), and Odobenidae (walrus).

Placenta: An organ that grows in the mother's uterus and lets the mother and developing offspring share food and oxygen through the blood.

Placental mammal: Any species of mammal that carries embryonic and fetal young in the womb through a long gestation period, made possible via the placenta, a filtering organ passing nutrients, wastes, and gases between mother and young.

Plantigrade: Walking on the heel and sole of the foot, instead of on the toes. Plantigrade species include bears and humans.

Plate tectonics: Geological theory holding that Earth's surface is composed of rigid plates or sections that move about the surface in response to internal pressure, creating the major geographical features such as mountains.

Poach: To hunt animals illegally.

Pod: In animal behavioral science (and in some zoology uses) the term pod is used to represent a group of whales, seals, or dolphins.

Pollen: Dust-like grains or particles produced by a plant that contain male sex cells.

Pollination: Transfer of pollen from the male reproductive organs to the female reproductive organs of plants.

Pollinator: Animal which carries pollen from one seed plant to another, unwittingly aiding the plant in its reproduction. Common pollinators include insects, especially bees, butterflies, and moths; birds; and bats.

Polyandry: A mating system in which a single female mates with multiple males.

Polyestrous: A female animal having more than one estrous cycle (mating period) within a year.

Polygamy: A mating system in which males and females mate with multiple partners.

Polygyny: A mating system in which a single male mates with multiple females.

Predator: An animal that eats other animals.

Prehensile: Able to control and use to grasp objects, characteristically associated with tails. Prehensile tails have evolved independently many times, for instance, in marsupials, rodents, primates, porcupines, and chameleons.

Prey: Organism hunted and eaten by a predator.

Primary forest: A forest characterized by a full-ceiling canopy formed by the branches of tall trees and several layers of smaller trees. This type of forest lacks ground vegetation because sunlight cannot penetrate through the canopy.

Promiscuity: Mating in which individuals mate with as many other individuals as they can or want to.

Puberty: The age of sexual maturity.

Q

Quadruped: Walking or running on four limbs.

R

Rabies: A viral infection spread through the bite of certain warm-blooded animals; it attacks the nervous system and can be fatal if untreated.

Rainforest: An evergreen woodland of the tropics distinguished by a continuous leaf canopy and an average rainfall of about 100 inches (250 centimeters) per year.

Regurgitate: Eject the contents of the stomach through the mouth; to vomit.

Rookery: A site on land where seals congregate to mate and raise the young.

Roost: A place where animals, such as bats, sit or rest on a perch, branch, etc.

S

Savanna: A biome characterized by an extensive cover of grasses with scattered trees, usually transitioning between areas dominated by forests and those dominated by grasses and having alternating seasonal climates of precipitation and drought.

Scavenger: An animal that eats carrion, dead animals.

Scent gland: Formed from modified, or changed, sweat glands, these glands produce and/or give off strong-smelling chemicals that give information, such as marking territory, to other animals.

Scent mark: To leave an odor, such as of urine or scent gland secretions, to mark a territory or as a means of communication.

Scrotum: The external pouch containing the testicles.

Scrub forest: A forest with short trees and shrubs.

Scrubland: An area similar to grassland but which includes scrub (low-growing plants and trees) vegetation.

Seamount: An underwater mountain that does not rise above the surface of the ocean.

Seashore: When referring to a biome, formed where the land meets the ocean.

Secondary forest: A forest characterized by a less-developed canopy, smaller trees, and a dense ground vegetation found on the edges of forests and along rivers and streams. The immature vegetation may also result from the removal of trees by logging and/or fires.

Semiaquatic: Partially aquatic; living or growing partly on land and partly in water.

Semiarid: Very little rainfall each year, between 10 and 20 inches (25 to 51 centimeters).

Sexually mature: Capable of reproducing.

Solitary: Living alone or avoiding the company of others.

Species: A group of living things that share certain distinctive characteristics and can breed together in the wild.

Spermaceti: A waxy substance found in the head cavity of some whales.

Steppe: Wide expanse of semiarid relatively level plains, found in cool climates and characterized by shrubs, grasses, and few trees.

Streamline: To smooth out.

Succulent: A plant that has fleshy leaves to conserve moisture.

Suckle: To nurse or suck on a mother's nipple to get milk.

Syndactyly: A condition in which two bones (or digits) fuse together to become a single bone.

T

Tactile: Having to do with the sense of touch.

Talon: A sharp hooked claw.

Taxonomy: The science dealing with the identification, naming, and classification of plants and animals.

Teat: A projection through which milk passes from the mother to the nursing young; a nipple.

Temperate: Areas with moderate temperatures in which the climate undergoes seasonal change in temperature and moisture. Temperate regions of the earth lie primarily between 30 and 60° latitude in both hemispheres.

Terrestrial: Relating to the land or living primarily on land.

Territorial: A pattern of behavior that causes an animal to stay in a limited area and/or to keep certain other animals of the same species (other than its mate, herd, or family group) out of the area.

Thicket: An area represented by a thick, or dense, growth of shrubs, underbrush, or small trees.

Threatened: Describes a species that is threatened with extinction.

Torpor: A short period of inactivity characterized by an energy-saving, deep sleep-like state in which heart rate, respiratory rate and body temperature drop.

Traction: Resistance to a surface to keep from slipping.

Tragus: A flap of skin near the base of the external ear.

Tributary: A small stream that feeds into a larger one.

Tropical: The area between 23.5° north and south of the equator. This region has small daily and seasonal changes in temperature, but great seasonal changes in precipitation. Generally, a hot and humid climate that is completely or almost free of frost.

Tundra: A type of ecosystem dominated by lichens, mosses, grasses, and woody plants. It is found at high latitudes (arctic tundra) and high altitudes (alpine tundra). Arctic tundra is underlain by permafrost and usually very wet.

Turbulent: An irregular, disorderly mode of flow.

U

Underfur: Thick soft fur lying beneath the longer and coarser guard hair.

Understory: The trees and shrubs between the forest canopy and the ground cover.

Ungulates: Hoofed animals, such as deer and elk.

Urine washing: A monkey behavior in which it soaks its hands with urine, then rubs the liquid on its fur and feet so as to leave the scent throughout its forest routes.

Uterus: A pear-shaped, hollow muscular organ in which a fetus develops during pregnancy.

V

Vertebra (pl. vertebrae): A component of the vertebral column, or backbone, found in vertebrates.

Vertebrate: An animal having a spinal column (backbone).

Vertical: Being at a right angle to the horizon. Up and down movements or supports.

Vestigial: A degenerate or imperfectly developed biological structure that once performed a useful function at an earlier stage of the evolution of the species.

Vibrissae: Stiff sensory hairs that can be found near the nostrils or other parts of the face in many mammals and the snouts, tails, ears, and sometimes feet of many insectivores.

Vocalization: Sound made by vibration of the vocal tract.

Vulnerable: An IUCN category referring to a species that faces a high risk of extinction.

W

Wallaby: An Australian marsupial similar to a kangaroo but smaller.

Wean: When a young animal no longer feeds on its mother's milk and instead begins to eat adult food.

Wetlands: Areas that are wet or covered with water for at least part of the year and support aquatic plants, such as marshes, swamps, and bogs.

Woodlands: An area with a lot of trees and shrubs.

Y

Yolk-sac placenta: A thin membrane that develops in the uterus of marsupials that does not fuse with the mother's uterus and results in short pregnancies with the young being born with poorly developed organs.

Getting to Know Mammals

MAMMALS

Mammals are found on all continents and in all seas. It isn't easy to tell that an animal is a mammal. A combination of special features separates mammals from other animals.

Mammal milk

Only mammals can feed their young with milk produced by their body. This milk comes from special glands called mammae. A female may have two mammary glands or as many as a dozen or more. Mammal milk is very healthy for infants and immediately available.

Body temperature

Mammals are warm-blooded, meaning they keep a constant body temperature. To keep their temperature fairly constant, a mammal needs some protective covering. Hair, made of a protein called keratin, serves several functions. One function is insulation, controlling the amount of body heat that escapes into the mammal's environment through the skin.

Mammal hair

All mammals have hair at some time of their life. Some have a lot, such as gorillas, and some have very little, such as the naked mole rats. There are three types of hair: a coarse long topcoat, a fine undercoat, and special sensory hairs, or whiskers.

In some mammals, hair has unusual forms. Porcupines have stiff, sharp, and thickened hairs called quills. Anteaters have

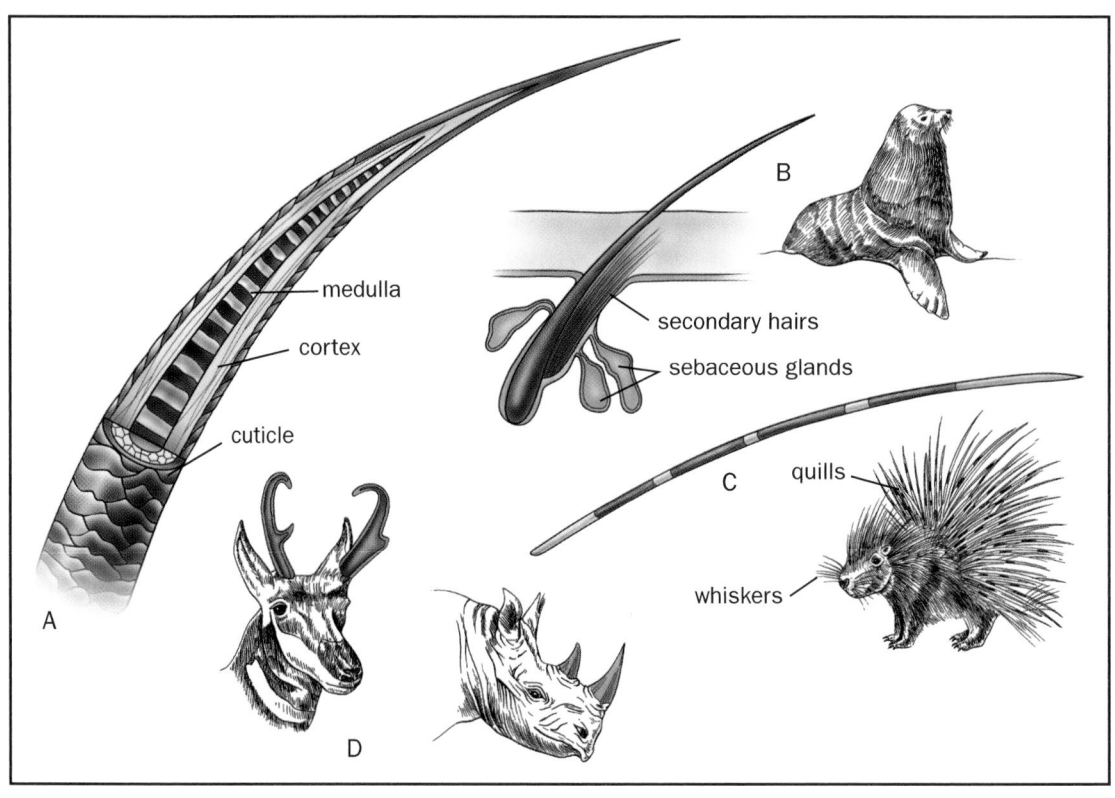

medulla

cortex

cuticle

A

B

secondary hairs

sebaceous glands

C

quills

whiskers

D

A. Cross section of a hair. B. Hairs may provide insulation and waterproofing. Specialized hair includes quills, whiskers (C), and horns (D). (Illustration by Patricia Ferrer. Reproduced by permission.)

sharp-edged scales made of modified hairs. These modified, or changed, hairs are protective against predators.

Mammals that live all or most of their lives in water, such as sea otters, may have a lot of dense, long hair, or fur. Others have much less hair, but a very thick hide, or skin, plus a thick layer of fat or blubber underneath the hide.

Hair color and pattern may vary. Males and females may have different fur colors. Special color patterns, such as a skunk's black and white fur, act as warnings. Hair color can also serve as camouflage, enabling the mammal to blend into its background.

Some mammals have fur color changes in summer and winter. Colors can be entirely different. Snowshoe rabbits and weasels can be brownish in summer, and almost pure white in winter. But this only happens if there is snow where they live. If it seldom snows, weasels and snowshoe rabbits stay brown.

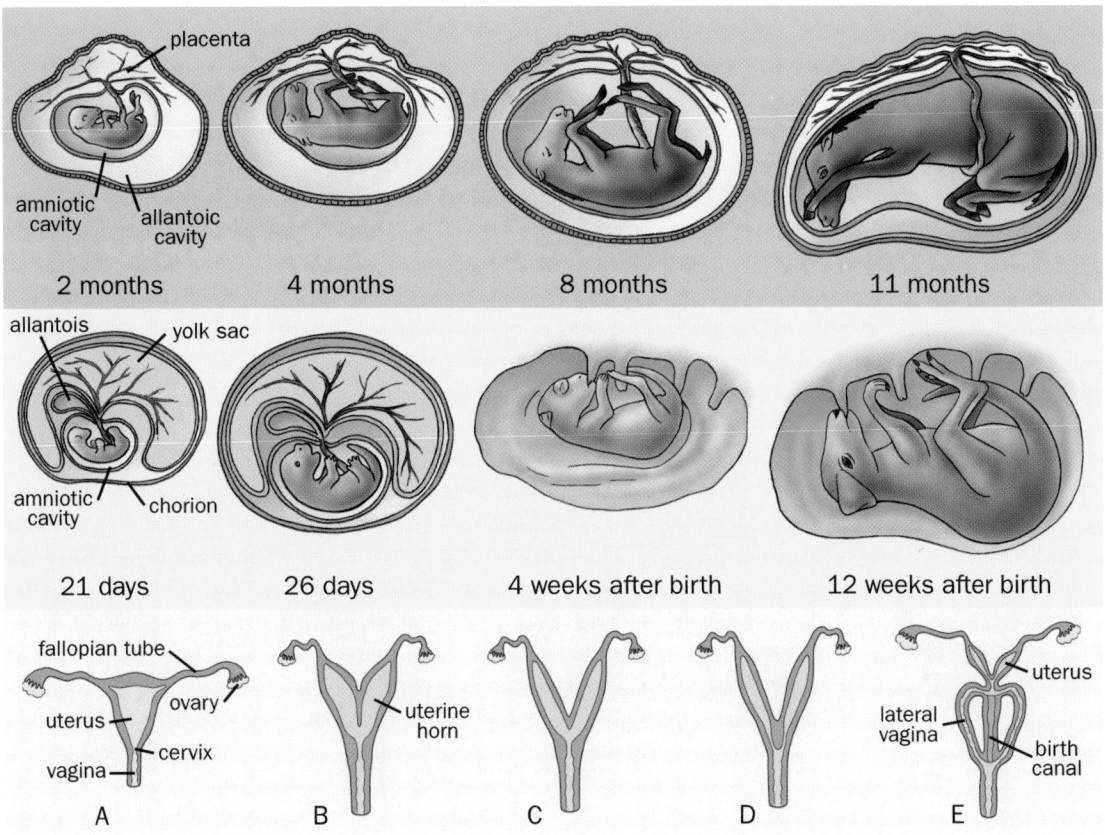

Top: Placental mammal development. Middle row: Marsupial mammal development. Types of uterus: A. Simplex; B. Bipartite; C. Bicornuate; D. Duplex; E. Marsupial. (Illustration by Patricia Ferrer. Reproduced by permission.)

Reproduction

Mammals have two genetic sexes, male and female. Ninety percent of mammals are placental (pluh-SENT-ul). In placental mammals, the baby develops, or grows, within the mother's body before it enters the world. What about the other 10 percent? These mammals lay eggs. There are only three egg-laying mammals alive today.:

Other mammal features

Other bodily mammal features include their ability to breathe air through their lungs. Water-dwelling mammals, such as the whale and porpoise, do this too. Mammals have jaws, usually with teeth. Mammals usually have four limbs. Mammals have a four-chambered heart. Mammals have vertebrae, or back bones, unlike invertebrates such as insects, in which there is an outside shell or structure called an exoskeleton.

This life-sized woolly mammoth model is kept in the Royal British Columbia Museum. Woolly mammoths were as tall as 10 feet (3 meters). (© Jonathan Blair/Corbis. Reproduced by permission.)

FOSSIL MAMMALS

Fossils are body parts of animals that lived very long ago. Not many long-ago mammals are preserved as fossils. But some entire mammal fossils have been discovered, such as a 10-foot (3-meter) woolly mammoth preserved in Siberian frozen ground, and an Ice Age woolly rhinoceros discovered in Poland, preserved in asphalt.

Many long-ago mammals lived in a warm, wet world. They ate soft, leafy plants. The earliest known mammals were possibly shrew-like creatures living about 190 million years ago. Later larger mammals occurred, then disappeared, or became extinct. These include the mesohippus, a three-toed horse only 24 inches (60 centimeters) high; a giant pig with a head that was 4 feet (1.22 meters) in length; and the smilodon, a huge saber-toothed cat with canine teeth that were 8 inches (20.3

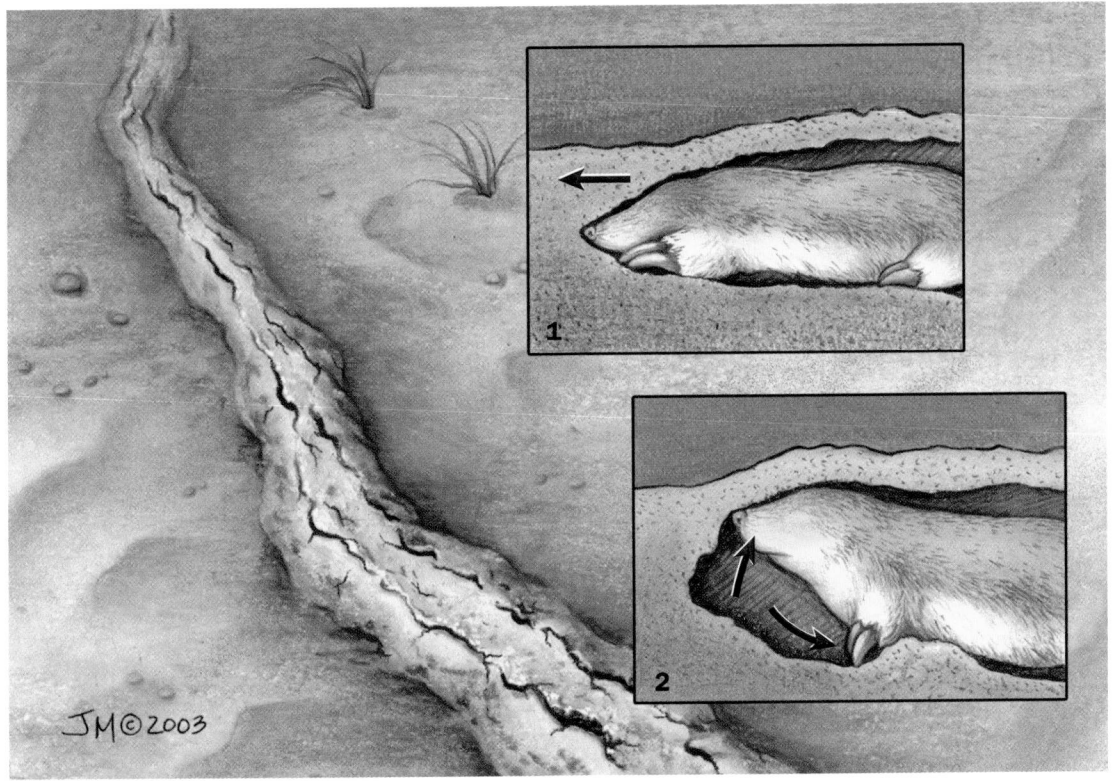

The Grant's desert mole uses its powerful forelimbs to burrow through the sands of the Namib Desert in southern Africa. The golden mole moves forward (1), and enlarges the tunnel by pushing dirt up with its head and back with its claws (2). (Illustration by Jacqueline Mahannah. Reproduced by permission.)

centimeters) in length. By about 15,000 years ago, long-ago people were hunting mammals with stone-pointed spears. Most of the animals they hunted are extinct for various reasons, some known, and some unknown.

WHERE MAMMALS LIVE

Underground mammals

Some small mammals spend all or most of their lives living underground. These include many species of prairie dogs, chipmunks, moles, groundhogs, Greenland collared lemmings, and Peruvian tuco-tucos. Each of these mammals has a special body design enabling it to survive underground.

Moles have large, powerful shoulders and short, very powerful forelimbs. Spade-like feet have claws, enabling quick digging. Hind feet have webbed toes, enabling the mole to kick soil backwards effectively. Velvety-type fur enables a mole to slip easily through its tunnels. And, although moles

A RECENT DISCOVERY

A bright orange, mouse-like mammal, weighing 0.5 ounces (15 grams) and measuring 3.12 inches (8 centimeters) plus a long tail, has recently been discovered in the Philippines. It has whiskers five times longer than its head. It can open and eat very hard tree nuts that no other mammal in the area can eat.

have almost no eyes, they can rely on touch, smell, and sensitivity to vibration to find underground insects and earthworms.

Sea mammals

Some mammals live in the sea, including manatees, whales, seals, and dolphins. While some need air every few minutes, a sperm whale can remain underwater for an hour and a half. How is this possible? Some sea mammals have a very low metabolism. They don't use up the their oxygen quickly and can store large amounts of oxygen in their bodies.

Tree mammals

Some mammals spend all or most of their lives in trees. Tree-dwelling mammals are often hidden from sight by leaves, vines, and branches. Tree-dwelling mammals include the Eastern pygmy possum, which nests in small tree hollows; the koala; Lumholtz's tree kangaroo, which leaps from branch to branch; the three-toed sloth; and the clouded leopard.

Flying mammals

The only truly flying mammals are bats. The sound of bat wings was first heard about 50 million years ago. Some bats are large, with a wingspan almost 7 feet (21.3 meters) wide. Some are small, as the Philippine bamboo bat, whose body is just 2 inches (5.08 centimeters) long.

Other mammals only appear to fly, such as the southern flying squirrel and the colugo, or Malayan flying lemur. These mammals have gliding membranes, skin folds from body front to legs, that, when spread out, act almost like a parachute. For example, the feathertail glider, a tiny possum, crawls along narrow branches. At branch end, it leaps out and slightly downward. Spreading its gliding membranes, it speeds through the air, landing on a nearby tree.

Mountain mammals

Some mammals spend most of their lives on mountain peaks. These include Asian corkscrew-horned markhor goats, North

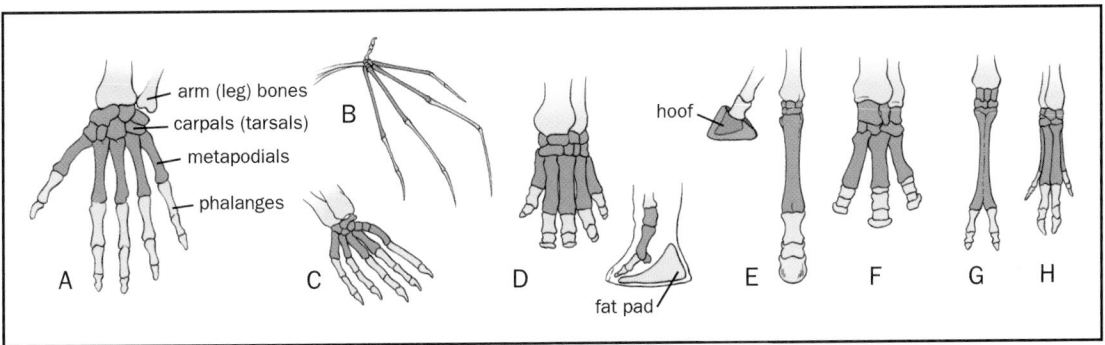

American Rocky Mountain bighorn sheep, and Siberian ibex. Siberian ibex can stand anyplace on any pinnacle with just enough room for its four feet. North American mountain goats can climb up a mountain peak, almost going straight up. Specially shaped hooves help.

Other high mountain dwelling mammals include snow leopards and Asian pikas that can survive at 19,685 feet (6,000 meters). Gunnison's prairie dogs do well up to 11,500 feet (3,505 meters).

Desert mammals

Some mammals spend most of their lives in arid, or very dry areas. Not all deserts are sandy like Death Valley or the Sahara. Some are rocky. Other arid areas are mountainous. Desert dwelling mammals include the North African elephant shrew, white-tailed antelope squirrel, and the desert kangaroo rat. No mammal can live without water. Desert rodents have a way to extract, or get, water from their own body functions. Rodents may also get water by eating plants, seeds, roots, and insects that contain water.

Larger mammals live in arid regions too. The striped hyena can survive in stony desert as long as it is within 6 miles (9.7 kilometers) of water. Fennecs, a very small fox living near sand dunes, can go a long time without drinking. Camels can use body fluids when no water is available.

WHAT DO MAMMALS EAT?

Insect-eaters

Some mammals have mostly insect meals. Insect-eating mammals include the moles, aye-ayes and aardvarks. The aardvark

Mammals' hands and feet differ depending on where the animal lives and how it gets around. A. A hominid hand is used for grasping objects; B. A bat's wing is used for flight; C. A pinniped's flipper helps move it through the water. Hoofed animals move around on all fours: D. Elephant foot; E. Equid (horse family) foot; F. Odd-toed hoofed foot; G. Two-toed hoofed foot; H. Four-toed hoofed foot. (Illustration by Patricia Ferrer. Reproduced by permission.)

has a sticky tongue that can reach out as long as 1 foot (0.3 meters) to capture its ant and termite meals.

Plant eaters

Some mammals eat nothing but plants. Plant eaters include pandas, the West Indian manatee, and the red-bellied wallaby. Some mammals have a single stomach that breaks the plant food down into small pieces. Other mammals, such as cows and camels, have a large stomach made of several parts. Each part does a separate job of breaking down difficult-to-digest plants.

Some mammals eat both plants and fruit. These include the 14-ounce (400-gram) Eurasian harvest mouse, the 100-pound (45-kilogram) South American capybara, and the African elephant. An elephant can eat up to 500 pounds (227 kilograms) of grass, plants, and fruit per day.

Meat eaters

Mammals eating mostly meat or fish are carnivorous. Carnivorous mammals have long, pointed, and very strong incisor teeth. Carnivores include polar bears, hyenas, walruses, and Eu-

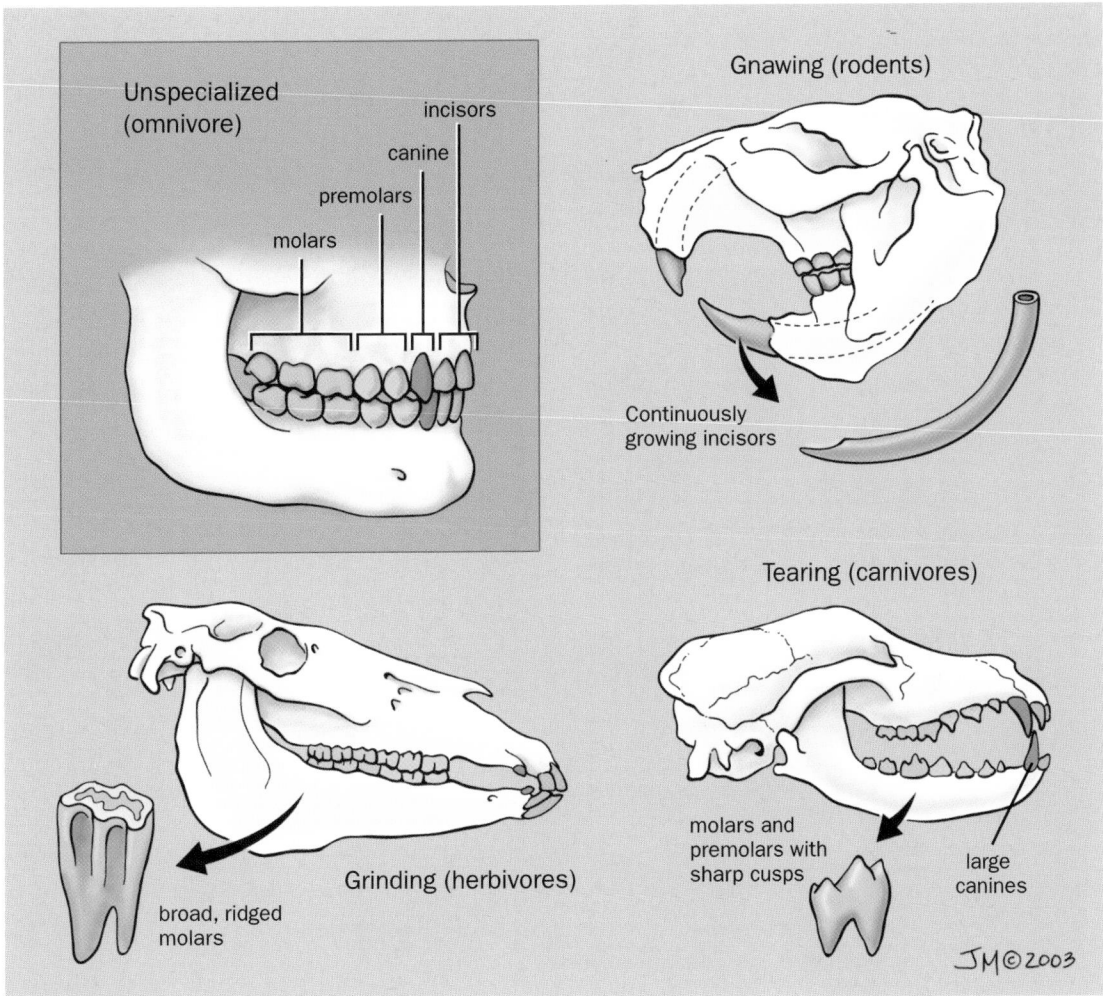

Mammals have different tooth shapes for different functions. Herbivores typically have large, flattened teeth for chewing plants. Rodents' ever-growing incisors are used for gnawing. Carnivores have teeth for holding and efficiently dismembering their prey. (Illustration by Jacqueline Mahannah. Reproduced by permission.)

ropean wild cats. The European wild cat may be an ancestor of our house cats.

Omnivores

Some mammals eat just about anything. They are omnivorous. Omnivorous mammals include wolverines, raccoons, and wild pigs. Wild pigs are the ancestors of our domestic pigs.

MAMMAL SLEEPING HABITS

Day or night

Some mammals sleep during the night, others sleep during the day. The night sleepers are diurnal, active during the day.

THE BIGGEST, THE TALLEST, AND THE SMALLEST

The largest and heaviest mammal alive today is the blue whale. One adult female measured 110.2 feet (33.6 meters). Blue whale weight can reach 268,400 pounds (121,853 kilograms).

The largest living land animal is the African bush elephant. From trunk tip to tail tip, a male has measured 33 feet (10 meters). Body weight was 24,000 pounds (10,886 kilograms).

The smallest non-flying mammal is the Savi's white-toothed pygmy shrew. An adult's head and body together measure only 2 inches (5.1 centimeters) long. Maximum weight is 0.09 ounces (2.5 grams).

How small is this? This pygmy shrew can travel through tunnels left by large earthworms!

The smallest flying mammal is the rare Kitti's hog-nosed bat, or "bumblebee bat," from Thailand. Head and body length is just 1.14 to 1.29 inches (29 to 33 millimeters). Weight is just 0.06 to 0.07 ounces (1.75 to 2 grams). This tiny bat was only discovered in 1973.

The tallest living animal is the giraffe. The average adult male, or bull, is 16 feet (4.9 meters) high, from front hoof to head horn tip. This size male weighs 2,376 to 2,800 pounds (1,078 to 1,270 kilograms).

The day sleepers are nocturnal, active at night. They may have special night vision. Many desert animals are nocturnal, moving about when it is cooler.

Hibernation

Some bat species hibernate through an entire winter. Hibernation is like a very long deep sleep. When a mammal hibernates, it uses up body fat that has accumulated from food eaten in good weather. Hibernators include the North African jird, groundhogs or woodchucks, and several dormice species. Dormice enter a tree hollow or ground burrow in autumn, and don't come out until springtime.

Bears don't truly hibernate. Their sleep isn't deep. They slow down quite a bit, and nap a lot, but do not sleep through an entire winter.

A new hibernating pattern has just been discovered. Madagascar fat-tailed lemurs hibernate in tree holes when winter daytime temperatures rise above 86° Fahrenheit (30° Celsius). They sleep for seven months. Scientists belief these dwarf lemurs find less food in what is the dry season in Madagascar, so they go to into deep sleep to preserve energy until a better food supply appears.

REPRODUCTION

Mating

Some mammals mate for life, such as wolves and sometimes coyotes. More commonly, a male may mate with several females each breeding period. Or a female may mate with several males.

Some mammals have one litter each year. Others have a litter only every two or three years. But the North American meadow mouse can have seventeen litters per year. That's a group of babies about every three weeks!

There may be one or more infants in a litter. Bats, giraffes, and two-toed sloths have just one baby per year. However, the Madagascar tenrec can produce thirty-two babies in just one litter.

Opossums are marsupial animals. The mother has a pouch in which the young continue to develop after they're born. (© Mary Ann McDonald/Corbis. Reproduced by permission.)

Child care

All mammal infants need protection. They are very small compared to their parents. They may be blind and hairless. Usually females provide care. However, in a few mammal species, such as the golden lion marmoset, the male does most of the care.

Female marsupial mammals, such as opossums, koalas, and kangaroos, have a pouch, like a pocket, on the front or under the body. Their tiny babies are incompletely developed when they are born. At birth, an opossum baby is about the size of a dime. It crawls immediately into its mother's pouch and stays there until ready to survive outside. The pouch contains mammary glands so babies can feed.

SOCIAL LIFE

Solitary mammals

Some mammals are solitary. They keep company with another of the same kind only when mating or when raising young. Solitary mammals include the giant anteaters, European bison, and right whales.

Japanese macaques are social animals, and groom each other regularly. (© Herbert Kehrer/OKAPIA/Photo Researchers, Inc. Reproduced by permission.)

Group living

Many mammals live in groups. In large groups, some eat, some rest, and some keep guard. Baboons, for example, may have from twenty to 300 animals in a group. One or more adult males lead each group. If a predator, such as a leopard, approaches, the males take action against it, while the females and young escape.

Some mammals travel in herds. Musk oxen travel in closely packed herds of fifteen to 100 individuals. These herds include males and females. Bighorn sheep females travel in herds of five to fifteen, with a dominant ewe, or female, as the leader.

Pack mammals get their food by cooperation. They work together to bring down much larger prey. Dingoes, killer whales, and lions hunt in packs.

MAMMALS AND PEOPLE

Domesticated mammals

About 14,000 years ago, humans began controlling, or domesticating, certain animals. This made humans' lives easier.

Horses have been domesticated for practical uses, such as transportation, and for entertainment, such as horse riding and racing. (© Kevin R. Morris/Corbis. Reproduced by permission.)

Rats can spread diseases that affect livestock and people. In addition, they eat and contaminate feed and their gnawing destroys buildings. (Jane Burton/Bruce Coleman, Inc. Reproduced by permission.)

The earliest domesticated mammal was probably the dog. Some scientists think hunters adopted wolf cubs and trained them to smell out game, animals they hunted for food.

People use mammals for many purposes. Cows provide meat, milk, cheese, butter, and hide. Camels, yaks, and Indian elephants carry or pull heavy items. Water buffaloes do hauling and can provide milk. Horses provide transportation and racing activities. Other domesticated animals include rabbits, pigs, goats, sheep, cavies, and capybaras.

People keep animals as pets. Common mammal pets are dogs, cats, guinea pigs, and hamsters.

Pest mammals

Some mammals are considered pests. These include rats, mice, and, depending where they live, gophers, rabbits, and ground squirrels. Rats can transmit disease-carrying fleas. Rabbits and gophers eat garden and food plants.

ENDANGERED MAMMALS

Mammals in danger

Of about 5,000 mammal species currently existing, over 1,000 are seriously endangered. Few wild mammals can live outside their natural habitat. When land is cleared for farming or housing, animals making homes there must leave, if there is any place for them to go. If not, they die from starvation or (because they are easily seen) from predators. Slowly, or quickly, the mammal species disappears.

Many human habits lead to endangerment. Hunting for amusement, killing for fur or body parts, native and commercial killing for food, fishing gear entrapment, land-destructive wars, and the illegal pet trade all take their toll. So do chemicals.

Some mammals are probably on the way to extinction, or total elimination. There are only about sixty Java rhinoceros left in the world. The Seychelles sheath-tailed bat has only about fifty individuals remaining. Yellow-tailed woolly monkeys number no more than 250 individuals. Mediterranean monk seals may be killed by scuba divers, and number only 600 individuals.

Saving endangered animals

Today many people are trying to save endangered animals. Methods include zoo breeding, establishing forest reserves, and training native populations that animals can be an economic benefit. Ecotourism, people visiting a country to see its animals in their natural habitat, is increasing. There are laws against importing and exporting endangered species. And, in some parts of the world, there are laws against land destruction.

Some mammals have possibly been rescued from immediate extinction. The American bison once roamed the North American prairies, numbering about 50 million. After slaughter by soldiers and settlers for food and sport, by 1889 only 541 remained alive. Now, in the United States, there are about 35,000 in protected areas. California northern elephant seals were once reduced to fewer than 100 members due to hunting. Today, protected, there are about 50,000. The ibex was once hunted for supposedly curative body parts and few were left. But in 1922, a National Park was established in the Italian Alps, where several thousand now live. The Mongolian wild horse, once thought to be extinct, now has a special reserve in Mongolia.

Too late to save

Some mammals became extinct only recently. Recently extinct animals include Steller's sea cows, which became extinct in about 1768. The Tasmanian wolf was last seen in 1933, eliminated by bounty hunters. The African bluebuck disappeared from Earth in 1880. The quagga, from southern Asia, was hunted for hides and meat. The last known quagga, a relative of the zebra, died in a Dutch zoo in 1883.

FOR MORE INFORMATION

Books

Boitani, Luigi, and Stefania Bartoli. *Guide to Mammals.* New York: Simon and Schuster, 1982.

Booth, Ernest S. *How to Know the Mammals.* Dubuque, IA: Wm. C. Brown Company Publishers, 1982.

Embery, Joan, and Edward Lucaire. *Joan Embery's Collection of Amazing Animal Facts.* New York: Dell Publishing, 1983.

Jones, J. Knox Jr., and David M. Armstrong. *Guide to Mammals of the Plains States.* Lincoln, NE: University of Nebraska Press, 1985.

Kite, L. Patricia. *Raccoons.* Minneapolis: Lerner Publications Company, 2004.

Kite, L. Patricia. *Blood-Feeding Bugs and Beasts.* Brookfield, CT: Millbrook Press, 1996.

Line, Les, and Edward Ricciuti. *National Audubon Society Book of Wild Animals.* New York: H. L. Abrams, 1996.

Nowak, Ronald M., and John L. Paradiso. *Walker's Mammals of the World.* Baltimore and London: The Johns Hopkins University Press, 1983.

Vogel, Julia, and John F. McGee. *Dolphins (Our Wild World.* Minnetonka, MN: Northword Press, 2001.

Walters, Martin. *Young Readers Book of Animals.* New York, London, Toronto, Sydney, and Tokyo: Simon & Schuster Books for Young Readers, 1990.

Whitaker, John O. Jr. *National Audubon Society Field Guide to North American Mammals.* New York: Alfred A. Knopf, 2000.

Wilson, D. E., and D. M. Reeder. *Mammal Species of the World.* Washington, DC: Smithsonian Institution Press, 1993.

Wood, Gerald L. *Animal Facts and Feats.* New York: Sterling Publishing, 1977.

Woods, Samuel G., and Jeff Cline. *Amazing Book of Mammal Records: The Largest, the Smallest, the Fastest, and Many More!* Woodbridge, CT: Blackbirch Press, 2000.

Periodicals

Allen, Leslie. "Return of the Pandas." *Smithsonian Magazine* (April 2001): 44–55.

Chadwick, Douglas H. "A Mine of Its Own." *Smithsonian Magazine* (May 2004): 26–27.

Cheater, Mark. "Three Decades of the Endangered Species Act." *Defenders* (Fall 2003): 8–13.

Conover, Adele. "The Object at Hand." *Smithsonian Magazine* (October 1996).

Gore, Rick. "The Rise of Mammals." *National Geographic* (April 2003): 2–37.

Mitchell, Meghan. "Securing Madagascar's Rare Wildlife." *Science News* (November 1, 1997): 287.

Pittman, Craig. "Fury Over a Gentle Giant." *Smithsonian Magazine* (February 2004): 54–59.

"Prehistoric Mammals." *Ranger Rick* (October 2000): 16.

Sherwonit, Bill. "Protecting the Wolves of Denali." *National Parks Magazine* (September/October 2003): 21–25.

Sunquist, Fiona. "Discover Rare Mystery Mammals." *National Geographic* (January 1999): 22–29.

Weidensaul, Scott. "The Rarest of the Rare." *Smithsonian Magazine* (November 2000): 118–128.

"Wildlife of Tropical Rain Forests." *National Geographic World* (January 2000): 22–25.

Web sites

Animal Info. http://www.animalinfo.org/ (accessed on June 6, 2004).

"Class Mammalia." Animal Diversity Web. http://animaldiversity.ummz.umich.edu/site/accounts/information/Mammalia004 (accessed on June 5, 2004).

"Hibernating Primate Found in Tropics." CNN Science & Space. http://www.cnn.com/2004/TECH/science/06/24/science.hibernation.reuit/inex.html (accessed on June 24, 2004).

"Ice Age Mammals." National Museum of Natural History. http://www.mnh.si.edu/museum/VirtualTour/Tour/First/IceAge/index.html (accessed on June 6, 2004).

"Mammary Glands." Animal Diversity Web. http://animaldiversity.ummz.umich.edu/site/topics/mammal_anatomy/mammary_glands.html (accessed on June 6, 2004).

PANGOLINS
Pholidota

Class: Mammalia
Order: Pholidota
One family: Manidae
Number of species: 7 species

PHYSICAL CHARACTERISTICS

Pangolins are unique looking animals covered with large, horny, overlapping scales. They were often referred to as scaly anteaters in the past. Typically, there are eighteen rows of scales. The scales are often described as looking similar to shingles on a roof. The weight of the scales and skin make up about 20 percent of the total body weight of most species. Scale color can be dark brown, dark olive-brown, pale olive, yellow-brown, or yellowish.

These animals have a small, pointed head that is smooth. Their eyes and ears are small. The tail is broad and long, ranging from 10 to 35 inches (26 to 88 centimeters). Limbs are short, small, and powerful. The front feet are longer and stronger than the hind feet. There are five curved claws on each foot.

Only the snout, chin, throat, neck, sides of the face, inner sides of the limbs, and the belly are not covered with scales. In some species the outer surface of the forelegs are also not covered. The parts of the body that are without scales are covered lightly with hair. The hairs of the scaleless areas are whitish, pale brown to reddish brown, or blackish. The skin is grayish with a blue or pink color in some areas. In the Asian species, there are both Asian and African species, there are three or four hairs at the base of each scale. The African species have no hair at the base of the scales.

In size, pangolins have a head and body length combined of 12 to 35 inches (30 to 90 centimeters). Females are generally smaller than males.

These animals have no teeth. To grab food they have a long and muscular tongue, able to extend a great distance. In the smaller species, the tongue measures about 6 to 7 inches (16 to 18 centimeters). In larger species the tongue stretches about 16 inches (40 centimeters). The tongue is sticky and either round or flat, depending on the species.

GEOGRAPHIC RANGE

Pangolins are found in the tropical, hot and humid climate, and subtropical areas of Africa and Asia.

HABITAT

Pangolins live in a variety of habitats, including forests, thick bush, sandy areas, and open grasslands. Some species of pangolins are arboreal, live in trees, and shelter in tree hollows. Other species live on the land and stay in burrows, holes, dug either by other animals or themselves.

DIET

Pangolins eat almost exclusively on ants and termites. They snatch up individual insects, and also dig up entire ant hills and termite nests.

BEHAVIOR AND REPRODUCTION

Pangolins move about slowly and deliberately. They often walk only on their hind legs. The smaller species are classified as arboreal and the larger ones as living on the land. Some species can live both on the ground and in trees. Most of these animals climb well and some also swim. These animals are solitary or sometimes found in pairs.

When they feel threatened, pangolins can roll themselves into a ball to defend themselves. When they are in a rolled-up position, the sharp-edged scales act as armor, shielding any unprotected skin and warding away predators, animals that hunt them for food. Once they are rolled into a ball it is very difficult to unroll them. A pangolin has been observed curling itself into a ball and then rolling down a slope, traveling 98 feet (30 meters) in 10 seconds. Pangolins can also spray potential predators with a strong, foul smelling fluid that comes from the anal region.

Almost all pangolins are nocturnal, meaning they are active at night. Only one species is active during the day. The species that live on land use their powerful claws to make burrows and can make an 8-foot (2.4-meter) deep tunnel within three to five minutes. The arboreal pangolins use their long tails to balance and hang. Arboreal pangolins roll up in a ball in a tree hollow at night to sleep.

These animals have a well-developed sense of smell that they use to locate prey, animals hunted for food. In general, they have poor eyesight. As pangolins do not have teeth, they grab the prey with their long sticky tongue. They use their front claws to tear open anthills or termite mounds. The food enters their stomach whole, and is broken apart in the lower area of the stomach. All species drink water frequently, and lap it up by rapidly darting out their tongue.

DINNER AROMA

Pangolins are picky eaters and they depend upon their well-developed sense of smell to locate their preferred foods. Each animal produces a specific smell. One report found that pangolins appear to eat only nineteen species of ants and termites. They especially favor formacid ants, a family of ants that includes fire ants and harvester ants.

Most pangolins are born between November and May, although findings have suggested that some pangolins can breed throughout the year. Gestation, length of pregnancy, is approximately 120 to 150 days. Generally, female pangolins have a single offspring. At the time of birth, scales are soft, flexible and do not overlap, but they harden after two days. Young pangolins can walk soon after birth. Offspring are carried on the mother's tail or back. A threatened mother will fold her tail and keep her baby under her body. Male pangolins may also share a burrow with females and the young, a characteristic not common among most mammals.

Babies are nursed for three to four months, and they begin to eat termites at about one month. Young pangolins first eat insects they find between the mother's scales. At about five months old offspring become independent.

PANGOLINS AND PEOPLE

People hunt and kill pangolins for several reasons. These animals are considered a delicacy and eaten as food in parts of Africa. They are also believed to hold magical powers. The scales are made into a ring as a charm against rheumatic fever, a disease that can damage the heart, and it used to treat other diseases. Certain groups of people mix the scales with bark from certain trees because it is believed to ward off witchcraft and evil spirits. Sometimes the scales are burned to keep wild animals away. Some tribes believe that pangolins flesh has aphrodisiac, enhancing sexual desire, values. And in certain areas, pangolins are sacrificed for rainmaking ceremonies.

CONSERVATION STATUS

Four species of pangolins are listed as Near Threatened, not currently threatened, but could become so, in the World Conservation Union (IUCN) Red List. Deforestation, the clearing of forests, has destroyed these animals natural habitat and caused a decrease in their population. In many areas, pangolins are legally protected animals. Aside from humans, leopards, lions, and tigers, are the main predatory threat of pangolins.

Ground pangolin (*Manis temminckii*)

GROUND PANGOLIN
Manis temminckii

Physical characteristics: Ground pangolins, also called Cape pangolins, have a combined head and body length of 20 to 24 inches (50 to 60 centimeters), and a tail length that ranges from 14 to 20 inches (35 to 50 centimeters). They have no external ears. The body and tail of these animals are covered with scales that are a grayish brown to dark olive brown. The scales are sharp and moveable. Skin is whitish with fine, dark hairs. Specialized thick eyelids protect their small eyes.

These animals have hind feet with blunt claws that are padded, like those of an elephant. Their forefeet have large, digging claws. Males are generally larger than the females.

Geographic range: Ground pangolins are found in Africa, specifically from Chad and Sudan in central Africa, down through Kenya

Ground pangolins live in forests, thick brush, and grasslands. During the day these animals sleep in burrows that they dig. (© Nigel J. Dennis/Photo Researchers, Inc. Reproduced by permission.)

and Tanzania, to the northern parts of South Africa. The ground pangolin is the most common and most widely distributed pangolin in Kenya and Tanzania.

Habitat: Ground pangolins live in forests, thick brush, and grasslands. They live in areas with both high and low rainfall amounts.

Diet: Ground pangolins feed on certain species of termites and ants. They tear open termite mounds and anthills, both on the ground and in trees.

Behavior and reproduction: This nocturnal species lives on the land, yet occasionally climbs trees and bushes. Ground pangolins can move quickly, up to 160 feet (50 meters) per minute. They often do move slowly, walking on the hind legs. They keep their body horizontal to the ground when moving, using their tail for balance as it drags behind them. During the day these animals sleep in burrows that they dig.

Ground pangolins locate prey by smell and feed frequently—about ninety times every night. Pangolins are known to crack pieces of termite-infested wood across their chests to get to their prey. They also scratch in animal droppings for ants. When the baby is two to four weeks old the mother will carry it around on her back or tail. Offspring will feed by themselves at about three months old.

Ground pangolins and people: The pangolins are prized for the supposed medicinal properties of their various body parts.

Conservation status: The IUCN lists ground pangolins as Near Threatened. ■

FOR MORE INFORMATION

Books:

Clutton-Brock, Juliet, and Don E. Wilson, ed. *Smithsonian Handbooks: Mammals.* New York: Dorling Kindersley Publishing, 2002.

Jordan, E. L. *Animal Atlas of the World.* Maplewood, NJ: Hammond Incorporated, 1969.

Macdonald, David, ed. *The Encyclopedia of Mammals.* New York: Facts on File Publications, 1984.

Nowak, Ronald M. *Walker's Mammals of the World,* 5th ed. Baltimore and London: The Johns Hopkins University Press, 1991.

Periodicals:

"Pangolins in Profile." *Asia Africa Intelligence Wire* (August 4, 2002).

"Wildlife Markets and Disease Transmission: The Problem Is, Pigs Do Fly." *Life Science Weekly* (July 28, 2003): 24.

Wise, Jeff. "Get Your Pangolins Here." *Esquire* (July 1994): 30.

Web sites:

Myers, Phil. "Pholidota." Animal Diversity Web. http://animaldiversity. ummz.umich.edu/site/accounts/information/Pholidota.html (accessed on May 22, 2004).

"Pangolin or Scaly Anteater." NepalNet. http://www.panasia.org.sg/ nepalnet/ecology/pangolin.htm (accessed on May 22, 2004).

"Pangolin, Temnick's ground." U.S. Fish and Wildlife Service. http:// ecos.fws.gov/species_profile/SpeciesProfile?spcode=A060 (accessed on May 22, 2004).

"Pholidota." American Zoo. http://www.americazoo.com/goto/index/ mammals/pholidota.htm (accessed on May 22, 2004).

"Wildlives: African Animals." African Wildlife Foundation. http://www. awf.org/wildlives/178 (accessed on May 5, 2004).

RODENTS

Rodentia

Class: Mammalia

Order: Rodentia

Number of families: 28 families

order

PHYSICAL CHARACTERISTICS

Rodents make up the largest group of mammals, representing approximately 43 percent of all mammalian species. Families in the order Rodentia include rats, mice, porcupines, hamsters, beavers, squirrels, chipmunks, lemmings, muskrats, and guinea pigs (rabbits are not rodents). These families range in size from the pygmy mice, which are 4.7 inches long (12 centimeters) and weigh 0.1 ounces (4 grams), to the capybara, which is 39.4 inches long (100 centimeters) and can weigh 110 pounds (50 kilograms). Most rodents are relatively small animals, such as mice, rats, and squirrels.

While there is a broad range of characteristics among the families, the feature that sets rodents apart from other family members is their teeth. Rodents have one pair of upper incisors (the chisel-shaped teeth at the front of the mouth), and one pair of lower incisors. These teeth grow continually throughout their life. The outer surfaces of the incisors have a thick enamel (hard white substance) layer. Behind the incisors is a large gap in the tooth rows. There are no canines, spade-shaped teeth located next to the incisors. Typically there are only a few molars at the rear of the jaws. The number of teeth rarely is more than twenty-two.

The name Rodentia comes from the Latin verb *rodere* meaning to gnaw, a name suitable for a rodent that is constantly gnawing! Rodents' incisor teeth grow throughout their life and they grind their incisor teeth together to wear them down. If for some reason the rodent is unable to wear its incisors down, the tips may grow past each other and continue to grow outward into spiral. This may result in the upper teeth piercing the roof of the mouth, and the lower teeth growing upward in front of the nose, which could kill the animal.

In general, rodents have a compact body with short legs. They typically have four to five digits on each of the front feet and three to five digits on the rear feet. Generally, the sole of the foot is bare. Some rodents, such as hamsters and pocket gophers, have cheek pouches, which allow the animals to store and transport food. The tails of some rodent species break off when these animals are caught by the tail, which allows them to escape. The tail will partially grow back.

Other physical characteristics of rodents vary widely depending upon the species and where it lives. For example, rodents that live in the desert, such as American kangaroo rats, Australian hopping mice, and north African jerboas, have long, narrow hind legs and feet with a long tail used for hopping over the sandy desert floor. They all have well-developed hearing, small front limbs, and pale coloration. Animals that live in and around the water, such as the capybara and beaver, may have webbed or partially webbed feet and tails modified for swimming.

GEOGRAPHIC RANGE

Rodents are found in all parts of the world, including the Arctic tundra, desert, and oceanic islands. About 70 percent of all rodents are rats and mice, and these animals are found on every continent.

HABITAT

The habitats of rodents are varied and numerous, from arid (extremely dry) deserts to the arctic tundra. There are rodents that live predominantly underground, others that live on land, and others are primarily arboreal (living in trees). Some species spend most of their life in the water, while others live in the desert. Some live close to humans in urban areas and even houses, while others make their home deep inside wetlands and rainforests. Rodents can be found in almost every habitat and on every continent except Antarctica.

DIET

All the families of rodents eat a wide range of foods. Most rodents are herbivorous, plant eaters, eating a wide range of plant materials, including seeds, stems, leaves, roots, and flowers. Many of these species eat primarily seeds. Some species, such as the grasshopper mouse, eat insects and spiders. Other species, such as the Australian water rat, are primarily carnivorous (meat-eating), preying (eating animals for food) on small fish, frogs, and mollusks. Many are to some degree omnivorous, eating both plants and animals. Still others have highly specialized meals, eating only a few species of invertebrates, animals without a backbone, or fungi.

BEHAVIOR AND REPRODUCTION

Rodents show a wide range of lifestyles and habits, depending upon the family and species. There are rodents that form burrows (holes or tunnels), such as gophers and moles; those that live in trees, such as the commonly called flying squirrels; rodents that spend most of their time in water, such as the capybara; and those that are specialized to life in the desert, such as kangaroo rats and jerboas.

Many rodents are social animals, living in large groups and interacting with one another frequently. Prairie dogs, naked mole-rats, and ground squirrels all live in these large colonies (groups). Other rodents live in smaller colonies. The beaver lives in a colony made up of the adult male and female, and their offspring. Each colony lives in a specific territory.

The prairie dog, for example, lives in a set area that can contain hundreds of these small animals (they look similar to squirrels, not dogs). These colonies or towns are broken up into certain neighborhoods. The prairie dogs post guards, they baby-sit and they help build one another's homes. There is a great deal of playing, mutual grooming, and vocal communication among the prairie dogs.

Some rodents are solitary, such as porcupines, pocket gophers, and pocket mice. Many desert species are solitary. Some of these species that burrow, dig, will construct and live in their own burrow system. However, during the mating season there may be more than one individual, or a mother and her offspring may live together.

Most rodents are active throughout the year. Some species, such as ground squirrels, may hibernate for several months. Species communicate with one another using sounds, smells, and sights. For example, squeaks, grunts, and calls can be used as alarm calls in mating and when a parent is searching for its young.

Many rodents have large numbers of offspring, which is one of the primary reasons they make up the largest group of mammals. Rodent reproduction can be divided into two forms. One group of families has a short gestation (pregnancy) period, produces multiple litters per year, and has large numbers of helpless offspring. Gestation periods can range from seventeen to forty-five days and the number of litters can be up to four. Rodents in this group include mice, rats, and pocket gophers. The other group of families has longer gestation periods (60 to 238 days), fewer litters per year (generally one to two), and have a relatively fewer number of offspring.

The mating system of rodents depends upon the species. A few species of rodents are monogamous (muh-NAH-guh-mus), such as the Patagonian mara, which forms male-female pairs that can last for multiple mating seasons. Other species have a harem-based (HARE-um based) mating system, one male with a set group of females for the mating season. Many rodents are promiscuous (prah-MISS-kyoo-us), meaning they mate randomly.

RODENTS AND PEOPLE

Rodents play a vital role in the ecosystem. They serve as the prey for many animals and some animals will use their burrows for shelter and protection.

People have caused the loss of population of many species of rodents by destroying their natural habitat, harming them directly, or introducing species that prey on rodents. Many species of rodents are considered pests and even dangerous to humans. Rodents cost billions of dollars in lost crops each year, eating the grain stored during the winter and the seeds of plants. Beavers can cause destruction by damming up creeks, causing water to back up into areas where its not wanted.

Rats carried the fleas that caused the plagues of Europe. Rats and mice help spread other deadly diseases as well, such as bubonic (byoo-BON-ik) plague and typhus (TIE-fus).

THE APPEARANCE OF MODERN RATS

Fossils show that the first rodents began scampering about an estimated fifty-four million years ago in Asia and North America. These original rodents were themselves descendants of rodent-like ancestors called anagalids, which also gave rise to the rabbits. It was not until about five million years ago that the modern Muridae family of rodents came on the scene. The murids (MYOO-rids) now make up more than half of all rodent species, including rats, mice, and hamsters. These mammals have flourished due to multiple, large litters and their ability to adapt quickly to environmental changes.

Rodents are important as sources of food for many people. Roasted, stuffed, or fried guinea pig, for example, is a popular dish in Ecuador, Peru, and other South American countries. In many parts of the world they have an economical importance for their fur, such as the chinchilla of South America, a rodent almost extinct in the wild but thriving in captivity.

Rodents such as mice and rats are also used extensively in medical research because their bodily processes are similar to humans' and they have a rapid reproduction rate. They are used to study many diseases and test medicines. People also use these and other rodents, such as guinea pigs, to test the safety of cosmetic and human food products. Many people also keep the small and "cute" rodents as pets.

CONSERVATION STATUS

The IUCN lists 669 species of rodents under varying degrees of threat and endangerment (facing varying risks of extinction in the wild) as of 2004. There are 32 species that are listed as

Extinct (died out). Loss of habitats and the introduction of species are the two main reasons for the loss of populations.

FOR MORE INFORMATION

Books:

Clutton-Brock, Juliet, and Don E. Wilson, eds. *Smithsonian Handbooks: Mammals.* New York: Dorling Kindersley Publishing, 2002.

Jordan, E. L. *Animal Atlas of the World.* Maplewood, NJ: Hammond Incorporated, 1969.

Macdonald, David, ed. *The Encyclopedia of Mammals.* New York: Facts on File Publications, 1984.

Nowak, Ronald M. *Walker's Mammals of the World,* 5th ed. Baltimore and London: The Johns Hopkins University Press, 1991.

Nowak, Ronald M. "Order Rodentia." *Walker's Mammals of the World 5.1 Online.* Baltimore: Johns Hopkins University Press: 1997. http://www.press.jhu.edu/books/walkers_mammals_of_the_world/rodentia/rodentia.html (accessed on July 8, 2004).

Periodicals:

Adams, Jonathan. "A Nose for Trouble (trained rats)." *Newsweek International* (January 12, 2004): 42.

Dickson-Ramos, Holly. "The World's Largest Rodent." *Faces: People, Places, and Culture* (January 2004): 36.

Marchand, Peter J. "A Squirrel's Glide to a Long Life." *Natural History* 110, no. 8 (October 2001): 18.

Ostfeld, Richard S. "Little Loggers Make a Big Difference: The Tastes of Two Small Rodents—the Meadow Vole and the White-Footed Mouse—Can Determine What Trees Grow in a Forest." *Natural History* (May 2002): 64.

Travis, John. "Mining the Mouse: A Rodent's DNA Sheds Light on the Human Genome." *Science News* (February 22, 2003): 122.

"World's Largest Rodent Risks Extinction." *United Press International* (September 20, 2002): 1008263 .

Web sites:

Myers, P. "Order Rodentia (Rodents)." Animal Diversity Web. http://animaldiversity.ummz.umich.edu/site/accounts/information/Rodentia.html (accessed on July 8, 2004).

Davis, William B., and David J. Schmidly. "Order: Rodentia." *The Mammals of Texas—Online Edition.* http://www.nsrl.ttu.edu/tmot1/ordroden.htm (accessed on July 8, 2004).

Lockwood, Burleigh. "Order: Rodentia." The Chaffee Zoo. http://www.chaffeezoo.org/animals/rodentia.html (accessed on July 8, 2004).

"Introduction to the Rodentia." University of California Berkeley, Museum of Paleontology. http://www.ucmp.berkeley.edu/mammal/rodentia/rodentia.html (accessed on July 8, 2004).

"Rat and Mouse FAQs." The Rat & Mice Club of America. http://www.rmca.org/Resources/faqs.htm (accessed on July 8, 2004).

MOUNTAIN BEAVER

Aplodontidae

Class: Mammalia

Order: Rodentia

Family: Aplodontidae

One species: Mountain beaver
(*Aplodontia rufa*)

family

C H A P T E R

PHYSICAL CHARACTERISTICS

This animal is also commonly called sewellel, named after the Chinook (American Indian tribe) word for a robe made from its pelts. There is only one species of mountain beaver and they are not closely related to the true beaver. These animals are about the same size as a squirrel, with a head and body length of 14.3 inches (36 centimeters), and a tall length of approximately 1.2 inches (3 centimeters).

They have a thickset, heavy body and short limbs. Eyes and ears are small. The head is broad and relatively flat. The neck is short and thick. All the limbs have five well-developed claws. These animals appear nearly tail-less because the tail is so short. They have strong incisors (chisel-shaped teeth at the front of the mouth).

The fur on these animals is thick, short, and typically a grayish, dark brown or reddish brown color, with sparse guard hair, which are coarse hairs that form the outer fur. Lighter, thick fur lies underneath, which is called the underfur. Guard hairs protect the underfur. Its belly is a slightly paler color, a white or chestnut brown. There is a small white patch of short fur at the bottom of its ears.

GEOGRAPHIC RANGE

Mountain beavers are found in North America along the Pacific Coast. They live in southwestern British Columbia to northwestern California, in certain coastal areas as far south as San Francisco Bay, and in the Sierra Nevada of eastern California.

phylum

class

subclass

order

monotypic order

suborder

▲ **family**

HOST TO WORLD'S LARGEST FLEAS

The largest flea in the world, the rare *Hystricopsylla schefferi,* is known from collections plucked from mountain beavers and their burrows. These fleas can grow up to one-third of an inch (9 millimeters) in length!

HABITAT

Mountain beavers generally live in moist forests, especially near streams, which are dense with herbs and shrubs. They are found on mountains with deciduous forest to areas at sea level, and also in coniferous forests. Mountain beavers must live in places with deep soils so that they can burrow (dig holes or tunnels).

DIET

Mountain beavers are herbivores (plant-eaters) and feed on almost any plant material. These animals eat leaves, branches, bark, and twigs. They also drink large amounts of water.

BEHAVIOR AND REPRODUCTION

These animals spend much of their time along the banks of rivers and streams. They frequently wash themselves by dipping their front feet into the water and then scrubbing their body. These animals are strong swimmers.

Mountain beavers live alone or in small colonies. They may live in the same area as other mountain beavers that are sometimes referred to as colonies (groups). The concentration of these animals is most likely due to the fact that the colony sites make good habitats.

These animals have small home ranges, about 0.6 acres (0.25 hectares). Within this range mountain beavers build complex burrows with chambers for food storage, sleeping, and shelter. The burrows are long and close to the surface. The majority of a mountain beaver's time is spent in the underground burrows. They emerge only to forage or during the brief period of time when the young animals leave the nest to establish their own burrow sites. Other animals may also use their burrow system. The tunnels are cleaned and worked on regularly. If a tunnel is flooded by rain, the mountain beaver will swim in it.

Mountain beavers are primarily nocturnal, active at night. They are occasionally active for short periods of time during the daytime, especially in the autumn. When foraging for food, they seldom wander more than a few feet (meters) from their burrow. Although food is sometimes eaten above ground, it is generally brought to the burrow. It cuts off the plants desired

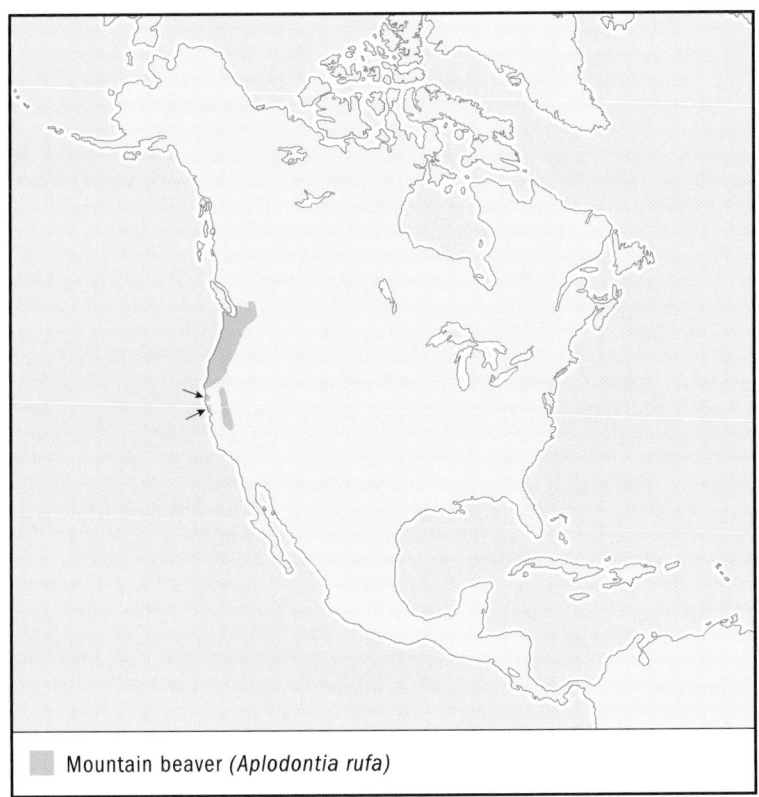

Mountain beaver *(Aplodontia rufa)*

and drags it to the mouth of the burrow. The food is placed over some logs or some rocks to wilt, then is either stored or eaten. It eats holding its food in its front feet like a raccoon.

While not a great climber, the mountain beaver climbs shrubs and small trees to cut off small limbs and twigs. It cuts off the branches as it climbs. Occasionally, it will let the small limbs and twigs drop to the ground. More typically, the mountain beaver will carry the wood down by climbing down the tree headfirst.

Mountain beavers do not hibernate (slow down their body temperature to conserve energy) and are active year round. In the cooler months they rarely appear above ground and at this time, eat supplies of stored food. In the winter when vegetation is sparse, the beavers will eat bark and small twigs.

Mountain beavers have a brief breeding season. Pregnant females have been collected from late February to early April. Gestation (length of pregnancy) typically lasts twenty-eight to thirty days. Females generally have one litter per year, bearing two or three offspring, and rarely four. Newborns' eyes are

Mountain beavers spend most of their time in their complex burrows, which have chambers for food storage, sleeping, and shelter. The burrows are long and close to the surface. (Joseph Van Wormer/Bruce Coleman Inc. Reproduced by permission.)

tightly closed and may not open fully until about fifty days later. After about eight weeks, offspring are nearly half-grown and able to leave the nest. Offspring reach sexual maturity late in the second year of life.

MOUNTAIN BEAVERS AND PEOPLE

Humans have caused this family to decrease in population by destroying its natural habitat through development and other activities. In the Pacific Northwest, mountain beavers are considered a pest by many foresters and gardeners because they eat seedlings and young trees. They can also cause damage to trees by peeling off the bark. To prevent damage to their crops and gardens, people may use herbicides (substance used to kill or control plants) and traps, factors that contribute to the decline of mountain beavers.

CONSERVATION STATUS

The World Conservation Union (IUCN) lists the mountain beaver as Near Threatened, not currently threatened, but could become so. Two of the seven subspecies of mountain beavers are listed as Vulnerable (facing a high risk of extinction in the wild) by the IUCN.

FOR MORE INFORMATION

Books:

Clutton-Brock, Juliet, and Don E. Wilson, eds. *Smithsonian Handbooks: Mammals.* New York: Dorling Kindersley Publishing, 2002.

Macdonald, David, ed. *The Encyclopedia of Mammals.* New York: Facts on File Publications, 1984.

Nowak, Ronald M. "Sewellel or Mountain Beaver." *Walker's Mammals of the World 5.1 Online.* Baltimore: Johns Hopkins University Press, 1997. http://www.press.jhu.edu/books/walkers_mammals_of_the_world/ rodentia/rodentia.aplodontidae.aplodontia.html (accessed on May 3, 2004).

Periodicals:

Drew, Lisa. "Creatures that Time Forgot." *National Wildlife* (June–July, 2002).

Valadka, Andrius. "Meet One of Nature's Survivors: The Mountain Beaver (*Aplodontia rufa*) is the World's Oldest Living Rodent." *Nature Canada* (Summer 1988): 6–7.

Web sites:

Newell, T. "*Aplodontia rufa.*" Animal Diversity Web. http://animaldiversity. ummz.umich.edu/site/accounts/information/Aplodontia_rufa.html (accessed on May 17, 2004).

Altig, Ron. "Mountain Beaver: *Aplodontia rufa.*" Enature.com. http://www. enature.com/fieldguide/showSpeciesSH.asp?curGroupID=5&shapeID=1 038&curPageNum=1&recnum=MA0073 (accessed on May 15, 2004).

Landes, Charles. "The Mountain Beaver (*Aplodontia*." Mount Rainier Nature News Notes (Nature Notes). http://www.nps.gov/mora/notes/ vol3-3a.htm (accessed on May 15, 2004).

"Lewis and Clark Expedition: Scientific Encounters." National Park Service. http://www.cr.nps.gov/nr/travel/lewisandclark/encounters.htm (accessed on May 13, 2004).

"Mountain Beaver." American Zoo. http://www.americazoo.com/goto/ index/mammals/139.htm (accessed on May 13, 2004).

CHAPTER

phylum

class

subclass

order

monotypic order

suborder

▲ family

PHYSICAL CHARACTERISTICS

Squirrels are some of the most familiar rodents. They are small to medium-sized animals with relatively long tails. Squirrels have five toes on the back feet and four on the front feet, with a well-developed claw on each digit. Eyes are relatively high on the head and spread apart to allow them a wide range of vision. Size, fur, shape, and tail features depend upon the type of squirrel. There are three general body forms in these animals: flying squirrels, ground squirrels, and tree squirrels.

Flying squirrels have large, bushy tails and bodies adapted for moving between trees. They are generally slim with long legs. A furred membrane, double layer of thin skin, extends between the wrist and ankle, which allows them to glide. They have large eyes. Their fur is soft and dense and is generally brown, gray, or blackish in color. The underside is a paler color.

Ground squirrels range widely in size. The marmots are the largest ground squirrels, with weights of up to 16.5 pounds (7.5 kilograms); the smallest are the American chipmunks, which weigh up to 5 ounces (142 grams). These squirrels are typically short legged with muscular bodies. Their tails are furry, but generally not as bushy as those of tree squirrels.

Tree squirrels have long, bushy tails, sharp claws and large ears. Some have well-developed ear tufts. Tree squirrels also range extensively in size, from the pygmy squirrels that is about the size of a mouse, to the fox squirrels that can measure 18 to 27 inches (46 to 69 centimeters). Their hind legs are extremely long and they have long curved claws. Their tails are almost as long as their bodies.

GEOGRAPHIC RANGE

Squirrels are found throughout the world, except in Australia, Madagascar, southern South America, and certain desert regions, such as in Egypt.

HABITAT

There are many types of flying squirrels found in south and southeast Asia, especially in tropical, hot and humid, forests. Some species live in northern temperate, not too hot or too cold, regions, up to the Arctic Circle.

Ground squirrels live in many different habitats, such as grassland, forests, meadows, and the arctic tundra. Chipmunks are the one type of ground squirrel that are often found in dense shrubs or closed forests.

Tree squirrels live in forests, woodlands, gardens, cities, and farmlands.

DIET

Most squirrels eat primarily plant materials. Tree squirrels and flying squirrels often eat nuts and seeds, and will occasionally also feed on fungi, eggs, insects, young birds, and small snakes. Ground squirrels also eat seeds, fruits, and nuts, but often have diets made up of large amounts of grasses and leafy materials.

BEHAVIOR AND REPRODUCTION

Most squirrels are active during the day, yet some species, such as all the flying squirrels, are nocturnal, active at night. Squirrels communicate by making shrill sounds. They also communicate by tail gestures, such as "flicking" the tail to indicate that another squirrel should go away. Most squirrels wrap their tail around themselves when resting. Squirrels build nests high in the trees called dreys, which are made of twigs and leaves. They line the inside of dreys with fur, feathers, or other soft material. The nest typically will have two exits. Squirrels also will build a nest called a den in the hollow of a tree.

Flying squirrels do not actually fly, as bats and birds do—they leap and glide. They leap from a high point, flattening their bodies and extending the legs widely, and then land at a lower point.

NEW TREES FROM FORGETFUL SQUIRRELS

For squirrels, a little forgetfulness can turn into a lot of trees. Every autumn, squirrels "squirrel away" numerous nuts. For example, it is estimated that each gray squirrel buries at least 1,000 nuts every fall, possibly as many as 10,000 nuts in one season. The squirrels can bury the nuts several inches deep. They locate their buried nuts by smell, and are able to find nuts buried under a foot or more of snow. But they can forget. It is estimated that millions of trees in the world are accidentally planted by squirrels that bury nuts and then forget where they hid them.

Some species can glide for as much as 1,476 feet (450 meters). The squirrels can even turn at a right angle to avoid a branch.

Ground squirrels make burrows, tunnels or holes, which they use to rest in during the heat of the day and escape predators, animals hunting them for food. Many of the ground squirrels hibernate, become inactive to conserve energy, for varying periods of time. Some squirrels can hibernate for up to nine months.

Tree squirrels are solitary animals, yet some African species travel in pairs or small groups. These squirrels build nests of leaves or needles in hollow trees or limbs. They are active and maneuver (mah-NOO-ver) easily in trees.

For ground squirrels, the breeding season follows shortly after hibernation. Some species will skip a year of breeding; others can reproduce more than once a year. Baby ground squirrels are generally born underground without fur. There are usually four in a liter. Flying squirrels typically give birth to small litters of one to two offspring, which are generally blind and naked at birth. Tree squirrels generally have a polygamous (puh-LIH-guh-mus) mating system, meaning the male and female can have more than one mate. Litter sizes vary, depending upon the habitat and food availability.

SQUIRRELS AND PEOPLE

People have hunted squirrels for their fur and meat, and for sport. While squirrels are generally considered playful and harmless creatures, these animals can destroy crops and some people consider them pests. Their burrows occasionally damage irrigation systems and can harm livestock, but these rodents also destroy undesirable weeds and insects. Some squirrels are also carriers of organisms that transmit human disease, such as the plague and Rocky mountain tick fever. People have caused a decline in many squirrel populations by destroying their habitats and hunting them.

CONSERVATION STATUS

The World Conservation Union (IUCN) lists two squirrel species as Critically Endangered, facing an extremely high risk of extinction in the wild; nine species as Endangered, facing a very high risk of extinction; twenty-six species as Vulnerable, facing a high risk of extinction in the wild; and thirty-four species as Near Threatened, not currently threatened, but could become so.

Southern flying squirrel (*Glaucomys volans*)

SOUTHERN FLYING SQUIRREL
Glaucomys volans

Physical characteristics: Southern flying squirrels are generally about 8 to 10 inches (20 to 25 centimeters) long, and have a black ring around their large eyes. They have gray fur with white bellies.

Geographic range: These squirrels are found in eastern Canada south through the eastern United States. Isolated populations stretch to Honduras.

Habitat: Southern flying squirrels live primarily in deciduous forests. They usually make their nests in tree hollows.

Diet: These squirrels eat nuts, seeds and berries. They will also eat bird eggs, bird nestlings, insects and occasionally dead mice.

A southern flying squirrel spreads its hands and feet, stretching the thin membrane that connects them to glide up to 80 yards (73 meters). (© Joe McDonald/Corbis. Reproduced by permission.)

Behavior and reproduction: Southern flying squirrels are nocturnal. These squirrels will form small groups in the winter and share a common nest to keep warm. They typically glide an estimated 20 to 30 feet (6 to 9 meters) from the top of one tree down to the trunk of another tree, though they may glide farther.

Southern flying squirrels mate in early spring and summer. Females give birth to two litters of two to seven offspring. Mothers will defend their young and move them to another nest if they are threatened.

Southern flying squirrels and people: These squirrels are considered gentle and are popular as pets.

Conservation status: Southern flying squirrels are not listed as threatened by the IUCN. They are generally common with some isolated populations threatened due to habitat loss. ■

Eastern chipmunk (*Tamias striatus*)

EASTERN CHIPMUNK
Tamias striatus

Physical characteristics: The largest of the chipmunks, eastern chipmunks are about 8.9 to 10.6 inches (22.5 to 26.8 centimeters) long. They have grayish to reddish brown fur, white fur on their bellies, and five stripes from the neck to their tail. Two of the stripes are white bordered by black stripes, and one black stripe is in the center. They also have light strips above and below their eyes, and pouched cheeks.

Geographic range: Eastern chipmunks are found in southeastern Canada and most of the northeastern United States, south to Mississippi and Virginia and west to North Dakota and Oklahoma.

Habitat: Eastern chipmunks generally live in open deciduous forests with rocks, logs, and stumps. They can also be found in more open, bushy areas.

Diet: Eastern chipmunks primarily eat nuts, acorns, seeds, mushrooms, fruits, berries, and corn. They also eat insects, bird eggs, snakes, snails and small mammals, such as young mice.

Behavior and reproduction: Eastern chipmunks construct elaborate burrow systems. They are solitary, prefer to burrow alone, except for offspring. In warmer months they spend much of their time gathering and storing large amounts of food—they can gather up to 165 acorns in a single day. These animals remain in their dens for the winter and sleep frequently. They wake up every few weeks to eat the food they have stored.

These chipmunks breed from late June to early July. Litter sizes average three to five offspring. In some areas a female may have a second litter. Offspring will come above ground five to seven weeks after birth.

Eastern chipmunks and people: There is no special connection between these chipmunks and people.

Conservation status: Eastern chipmunks are not considered threatened. ■

Black-tailed prairie dog (*Cynomys ludovicianus*)

BLACK-TAILED PRAIRIE DOG
Cynomys ludovicianus

Physical characteristics: Black-tailed prairie dogs have sharp teeth, a black-tipped tail, and are about 14 to 15.7 inches (35.5 to 39.8 centimeters) long. Their fur is brown, golden brown, or reddish brown, and whitish on the underside.

Geographic range: These prairie dogs are found in areas from Canada to Mexico. In Canada they are found in Saskatchewan; in the United States they live from Montana to eastern Nebraska, south to northern Mexico.

Habitat: Black-tailed prairie dogs live in open, flat and arid, extremely dry, grassy plains.

Black-tailed prairie dogs are very social, living together in underground burrows called "towns." (© George D. Lepp/Corbis. Reproduced by permission.)

Diet: These animals eat primarily leaves, stems, grass roots, weeds, and wildflowers. They will sometimes eat grasshoppers, beetles and other insects.

Behavior and reproduction: Black-tailed prairie dogs are extremely social. They dig a complex series of tunnels deep into the ground, which is called a town. Towns can spread over hundreds of acres and contain thousands of prairie dogs. They communicate to one another frequently, using yips, growls, chattering, barks and chirps.

Black-tailed prairie dogs have one litter a year. Breeding occurs from February to March. A month after mating, the female will have three to four offspring. Female prairie dogs are extremely protective of their young. They will often fight with other females to guard their territory and babies.

Black-tailed prairie dogs and people: Some farmers and ranchers consider black-tailed prairie dogs pests. Livestock can hurt a leg if they step into a prairie dog's burrow, and they may compete with livestock for food.

Conservation status: Black-tailed prairie dogs are listed as Near Threatened by the IUCN. ∎

Alpine marmot (*Marmota marmota*)

ALPINE MARMOT
Marmota marmota

Physical characteristics: Alpine marmots are relatively large with a head and body length of about 20 to 24 inches (50 to 60 centimeters). Their fur is thick and color varies from gray to yellow-brown to reddish. They have large heads; short, powerful legs; short, hairy tails; and a white bridge on their noses.

Geographic range: Alpine marmots are found in the French, Swiss and Italian Alps, South Germany, West Austria, the Carpathian mountains, and the Tatra Mountains. They have been introduced into the Pyrenees, east Austria, and Yugoslavia.

Habitat: These animals live in open mountainous grassland areas, at approximately 4,300 to 9,800 feet (1,300 to 3,000 meters).

The thumb of the alpine marmot has a nail instead of a claw to aid in digging. (© St. Meyers/ Okapia/Photo Researchers, Inc. Reproduced by permission.)

Diet: Alpine marmots feed primarily on a wide variety of vegetation, including grasses, flowers, bulbs and seeds. They may also eat insects, birds' eggs and occasionally each others' young.

Behavior and reproduction: Alpine marmots are social animals that form burrows. They live in family groups generally made up of an adult pair and their offspring from previous years. Colonies, groups, can be as small as two or three to as large as fifty, all living in one burrow system. During warmer weather they eat heavily, and then hibernate as a family from September to mid April or May. The last animal into the burrow, usually an adult male, plugs the entrance with hay and earth to keep the burrow warm and safe from predators. These animals have distinctive calls. One long whistle warns of a threat in the air, such as an eagle, while a series of whistles may warn of an approaching fox.

Female marmots are able to breed at the age of two. Breeding occurs once a year, a few days after they emerge from hibernation, but females do not typically reproduce as long as the offspring remain in the family group. Females have an average of three to four offspring.

Alpine marmots and people: Some people have long believed that alpine marmot fat rubbed into the skin could relieve arthritis. In Europe these animals have been a source of fur, meat, and fat for the last thousand years. The reliance of these animals for their food has decreased and some people consider them agricultural, farming, pests. They are also hunted for trophies in some areas, and hunting has caused the population of these animals to decline. Alpine marmots have become a symbol for the Alps.

Conservation status: Alpine marmots are not listed as a threatened species by the IUCN. ■

Gray squirrel (*Sciurus carolinensis*)

GRAY SQUIRREL
Sciurus carolinensis

Physical characteristics: Gray squirrels have a head and body length of 9.4 to 11.2 inches (24 to 29 centimeters). Fur color varies widely within the species, generally fur is black to pale gray with a white to pale gray belly. They have broad, bushy tails that are about the length of their head and body combined.

Geographic range: Gray squirrels are found in eastern and central United States, reaching southern Canada in the north. They have also been introduced into Texas, California, Quebec, Vancouver Island, and South Africa.

Habitat: Gray squirrels prefer forests and woodlands but they are often seen in urban parks and yards.

Diet: Gray squirrels eat primarily tree seeds and nuts, including acorns, hickory nuts, beechnuts, and butternuts. They also feed on berries, mushrooms, buds, and flowers.

The eastern gray squirrel, despite its name, can be colored gray or black. (© M. H. Sharp/Photo Researchers, Inc. Reproduced by permission.)

Behavior and reproduction: Gray squirrels climb and jump well. They are considered solitary. They have well-developed senses of sight, smell, and hearing and are alert, especially on the ground. They are active year round, sheltering in tree hollows during the winter months. In the fall, gray squirrels gather and bury, at random, a winter food supply. When food is needed, these squirrels sniff the ground to recover their supply.

Gray squirrels have two breeding peaks during the year, generally December to February and May to June. After a forty-four–day gestation period, females give birth to a litter of two to seven young. Offspring are blind and helpless at birth, becoming somewhat independent at eight to ten weeks old.

Gray squirrels and people: These squirrels are hunted for sport and food. They are considered attractive and enjoyable for many park visitors. For homeowners, these squirrels may enter their homes for shelter, dig up their gardens, or eat the seeds in their bird-feeders. They are also considered a pest in areas where they damage the trees by stripping them of bark.

Conservation status: Gray squirrels are not considered threatened by the IUCN. ■

FOR MORE INFORMATION

Books:

Clutton-Brock, Juliet, and Don E. Wilson, eds. *Smithsonian Handbooks: Mammals.* New York: Dorling Kindersley Publishing, 2002.

Macdonald, David, ed. *The Encyclopedia of Mammals.* New York: Facts on File Publications, 1984.

Periodicals:

Cohen, Jonathan. "Squirreley Fun." *Ranger Rick* (December 2001): 10.

Marchand , Peter J. "A Squirrel's Glide to a Long Life ." *Natural History* (October 2001): 18–19.

McMahan, Kim Hone. "Outwit, Baffle Squirrels ." *Knight Ridder/Tribune News Service* (June 5, 2003): K6208.

Nowak, Ronald M. "Squirrels, Chipmunks, Marmots, and Prairie Dogs." *Walker's Mammals of the World Online 5.1.* Baltimore: Johns Hopkins

University Press, 1997. http://www.press.jhu.edu/books/walkers_
mammals_of_the_world/rodentia/rodentia.sciuridae.html (accessed on
June 2, 2004).

Phillips, John E. "Calling All Squirrels: Get Vocal to Grab More Bushy-
tails." *Outdoor Life* (August 1, 2003): 89.

Tangley, Laura. "News of the Wild (Ground Squirrels Warning System)."
National Wildlife (August–September, 2002).

Web sites:

Jansa, S., and P. Myers. "Family Sciuridae." Animal Diversity Web. http://
animaldiversity.ummz.umich.edu/site/accounts/information/Sciuridae.
html (accessed on June 2, 2004).

"The Life of Mammals." BBC: Science and Nature: Animals.
http://www.bbc.co.uk/nature/animals/mammals (accessed on June 2,
2004).

"Mammal Guide." Animal Planet. http://animal.discovery.com/guides/
mammals/habitat/alpine/alpmarmot.html (accessed on June 1, 2004).

"Mammals." Canadian Museum of Nature. http://nature.ca/note-
books/english/mon2.htm (accessed on June 2, 2004).

"Sciuridae." Discover Life. http://www.discoverlife.org/nh/tx/Vertebrata/
Mammalia/Sciuridae/ (accessed on June 2, 2004).

The Squirrel Place. http://www.squirrels.org/ (accessed on June 2,
2004).

BEAVERS
Castoridae

Class: Mammalia
Order: Rodentia
Family: Castoridae
Number of species: 2 species

family

CHAPTER

PHYSICAL CHARACTERISTICS

Beavers are among the largest of the rodents. They have a combined head and body length of 31 to 58 inches (80 to 140 centimeters). The flat, paddle-like tail is about 9.8 to 17.7 inches (25 to 45 centimeters) long. The tail is broad and scaly. A typical beaver can weigh 33 to 75 pounds (15 to 33 kilograms), with a few beavers weighing in at 100 pounds (45 kilograms). Males and females are similar in size.

Beavers' bodies are stocky with short limbs. Each limb has five clawed digits. The back feet, which are larger than the front, are webbed. The claws on the hind feet's first and second toes are split, appearing as a double claw. They have long, curved incisors, chisel-shaped teeth at the front of the mouth, that are an orange-brown color. The incisors grow continuously.

Their eyes are small and their ears are short. Their ears are set far back on their heads, which are broad and rounded. Beavers can close both their ears and nostrils when underwater. Beavers have a skin fold inside their mouths, which allows them to grasp onto items in their teeth without water entering their throat.

Beavers' fur is dense, made up of a fine coat of soft fur, called underfur, beneath long guard hairs, coarse hairs that form the outer fur and protect the underfur. The short underfur helps the beaver with water shedding and insulation. Fur color is a glossy yellowish brown to black. Their bellies are slightly paler in color, ranging from a brown to yellowish brown. The tail and feet are black.

The family name "Castoridae" refers to beavers' castor glands, or "castors." A gland is a group of special cells that make substances so that other parts of the body can work. This pair of glands, along with a pair of anal glands, releases a pungent, musky odor. Both sets of glands lie at the base of the tail.

GEOGRAPHIC RANGE

Beavers are found in North America, northern Europe, and northern Asia. After a decrease in population, these animals have been reintroduced to Russia, Scandinavia, and Argentina. They are also found in Chile.

HABITAT

Beavers live primarily along streams, ponds, lakes, swamps and other waterways, in areas where they can build dams. They are found mainly in areas with a year-round water flow, but are found occasionally in roadside ditches, drainage ditches, and sewage ponds. They are have also become more common in urban areas.

DIET

Beavers feed primarily on the bark and outer layers of deciduous trees such as birch, willow, alder, sweet gum, magnolia, maple, and dogwood. They eat twigs, leaves, and roots of trees and shrubs. They also eat various parts of aquatic plants, especially the young shoots of water lilies. During the warmer months, they may add grasses, corn, and other plants to their diet.

BEHAVIOR AND REPRODUCTION

Beavers are generally nocturnal, active at night. They are active year round. These animals are semiaquatic, living partly on land and partly in water, and are graceful moving about in water. They use their webbed feet and paddle-like tails to swim.

Beavers are hard workers and are considered the engineers of the animal kingdom because of the complex dams and lodges they build. Dams can be extensive, reaching over 10 feet (3 meters) high and stretching hundreds of feet long. A typical dam is 65 to 98 feet (20 to 30 meters) long. Mud and stones may set the foundation, base, for the dam. Brush and poles are added with the butt ends facing upstream, and mud, stones, and soggy vegetation are used as plaster on top of the poles. A dam is built higher than the water level. With maintenance and upkeep,

COUSINS TO A MAMMOTH

Today's beaver had a mega cousin that lived millions of years ago and was one of the largest rodents ever known. The giant beaver was estimated at 7 to 8 feet (2.1 to 2.4 meters) long and weighed 450 to 700 pounds (204 to 318 kilograms). The giant beaver roamed North American marshlands until about 10,000 years ago, when they disappeared. The giant beaver ate plant materials and spent a lot of time in the water. Unlike today's beavers, giant beavers had ridged cutting teeth and did not build dams. Fossil evidence of the giant beaver ranges from Florida to northern Canada.

dams are used by several generations of beavers.

Beavers may create multiple homes in their territory. Homes can take the form of a burrow, hole or tunnel, along a bank to make a den, or a wood lodge. Built of sticks and mud, the dome-shaped lodge is generally surrounded by the water backed up by the dam. The lodge may eventually reach more than 6.6 feet (2 meters) above the surface of the water. Each home may have several underwater entrances, which must reach below the winter ice. In some areas, especially near large rivers, beavers dig complex dens instead of building lodges. Burrows also may have underwater entrances that lead to the dry areas.

Beavers live in colonies, groups, of four to eight related individuals. Generally, the colony consists of a mated pair of adults and young that are less than two years old. There is usually only a single breeding female in a colony. A single beaver colony sometimes maintains several dams to control water flow.

The oil that beavers' glands produce is used to mark their territory. This oil is also used to grease the beaver's fur coat to make it water repellent. Constant grooming and this oil keeps beavers' fur waterproof. It uses its second claw on its hind feet for grooming. Males and females display territorial behavior and will fight trespassing beavers. Communication is through postures, scent marking, tail slapping, and vocalizations, including a whistling or whining call.

In the winter, beavers anchor sticks and logs underwater to feed on during winter. If their pond freezes over, they swim beneath the ice and feed on previously stored food. The senses of hearing, smell, and touch are well developed.

Beavers usually mate for life and are monogamous, have one mate. If one of the pair dies, the beaver may then find another mate. Females are dominant. Mating takes place once a year from January to March. Gestation, pregnancy, is 100 to 110 days. Females generally have three to four offspring, called kits, but can have anywhere from one to nine. Offspring generally will nurse for two to three months.

BEAVERS AND PEOPLE

Beavers were once common throughout Europe, Asia, and North America before people began hunting them for their thick, glossy pelts, fur. People used these pelts for coats and hats. People also dined on beaver and used the scents produced by their castor glands for perfume. In Europe, beavers were almost hunted to extinction, no longer existing, by 1860 C.E.

Beavers also can affect the water flow of an ecosystem. By constructing dams and burrowing into banks, they increase the wetland area and overall growth in an area. This helps organisms around the area flourish. For people, beaver's altering of a landscape can be a nuisance. Damming can flood roads, crops, and homes.

CONSERVATION STATUS

Populations of beavers, once extremely low, are gaining in numbers. The Eurasian beaver is listed as Near Threatened, not currently threatened, but could become so, by the World Conservation Union (IUCN).

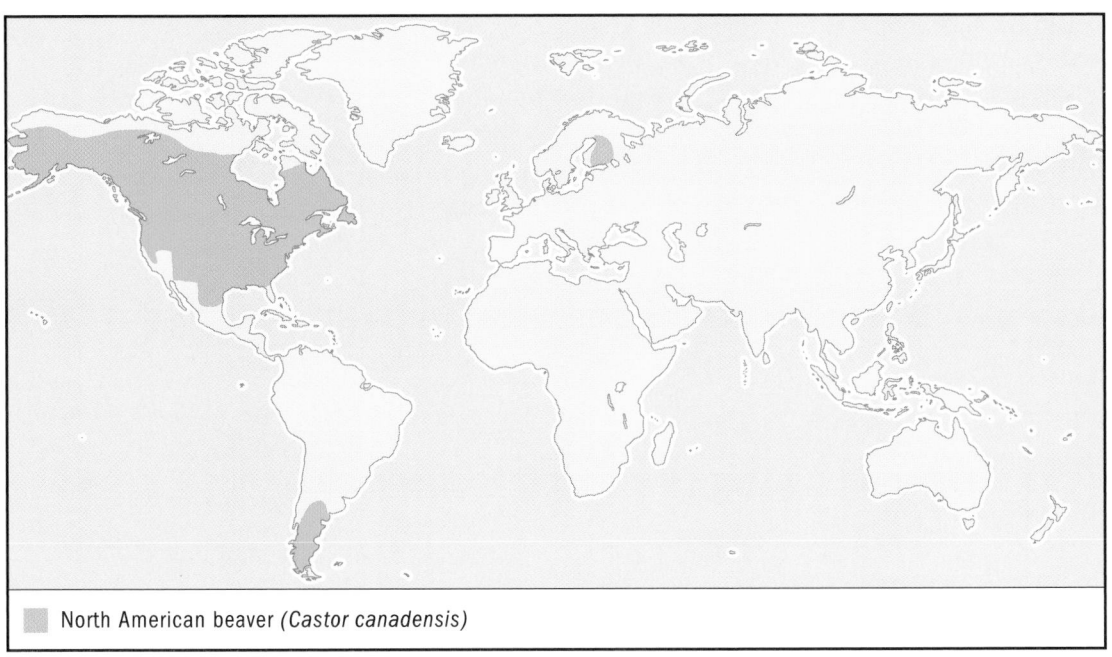

North American beaver (Castor canadensis)

NORTH AMERICAN BEAVER
Castor canadensis

Physical characteristics: Also commonly called simply the American beaver, the North American beaver weighs from 33 to 75 pounds (15 to 35 kilograms). They have yellowish brown to black fur.

Geographic range: North American beavers are found in Alaska, Canada, throughout the continental United States, and the extreme northern areas of Mexico. These animals are not found in desert regions or southern Florida. They have also been introduced in Finland, Russia, and Argentina.

Habitat: Like all beavers, the North American beaver is aquatic and lives near water in the form of a pond, stream, lake, or river.

Diet: North American beavers eat a variety of plant material. They prefer the cambium, the soft layer between the wood and bark, and leaves of trees such as aspen, birch, aspen, willow, cottonwood, and alder. Their diet also can include aquatic plants, such as pond weeds, water-lilies, and cattails. North American beavers also eat grasses, shrubs, and herbs.

Behavior and reproduction: North American beavers build more extensive dams that alter the landscape than their European counterparts. They are primarily nocturnal but are also frequently active during the day. As the weather gets cooler, beavers stockpile food for the winter by storing it underwater in their lodge or den. When they are able to break through the winter ice, these animals continue to cut down trees. In the northern areas, this underwater food storage may be the beaver's main food supply for months. In the southern areas, beavers are more active year around.

North American beavers and people: North American beavers are part of Native American myths. An Apache myth says that beavers have the magic of the medicine men. Beavers have played an integral role in the development of the United States and Canada. These animals were highly valued for the pelts. The beaver pelt became a unit of currency in colonial times, often leading to fights over trapping territories. The potential for profit, money, encouraged trappers to continue to move west, and settlers soon followed the trappers. Beavers were hunted so intensively throughout North America that the population was reduced by 90 percent by the late twentieth century.

North American beavers eat mostly cellulose, which is broken down by microorganisms in their cecum (SEE-kum), a part of the digestive system. (© Phil Schermeister/Corbis. Reproduced by permission.)

Altering its environment with dams and the creation of ponds benefits the beaver's ecosystem. The ponds help control runoff and help the fish and other organisms flourish. There are over fifty species of animals that live in beaver ponds. The damming of streams raises the level of the water. This causes the tree species that cannot survive in permanently wet soil to die, allowing for the spread of other species. Some people consider these animals a pest. The cutting of trees can damage crops and timber. Their creation of dams can cause flooding that can also harm woodlands and farms.

Conservation status: The IUCN does not list the North American beaver as a threatened species. ■

FOR MORE INFORMATION

Books:

Clutton-Brock, Juliet, and Don E. Wilson, eds. *Smithsonian Handbooks: Mammals.* New York: Dorling Kindersley Publishing, 2002.

Macdonald, David, ed. *The Encyclopedia of Mammals.* New York: Facts on File Publications, 1984.

Nowak, Ronald M. *Walker's Mammals of the World,* 5th ed. Baltimore and London: The Johns Hopkins University Press, 1991.

Periodicals:

Hair, Marty. "Busy Beavers Work to Build Homes." *Knight Ridder/Tribune News Service* (February 26, 2004): K5424.

Stewart, Doug. "I'll Be Dammed! Once Nearly Extinct, Beavers are Making a Comeback—Sometimes a Little Too Close to Home." *Time* (March 29, 2004): 42–43

Wilkinson, Todd. "The Benefits of Beavers." *National Parks* (January–February 2003): 30–32

Web sites:

Lindsey, Donald W., and Christy Brecht. "American Beaver." Discover Life. http://www.discoverlife.org/nh/tx/Vertebrata/Mammalia/Castoridae/Castor/canadensis/ (accessed on June 1, 2004).

Myers, P. "Castoridae." Animal Diversity Web. http://animaldiversity.ummz.umich.edu/site/accounts/information/Castoridae.html (accessed on June 1, 2004).

"North American Beaver, Canadian Beaver." BBC Science & Nature: Animals. http://www.bbc.co.uk/nature/wildfacts/factfiles/615.shtml (accessed on June 1, 2004).

"Rodents: Castorida." Animals Online. http://www.animals-online.be/rodents/bevers/european_beaver.html (accessed on June 1, 2004).

POCKET GOPHERS

Geomyidae

Class: Mammalia

Order: Rodentia

Family: Geomyidae

Number of species: 36 species

family

CHAPTER

PHYSICAL CHARACTERISTICS

Pocket gophers have stout, heavy set bodies that have a tube-like shape. The length of their bodies varies depending upon the species from 5 to 14 inches (13 to 36 centimeters). Males are generally larger than females. Their legs are relatively short and powerful. The five claws on their thick front legs are long, sharp, and curved. The third claw is the longest. Their hands are broad.

The pocket gopher does not appear to have a neck. They have short, almost hairless tails, which are extremely sensitive to the touch. Eyes and ears are small, and surrounded by numerous hairs that prevent soil from getting in. They have large and sharp incisors, chisel-shaped teeth at the front of the mouth. They also have whiskers that extend from their nose.

The "pocket" part of their name refers to fur-lined pouches, one on each side of their mouth, in which they carry food. The name gopher comes from the French word *gaufre* meaning waffle or honeycomb, and refers to the network of passages that it digs. The pouches open into the mouth and extend from the mouth region back to the shoulders. When filled with food, the pouches make the pocket gopher's head appear almost twice its size. Pocket gophers can turn these pouches inside out for cleaning.

Pocket gophers have loose and flexible skin. The skin is thick around the head and throat. Fur color varies widely, even within a species. The color generally matches the color of freshly turned soil, a light brown to almost black. Fur is generally soft, and is short in species living in hot environments.

GEOGRAPHIC RANGE

Pocket gophers are found in North America and extend into Central America. They are found from southern Canada through western North America, southward to northwestern Colombia in South America. One species occurs in the southeastern United States, in Alabama, Georgia, and Florida.

HABITAT

Pocket gophers live in almost any area that has soil that they can dig. They are found in meadows, forests, deserts, rainforests, and fields, from dry, extremely hot, climates at sea level to extremely cold climates in mountainous areas. They do not travel far, and occur in isolated areas. They spend most of their lives underground, though they surface at times to gather food. In certain parts of the country, the older animals may move to moister areas during dry periods.

DIET

Pocket gophers are herbivores, plant eaters. These animals feed primarily on the underground parts of plants, especially the roots, bulbs, and tubers. They also cut stems and carry them in their cheek pouches to their storage chambers.

BEHAVIOR AND REPRODUCTION

Pocket gophers are rarely seen because they spend almost their entire lives underground. Also, these animals are generally crepuscular (kri-PUS-kyuh-lur), active at dawn and dusk, and some are nocturnal, active at night. Pocket gophers do not hibernate, go into a resting state to conserve energy, and in general, are active year round.

These animals forage, look for food, through the ground, burrowing, or digging, a set of complex tunnels. Where the digging is easy, pocket gophers are able to tunnel as much as 200 to 300 feet (61 to 91 meters) in a single night. They dig primarily with their powerful front claws. They use their upper incisors to cut roots and loosen soil and rocks. They use their sensitive tail and whiskers to feel their way around in the dark.

Pocket gophers generally dig two kinds of tunnels. One type of tunnel is long, winding, and shallow. They use this type to get food from above. The second type of tunnel is deeper. They use these tunnels for shelter, with chambers for nests, food storage, and fecal, waste, deposits. The tunnels are usually marked above ground by small mounds of earth. When not in use, these animals plug up burrow entrances with dirt. Pocket gophers can run backward in their burrows almost as fast as they can run forward. Burrows may be occupied by the same animal for several years and spread over an acre (0.4 hectares) of ground.

Pocket gophers are extremely unsocial. They live alone in their burrow system. When one pocket gopher meets another, they squeal and hiss at one another, and their teeth chatter. They may fight violently. One is often killed in the fight.

The only time pocket gophers spend time with others of their species is during the mating season. Generally in the spring, the male leaves his den and briefly goes into the burrow of a female. Pocket gophers typically breed only once per year, although some species are capable of breeding in the spring and fall. Gestation, pregnancy, ranges from eighteen to more than thirty days, with the smaller species having the lower gestation times. Litter size varies from one to ten offspring. Until they are five weeks old the babies' eyes and ears are sealed shut. Offspring stay with the mother in the burrow for one to two months, and then each sets off to burrow its own system of tunnels.

POCKET GOPHERS AND CHEWING LICE

Studies have shown that relationships among species of pocket gophers mirror relationships among species of chewing lice, suggesting they have a long history of living together. Lice are small organisms that live, grow, and eat on other organisms. When pocket gophers mate, the lice on one gopher can jump to the other gopher to mate with the lice infesting it. Since pocket gophers mate only with their own species, the lice are limited to mating with other lice that live on that same species of pocket gopher. In this way, as pocket gophers formed separate species, the lice that live on them are also likely to form separate species.

POCKET GOPHERS AND PEOPLE

Pocket gophers play an important role in the ecosystem in which they live. They loosen and enrich the soil when they burrow. The occupied or abandoned burrows of these rodents are used extensively by other animals for shelter or foraging.

Some people consider these animals to be pests. In some areas, a single pocket gopher can destroy a family garden in less than a month. Their burrows can harm agricultural fields, causing extensive crop damage. They can consume a great deal of the underground parts of plants. Commercial farmers may trap and poison pocket gophers. Humans have also destroyed or altered these animals natural habitat, causing a decline in the population of some of these species. Some people in Latin America consider the meat of the pocket gopher to be a delicacy, luxury.

CONSERVATION STATUS

The World Conservation Union (IUCN) lists fifteen species of pocket gophers as threatened. The Oaxacan (wah-HAH-kan) pocket gopher and Querétaro pocket gopher are listed as Critically Endangered, facing an extremely high risk of extinction. The Michoacan pocket gopher is considered Endangered, facing a high risk of extinction.

Valley pocket gopher *(Thomomys bottae)*

VALLEY POCKET GOPHER
Thomomys bottae

Physical characteristics: The valley pocket gopher is also commonly know as Botta's pocket gopher, smooth-toothed pocket gopher, and western pocket gopher. Valley pocket gophers have a combined head and body length of 6 to 13 inches (15 to 33 centimeters). Claws on their front feet are relatively small. Fur color varies among individuals, ranging from pale gray to reddish brown to black. The belly is grayish white, white, light yellowish brown, or mottled, splotched. An identifying characteristic of these animals is a single indistinct groove on each incisor.

Geographic range: Valley pocket gophers are found in the western United States into northern Mexico. They can live at altitudes from sea level to 10,000 feet (3,000 meters).

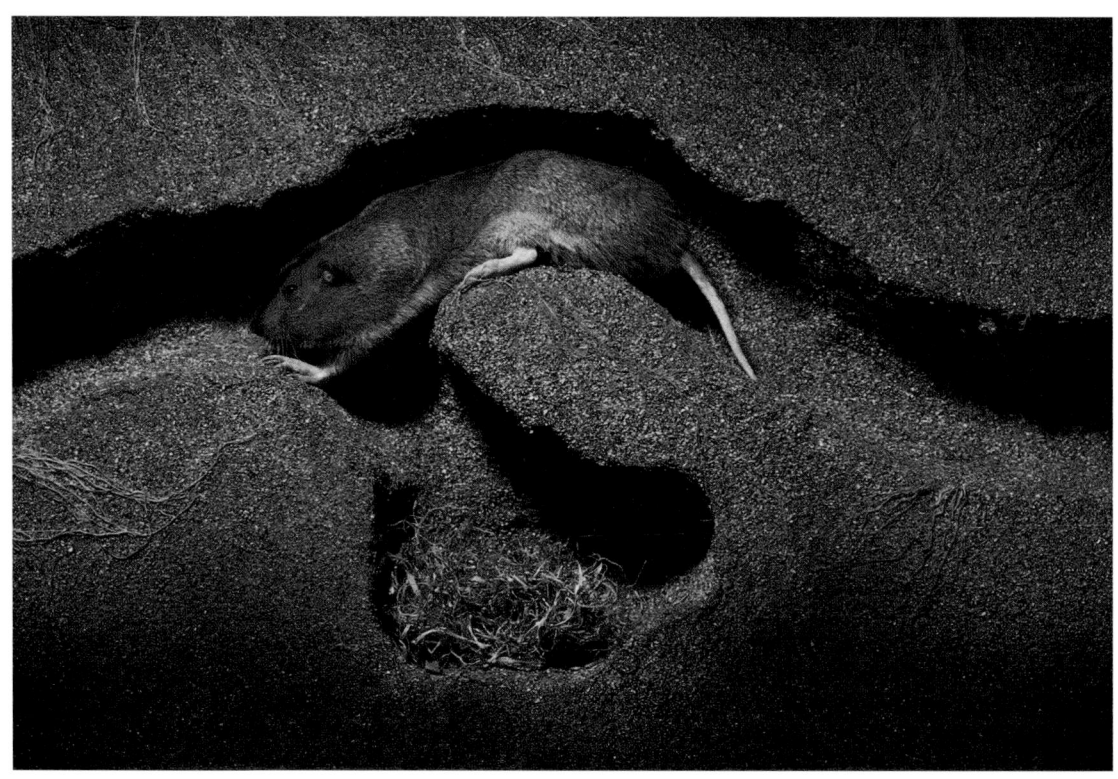

Valley pocket gophers spend 90 percent of their time below ground. By the roots, they can pull entire plants underground into their burrows. (© Tom McHugh/Photo Researchers, Inc. Reproduced by permission.)

Habitat: These animals can live in a wide range of habitats. They occur in soils ranging from loose sands to tight clays, and in dry deserts to mountainous meadows. They commonly live in valleys, woodlands, deserts, and agricultural fields.

Diet: Valley pocket gophers feed on below ground plants such as roots and tubers. They especially like the roots of alfalfa. From its root, pocket gophers can pull the entire plant into its burrow to eat or store the food. They will also come to the surface to feed and clip off vegetation near the entrance of their burrow.

Behavior and reproduction: Valley pocket gophers are solitary animals that are active throughout the year. They burrow a system of tunnels and spend about 90 percent of their time below ground.

During the breeding season males will briefly join females in their burrows. The main breeding season is in spring, however these animals will sometimes breed in the fall also. Females generally bear two to four offspring per litter.

Valley pocket gophers and people: Farmers and gardeners may consider these animals pests. Valley pocket gophers can be destructive to plants, and people will trap or poison them. Yet the burrowing activity of these animals cultivates the soil, and vegetation and many organisms are dependent upon their continued activity.

Conservation status: This species is not listed as threatened by the IUCN. ■

FOR MORE INFORMATION

Books:

Clutton-Brock, Juliet, and Don E. Wilson, ed. consultants. *Smithsonian Handbooks: Mammals.* New York: Dorling Kindersley Publishing, 2002.

Macdonald, David, ed. *The Encyclopedia of Mammals.* New York: Facts on File Publications, 1984.

Nowak, Ronald M. *Walker's Mammals of the World,* 5th ed. Baltimore and London: The Johns Hopkins University Press, 1991.

Nowak, Ronald M. "Pocket Gophers." *Walker's Mammals of the World Online 5.1.* Baltimore: Johns Hopkins University Press, 1997. http://www.press.jhu.edu/books/walkers_mammals_of_the_world/ rodentia/rodentia.geomyidae.html (accessed on July 7, 2004).

Periodicals:

Benedix, J. H. Jr. "A Predictable Pattern of Daily Activity by the Pocket Gopher *Geomys bursarius.*" *Animal Behaviour* (September 1994): 501–509.

Brower, Kenneth. "The Proof is in the Pellet." *Audubon* (March 2004): 78.

Web sites:

Myers, P. "Family Geomyidae (Pocket Gophers)." Animal Diversity Web. http://animaldiversity.ummz.umich.edu/site/accounts/information/ Geomyidae.html (accessed on July 7, 2004).

"Pocket Gophers." Colorado Division of Wildlife. http://wildlife.state.co. us/Education/mammalsguide/pocket_gophers.asp (accessed on July 7, 2004).

"The Pocket Gopher." Forest Preserve District of Cook County (Illinois). http://www.newton.dep.anl.gov/natbltn/400-499/nb493.htm (accessed on July 7, 2004).

POCKET MICE, KANGAROO RATS, AND KANGAROO MICE
Heteromyidae

Class: Mammalia

Order: Rodentia

Family: Heteromyidae

Number of species: 60 species

phylum

class

subclass

order

monotypic order

suborder

▲ **family**

PHYSICAL CHARACTERISTICS

Pocket mice, kangaroo rats, and kangaroo mice, sometimes called heteromyids (members of the family Heteromyidae), are small- to medium-sized rodents with external, fur-lined cheek pouches. The pouches open in front of the mouth and go back along the shoulders. They have fairly large eyes and short, rounded ears. Pocket mice use all four feet while walking, while kangaroo rats and mice use only their rear two feet for walking. Kangaroo rats and mice have long tails with white tips or tufts on the end, along with relatively short front limbs. Pocket mice have shorter, less noticeable tails. Kangaroo rats and mice have good hearing. Kangaroo rats and mice have soft and silky fur, while pocket mice have coats that range from silky to spiny. The coat color varies from light to dark, depending on species and habitat, often matching the soil color on which they live.

Adults are 1.7 to 14.6 inches (4.3 to 37 centimeters) long and weigh between 0.2 and 6.9 ounces (5 and 195 grams). Kangaroo rats weigh between 1.2 and 6.9 ounces (33 and 195 grams); kangaroo mice weigh between 0.4 and 0.6 ounces (10 and 17 grams); and pocket mice weigh between 0.2 and 3.0 ounces (5 and 85 grams).

GEOGRAPHIC RANGE

Heteromyids are found in the western United States, southwestern Canada, Mexico, Central America, and northern South America.

HABITAT

Heteromyids live in deserts, dry grasslands, and, in a few cases, wet and dry tropical forests. Desert pocket mice and kangaroo rats like arid, dry, climates that contain sand, scrubs, sagebrush, grasses, and chaparral. Kangaroo mice prefer sandy habitats. In all cases, heteromyids like areas that contain many seeds.

DIET

Heteromyids eat mostly seeds, but also eat green vegetation and, in some species, insects. Desert species can go without water for long periods of time. They leave their burrows at night to dig through soil with their forelimbs to gather seeds into their cheek pouches. When pouches are full, they return to one of their caches (KASH-uhz), hidden supply areas, which are used throughout the animal's home range. Heteromyids defend their territory aggressively when they have collected many seeds.

BEHAVIOR AND REPRODUCTION

Heteromyids are nocturnal, active at night, rodents. Kangaroo rats and mice move about mostly by hopping on their hind limbs, while pocket mice use all four of their limbs in a walking motion. They have a very basic social structure, mostly living alone except for females and young. They do interact with nearby neighbors, which are often relatives. Most species burrow tunnel systems with multiple chambers and surface openings.

Heteromyids have well-developed communication systems. Medium- and large-sized kangaroo rats communicate by drumming or thumping the ground with their large hind feet; familiar thumping identifies neighbors, while strangers are not recognized. Each species has its own set of drumming patterns, which are heard through the air and ground.

Male home territories overlap with those of other males and females. Females occupy a territory that contains no other females. They regularly bathe in sand, which helps to clean their hair and to deposit their scents onto the ground. Their scent informs other heteromyids and other animals about their sex, identity and mating status. When a predator, an animal that hunts other animals, is seen, heteromyids use their body coloring to hide and avoid them. If needed, they will run away along a crooked path. Desert heteromyids also have strong hearing that lets them hear approaching predators.

Males always travel to female territories during breeding season in order to mate. Mating relationships range from one male and one female, to several males competing for access to one breeding female. Larger and medium sized kangaroo rats drum their feet in order to chase away competing males. Females prefer to mate with males they know, but will mate with strangers if necessary. Males will mate with any females. Breeding occurs only when enough moisture is available for nursing females to provide milk to young. Females produce several litters, group of young animals born at same time from the same mother, each year, but the number depends on environmental conditions. Litter sizes range from one to nine, but average three to four in most species. They live ten years or longer.

POCKET MICE, KANGAROO RATS, KANGAROO MICE, AND PEOPLE

Kangaroo rats are considered keystone species because their burrows provide habitat for a variety of plants and animals. A keystone species is a species that is important in maintaining the biodiversity, the variety of different animals and plants, of an area.

CONSERVATION STATUS

Four species of pocket mice, kangaroo rats, and kangaroo mice are listed by the World Conservation Union (IUCN) as Critically Endangered, facing an extremely high risk of extinction in the wild. One species is listed as Endangered, facing a very high risk of extinction in the wild, and one species is Vulnerable, facing a high risk of extinction. The IUCN also lists nine species as Near Threatened, not currently threatened, but could become so. Many species are threatened with excessive destruction and fragmentation, breaking up, of habitat and the loss of plant life.

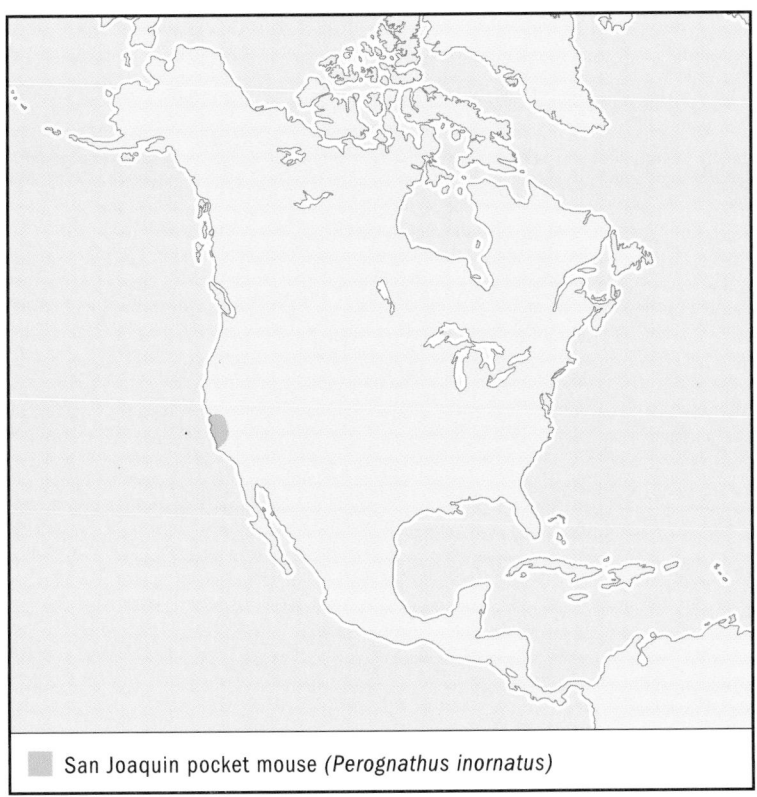

San Joaquin pocket mouse (*Perognathus inornatus*)

SAN JOAQUIN POCKET MOUSE
Perognathus inornatus

Physical characteristics: San Joaquin (san-wah-KEEN) pocket mice are small sand-colored mice with soft coats, sparse darker back hairs, and yellowish undersides. They do not have spiny hairs that are often found on other pocket mice species. A line separates the lighter belly hairs from the darker back hairs. San Joaquin pocket mice have short ears that sometimes have a base patch of lighter hair. Their hind feet have hair on the soles and their long tails are covered with hair with a small hair tuft on tip. They have external fur-lined cheek patches that are used for storing and transporting food. Adults are 5.0 to 6.3 inches (13 to 16 centimeters) long and weigh between 0.22 and 0.39 ounces (7 and 12 grams).

Geographic range: They are found in west-central California.

San Joaquin pocket mice not only eat seeds, but help to scatter them, which helps to maintain a healthy environment. (Illustration by Michelle Meneghini. Reproduced by permission.)

Habitat: San Joaquin pocket mice inhabit arid grasslands, deserts, and scrublands, especially areas with fine soils.

Diet: Their diet consists of seeds of grasses, shrubs, and forbs, broad-leaved herbaceous plants that grow in prairies and meadows. San Joaquin pocket mice forage, search for food, within shrub branches. They also eat soft-bodied insects such as cutworms and grasshoppers, and rarely drink water, getting almost all moisture through their food.

Behavior and reproduction: San Joaquin pocket mice do not travel far to forage, and stay away from open areas. They bathe by rubbing their sides and ventrum, external opening by which wastes pass in primitive mammals, in the sand. Their breeding season is from March to July. Females have at least two litters of four to six babies per litter.

San Joaquin pocket mice and people: San Joaquin pocket mice help to scatter seeds, which helps to maintain a healthy environment where it lives.

Conservation status: San Joaquin pocket mice are listed by the U.S. Fish and Wildlife Service as a species of special concern. Two subspecies, populations of a species in a specific area, are listed as Near Threatened. ■

Giant kangaroo rat (*Dipodomys ingens*)

GIANT KANGAROO RAT
Dipodomys ingens

Physical characteristics: Giant kangaroo rats are the largest members of heteromyids. They have long and powerful hind limbs that are used for hopping, and small and relatively weak front limbs that are used for digging. These animals have very long tails that are used for balance. Their dark tail has white lines along either side. They have large eyes, small rounded ears, and a somewhat rounded body. Their coat is sandy-colored with a white underside and a white stripe across the hindquarters. Adults are 12.3 to 13.7 inches (31 to 35 centimeters) long and weigh between 3.0 and 6.3 ounces (93 and 195 grams).

Geographic range: Giant kangaroo rats are found in San Joaquin Valley, California.

Habitat: They inhabit arid grasslands that contain sandy soils and are sparsely populated by desert shrubs.

Giant kangaroo rats use their strong hind limbs to hop around. They can jump up to 6 feet (2 meters) to escape from a predator. (© Richard R. Hansen/Photo Researchers, Inc. Reproduced by permission.)

Diet: Their diet consists of seeds, which are first stored in burrows. Sometimes seed heads are cured, preserved, in surface caches. They also eat insects and other vegetation.

Behavior and reproduction: Giant kangaroo rats are nocturnal animals, hiding in their burrows during the hottest parts of the day. Burrows are usually shallow tunnels that contain larger chambers, one that acts as a nest and the others used to store food. They are usually found alone, and move by hopping on their back legs. Their back, hind, legs let them jump over 6 feet (2 meters) when escaping predators. Their front limbs are smaller and used only for digging. They defend their territory, but live peacefully with their close neighbors.

Both sexes drum their hind feet in order to tell visitors to stay away, or to tell other giant kangaroo rats that predators, such as snakes and kit foxes, are around. Males drum their feet while competing with other males for the right to mate with a mature female. This mating sound may include up to 300 individual thumps that are repeated many times. The breeding season is from January to May. Females have more than one breeding cycle per year, and have an average of three breeding cycles in a breeding season. The gestation, pregnancy, period is thirty to fifty-five days. Typically, females are able to breed again three days after giving birth. Young are able to breed after only two to three weeks of being born.

Giant kangaroo rats and people: Giant kangaroo rats are considered keystone species.

Conservation status: Giant kangaroo rats are listed by the IUCN as Critically Endangered. They are also considered endangered by the California Fish and Game Commission and the U.S. Fish and Wildlife Service. Their populations have drastically decreased due to habitat loss as deserts are converted to agricultural lands. They no longer occupy over 95 percent of their former habitat, but are protected within the Carrizo Plain Natural Heritage Reserve and a number of federal lands. ■

FOR MORE INFORMATION

Books:

Feldhemer, George A., Lee C. Drickamer, Stephen H. Vessey, and Joseph F. Merritt. *Mammalogy: Adaptation, Diversity, and Ecology.* Boston: WCB McGraw-Hill, 1999.

Nowak, Ronald M. *Walker's Mammals of the World,* 6th ed. Baltimore and London: The Johns Hopkins University Press, 1999.

Vaughan, Terry A., James M. Ryan, and Nicholas J. Czaplewski. *Mammalogy,* 4th ed. Philadelphia: Saunders College Publishing, 2000.

Whitfield, Dr. Philip. *Macmillan Illustrated Animal Encyclopedia.* New York: Macmillan Publishing Company, 1984.

Wilson, Don E., and DeeAnn M. Reeder, eds. *Mammal Species of the World,* 2nd ed. Washington, DC and London: Smithsonian Institution Press, 1993.

BIRCH MICE, JUMPING MICE, AND JERBOAS

Dipodidae

Class: Mammalia

Order: Rodentia

Family: Dipodidae

Number of species: About 50 species

phylum

class

subclass

order

monotypic order

suborder

▲ family

PHYSICAL CHARACTERISTICS

The Dipodidae family includes small to medium-sized rodents that walk on two or four legs. In general, their back legs are slightly or much longer than their front legs. They have long tails, and the jerboas' tails often have a distinctive black-and-white "banner" at the end. These mammals' fur is either coarse or soft and colors range from soft brown to brownish yellow to purplish-brown. The Dipodidae rodents range in length from 1.8 to 9 inches (4.5 to 23 centimeters) and weigh from 0.2 to 15 ounces (6 to 415 grams). The birch mice and jumping mice walk on four legs and are small, mouselike creatures with long tails and small, narrow heads. Birch mice have four legs of equal length, while the back legs of jumping mice are somewhat longer than their front legs. Both birch mice and jumping mice have short, blunt claws. Jerboas can be small or medium sized, and jump or walk on their back legs. Unlike the birch mice and jumping mice, which are mainly nocturnal but are sometimes active during the day, jerboas are strictly night-time creatures. They can run very quickly through sparse brush. Their heads are large, with wide muzzles and flat snouts, and they have large eyes for better nighttime vision. Jerboas have compact, short bodies with short front legs and long, strong back legs. They can have either long or short claws and three, four, or five toes. All members of the Dipodidae family are remarkable for their jumping ability—probably an adaptation for evading predators in open country. Many of the mammals can cover 10 feet (3 meters) in a single jump, using their long tails to balance. In most species, the three central bones of the foot are fused, creating a single bone that provides major strength and support.

GEOGRAPHIC RANGE

The Dipodidae family is widespread throughout the world, and its species are present in North America, northern Africa, the Arabian Peninsula, Europe, and Asia, where they are believed to have originated.

HABITAT

Birch mice, jumping mice, and jerboas occupy a wide range of habitats around the world. Birch mice are most often found in thickets, forests, fields, moors, and steppes. Jumping mice tend to live in woodlands, grasslands, and alpine meadows, where they concentrate in the thick growth near streams, rivers, and marshes. Jerboas are adapted to desert environments and occupy moving sands, rocky plateaus, dry mountainsides, and even clay depressions. Many of the species will live in only very specific places, while others are less selective.

DIET

Birch mice and jumping mice eat berries, fungus, nuts, fruits, and insects. Jerboas are omnivores, and eat insects, fruits, seeds, bulbs, plant parts, and even other jerboas.

BEHAVIOR AND REPRODUCTION

Birch mice are able to mate after their first hibernation, and usually have one litter per year containing three to eleven pups. Their gestation period is two to five weeks, and parents care for the young for one month, which is quite long by rodent standards. In jumping mice, which (with a few exceptions) are also ready to mate after hibernation, mating pairs sometimes produce two or three litters. The gestation period is seventeen to twenty-three days and the litter size is usually two to nine pups. Among jerboas, some species breed only once a year during the spring and summer and produce litters of two to nine pups. Others breed in the spring and fall and can produce up to three litters a year, although their litter size is smaller (one to eight pups). In the majority of jerboa species, pups stay in the burrow for five to six weeks before emerging, probably because it takes extra time for them to develop the coordination required for bipedal movement.

Birch mice and jumping mice, while quadrupeds (animals that move about on all fours), also hop and use their tails to hang onto twigs and grasses. Jumping mice can hop up to 6 feet (1.8 meters) long and 3.3 feet (1 meter) high. Both types of mice are strong swimmers as well, and hop straight up when startled. Jerboas move on their hind feet exclusively and are very fast runners. The five-toed jerboa, for instance, can maintain speeds of 25 miles per hour (40 kilometers per hour).

Jumping mice and birch mice seldom dig, finding shelter under logs, in other animals' abandoned burrows, among roots, or under boards. Jerboas, on the other hand, typically dig and live in complex burrows with multiple chambers that they plug during the day to seal out heat and keep in moisture. Sometimes they have different burrows for daytime shelter and for nighttime escape from predators.

Most members of the Dipodidae family hibernate, but for how long and when varies widely based on geography and species. Birch mice hibernate for six or seven months of the year, and can lose up to half of their body weight. Species that breed in the spring and fall hibernate for shorter periods, while those that live in tropical regions experience only a few days of lethargy.

Species of this family are typically solitary and every individual has its own burrow for sleeping and hibernating. In general, these mammals seem tolerant of other individuals' presence, although females are reportedly more aggressive in defending their areas. Neighboring birch mice and jumping mice species even share shelter burrows, but jerboas actively avoid contact with other jerboas in overlapping areas. This is problematic in places where the abundance of jerboas results in population densities of forty to fifty individuals per 2.5 acres (1 hectare). Some jerboas mark their territories by rolling in sand, while others rub their genital areas on the ground.

None of the species in this family store food. Many of them, however, have specialized ways of finding prey, such as highly developed inner ears that help them hear tiny vibrations in the earth and powerful hind legs that allow them to jump extremely quickly into the air to catch passing insects.

BIRCH MICE, JUMPING MICE, JERBOAS, AND PEOPLE

While the Dipodidae family plays an important role in numerous ecosystems, they have very little interaction with or significance to humans.

CONSERVATION STATUS

Two species, the Armenian birch mouse and the Iranian jerboa, are listed as Critically Endangered, facing an extremely high risk of extinction, dying out, by the IUCN. Three other species are Endangered, facing a very high risk of extinction; three are Vulnerable, facing a high risk of extinction; and nine are considered Near Threatened, not currently threatened, but could become so.

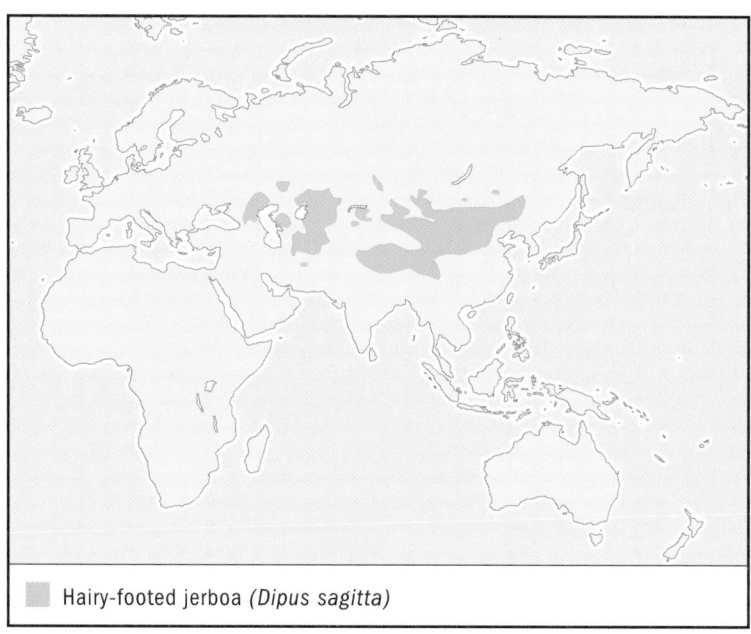

Hairy-footed jerboa (*Dipus sagitta*)

HAIRY-FOOTED JERBOA
Dipus sagitta

Physical characteristics: Also known as the feather-footed jerboa, rough-legged jerboa, and northern three-toed jerboa, the hairy-footed jerboa was first discovered in 1773. Its body ranges in length from 4.5 to 6 inches (11.5 to 14.5 centimeters), while its tail is typically 7 to 7.1 inches (17.5 to 18 centimeters) long. These mammals weigh between 2.4 and 4 ounces (69 to 104 grams). Underparts are white, and upperparts change from orangey and black in the winter to pale, sandy buff color in summer.

Geographic range: A resident of the Middle East, Asia, and Europe, the hairy-footed jerboa occupies ten isolated, large areas and several smaller fragments of habitat in the northern Iranian sand deserts, Turkmenistan, Uzbekistan, southwestern Kazakhstan, Mongolia, China, and eastern Russia.

Habitat: At the northern extreme of its range, the hairy-footed jerboa lives in sparsely vegetated areas of pine forests, but in general this mammal occupies sandy expanses of steppes, deserts, and semi-deserts.

In central Asia, this jerboa also lives in places with hard rocky or gravel-strewn surfaces.

Diet: While the hairy-footed jerboa subsists mainly on desert plant greens and seeds, it occasionally preys on insects as well.

Behavior and reproduction: Hairy-footed jerboas mate with more than one individual during the breeding season in spring. Female bear two or three litters per season, in spring and fall. The spring-born animals can mate at two-and-a-half to three months, and usually participate in the fall mating. Pregnancy lasts thirty-five days, and the number of young varies from one to eight. In springtime, female adults are usually still nursing their fall litter when they mate again.

Hairy-footed jerboas are solitary creatures, although they willingly tolerate overlapping home ranges. The vast majority of their contacts in nature (versus those in captivity) are non-aggressive. When captive, males and females form pairs and sleep together in a single nest.

Hairy-footed jerboas and people: There are no records of significant interactions between this species and humans.

Conservation status: The hairy-footed jerboa is common in all of its habitats, with the exception of one subspecies, which is listed as Vulnerable because of the expansion of steppes through areas of open sand dunes in southeastern Russia. ■

FOR MORE INFORMATION

Books:

Boitani, Luigi. *Simon and Schuster's Guide to Mammals.* New York: Fireside Books, 1990.

Corbet, G. B., and J. E. Hill. *A World List of Mammalian Species.* Oxford, U.K.: Oxford University Press, 1991.

Nowak, Ronald M. "Birch Mice and Jumping Mice." *Walker's Mammals of the World Online 5.1.* Baltimore: Johns Hopkins University Press, 1997. http://www.press.jhu.edu/books/walkers_mammals_of_the_world/rodentia/rodentia.zapodidae.html (accessed on June 13, 2004).

Nowak, Ronald M. "Jerboas." *Walker's Mammals of the World Online 5.1.* Baltimore: Johns Hopkins University Press, 1997. http://www.press.jhu.edu/books/walkers_mammals_of_the_world/rodentia/rodentia.dipodidae.html (accessed on June 13, 2004).

Simon, Noel. *Nature in Danger: Threatened Habitats and Species.* Oxford, U.K.: Oxford University Press, 1995.

Web sites:

"Family Dipodidae." Animal Diversity Web. http://animaldiversity.ummz.umich.edu/site/accounts/information/Dipodidae.html (accessed June 24, 2004).

Class: Mammalia

Order: Rodentia

Family: Muridae

Number of species: More than 1,326 species

family

CHAPTER

PHYSICAL CHARACTERISTICS

Rats, mice, and relatives, sometimes called murids (MYOO-rids; members of the family Muridae), are divided into seventeen subfamilies, including voles and lemmings, hamsters, Old World rats and mice, South American rats and mice, and many others. As a result of the large number of species, there is much variation in the physical characteristics of murids.

Voles and lemmings are small rodents with a broad, rounded head; small eyes and ears; thick, cylindrical body; and short legs and tail. Most species' fur is some shade of brown with paler underparts. Lemmings look a lot like voles, but most species are stockier, with heavier bodies and shorter tails. Adults are 3.5 to 24.5 inches (8.5 to 62 centimeters) long and weigh between 0.5 ounces and 4 pounds (15 grams to 1.8 kilograms).

Hamsters are mouse-like Old World rodents with large cheek pouches used to carry food; stout body; short legs; wide, (sometimes) furry feet; and short, furry tails. They have front paws with four digits and a short thumb, and hind feet with five digits. Their soft, thick fur varies in color (depending on the species) from gray to reddish brown, and their underparts can be white, gray, or black. They have excellent senses of hearing and smell, but poor eyesight (even though they have large, round eyes). Adults are 2 to 13.4 inches (5 to 34 centimeters) long and weigh between 0.9 and 31.7 ounces (25 to 900 grams).

Old World rats and mice have long tails (sometimes longer than the body) that are either furry or scaly; strong feet; long hind feet; and opposable digits on their front feet. Adults have

phylum

class

subclass

order

monotypic order

suborder

▲ **family**

a length of 1.9 to 14.7 inches (5 to 36 centimeters) and a weight of 0.2 to 52.9 ounces (5 grams to 1.5 kilograms).

South American rats and mice are small- to medium-sized rodents with brownish or blackish upper coats; very small or no external ears; grayish or whitish underparts; thinly haired tails that sometimes have a penciled tip; and relatively small feet. They have a head and body length of 2.4 to 11.4 inches (6.1 to 29.0 centimeters); tail length of 1 to 6.3 inches (3 to 16 centimeters); and weight of 0.4 to 18 ounces (12 to 510 grams).

All other rats, mice, and relatives vary widely in physical characteristics. Most species are small, usually with somewhat long tails and brownish fur.

GEOGRAPHIC RANGE

Rats, mice, and relatives are found throughout the world except for the extreme polar regions of Earth.

HABITAT

Rats, mice, and relatives live in many different habitats including open flatlands, savannas (flat grasslands), grasslands, prairies, steppes (treeless plains that are often somewhat dry and grass-covered), woodlands, forests, deserts, scrublands, foothills, jungles, rainforests, wetlands, cultivated lands and fields, and along waterways and water bodies. They are found from dry temperate (mild) climates to wet tropical environments.

DIET

Most species of rats, mice, and relatives eat at least a few of the following foods: grasses, seeds, grains, root vegetables such as bulbs and tubers, green plant parts, conifer needles, nuts, berries, fruits, insects and insect larvae (LAR-vee), fish, lizards, frogs, baby birds, crabs, tadpoles, salamanders, fungus, lichens, mosses, other small vertebrates (animals with a backbone) and invertebrates (animals without a backbone), and carrion (decaying animals).

BEHAVIOR AND REPRODUCTION

Rats, mice, and relatives are active during the day, at night, or both night and day (depending on the species). For their size, they can be very aggressive to predators and even to other members of their species. The rodents can be vocal, with various communicative sounds such as chattering, screaming, and whistling. They set up territories and defend them vigorously. Murids are sometimes found alone, but often are social, and are found traveling and sleeping together. They use nests for shelter and to raise their young. Some species breed throughout the year but others only during certain seasons. Murid rodents generally have high reproduction rates (lots of offspring) and large populations. Litters (groups of young born at the same time from the same mother) have one to seventeen offspring. Young are born blind and naked, although they develop fast, are weaned (stop drinking their mother's milk) quickly, and are able to reproduce within weeks or months.

RATS, MICE, RELATIVES, AND PEOPLE

Rats, mice, and relatives are generally considered pests in agricultural and forested lands. Large species are often trapped for their fur. Some species carry diseases that can sicken and kill people. Rats, mice, and relatives are frequently used as laboratory research animals. Some, such as hamsters and gerbils, are kept as pets. They are often important in maintaining a healthy ecosystem in their natural habitats.

CONSERVATION STATUS

Almost 450 species of murids are listed on the World Conservation Union's (IUCN) Red List. Of these, twenty-one are Extinct, died out; fifty are Critically Endangered, facing an extremely high risk of extinction in the wild; seventy-four are Endangered, facing a very high risk of extinction in the wild; and 110 are Vulnerable, facing a high risk of extinction in the wild.

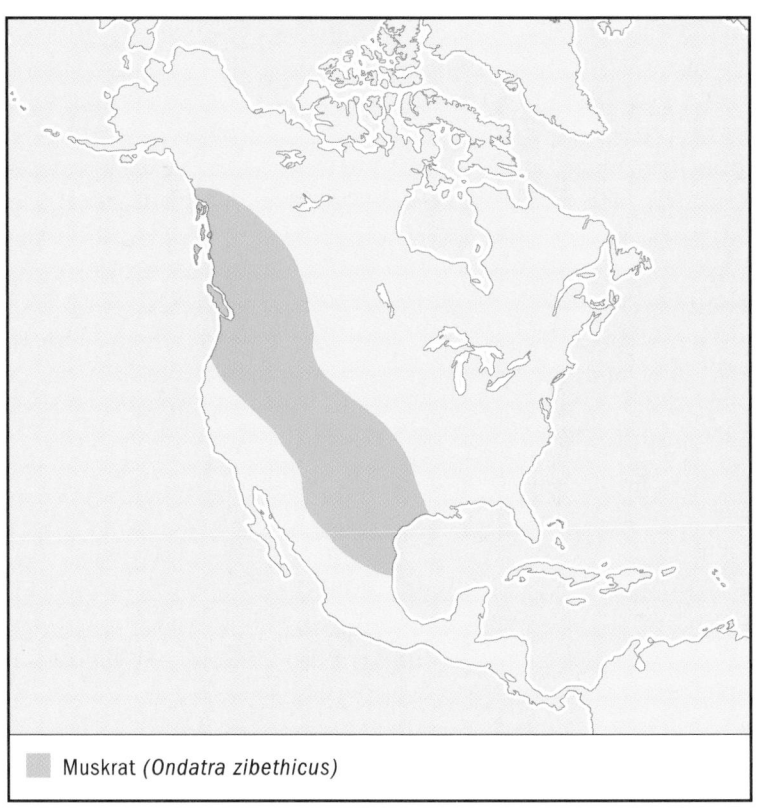

Muskrat (*Ondatra zibethicus*)

MUSKRAT
Ondatra zibethicus

Physical characteristics: The muskrat has dark brown upperparts and light grayish brown underparts. Adult head and body length is 15.5 to 24.5 inches (40 to 62 centimeters) and weight is 1.1 to 4 pounds (0.55 to 1.82 kilograms).

Geographic range: They range in the western part of North America, and have also been introduced into Europe, Asia, and South America.

Habitat: Muskrats are found around water, specially rivers, lakes, marshes, and lagoons.

Diet: They eat aquatic plants, invertebrates, and small vertebrates.

Behavior and reproduction: Muskrats either dig burrows in earthen banks or build large floating lodges of vegetation. They sometimes

live in families of several generations. Females have a gestation, pregnancy, period of twenty-five to thirty days, and then have a litter of four to eight young. Five or six litters are possible each year.

Muskrats and people: People hunt and raise muskrats for fur. They are often considered pests in some regions.

Conservation status: Muskrats are not threatened. ■

Muskrats are typically found near water, and eat aquatic plants and small animals. (© Alan D. Carey/The National Audubon Society Collection/Photo Researchers, Inc. Reproduced by permission.)

Norway lemming *(Lemmus lemmus)*

NORWAY LEMMING
Lemmus lemmus

Physical characteristics: Norway lemmings have brown to black fur. Adult head and body length is 3 to 7 inches (8 to 17.5 centimeters) and weight is 0.5 to 4.5 ounces (20 to 130 grams).

Geographic range: They are found in Scandinavia (the northern European region of Norway, Sweden, Denmark, Finland, Iceland, and the Faroe Islands).

Habitat: These lemmings inhabit open tundra and subarctic bog areas.

Diet: Their diet consists of mosses, lichens (LIE-kenz), bark, and some grasses.

Behavior and reproduction: Norway lemmings are mostly nocturnal (active at night). They travel long distances in mass migrations, and are active year-round, remaining mostly beneath snow cover. The gestation period is about sixteen days, with a litter of up to thirteen young and up to six litters produced each year.

Norway lemmings and people: Scandinavian people have made lemmings a popular animal in their myths and legends.

Conservation status: Norway lemmings are not threatened. ◼

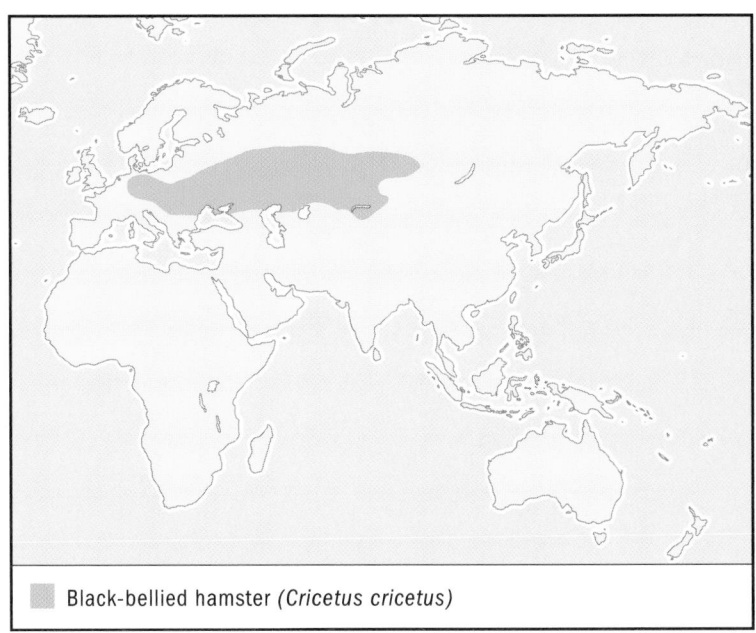

Black-bellied hamster (*Cricetus cricetus*)

BLACK-BELLIED HAMSTER
Cricetus cricetus

Physical characteristics: Black-bellied hamsters have a short hairless tail; a thick fur that is reddish brown above with white patches on the flanks, nose, cheeks, and throat; and black underparts. Males are larger than females. Adults are 8 to 12 inches (20 to 34 centimeters) long and weigh between 4.5 and 36.3 ounces (112 to 908 grams).

Geographic range: These hamsters are found in central and eastern Europe, from Belgium to the Altai region of Siberia.

Habitat: Black-bellied hamsters live in lowlands such as steppes, agricultural lands, and along riverbanks.

Diet: Their diet includes grains, beans, roots, green plant parts, insect larvae (especially beetle larvae), frogs, earthworms, and field mice. They often store cereal grains, seeds, peas, and potatoes in winter burrows.

Behavior and reproduction: Black-bellied hamsters generally live alone; are active at night; and hibernate in winter. Winter burrows can extend more than 6 feet (2 meters) below the soil surface. Older females with young have the most complex burrows with several entrance tunnels, numerous chambers for nesting and food storage, and a dead-end tunnel for waste disposal. Breeding takes place from June to August. A courting male enters a female's territory by marking an area with his secretions, running after the female, and making loud sniffing noises. The female drives away the male after mating. The gestation period is eighteen to twenty days, with a litter of four to twelve pups. Two litters are raised each year. They sometimes live to the age of eight years old.

Black-bellied hamsters and people: People hunt black-bellied hamsters for food and trap them for clothing. They are considered pests when around cornfields, but do help to control other pests such as mice and insects. The rodents are also used as laboratory animals.

Conservation status: Black-bellied hamsters are protected under European Community Habitats Directive as a threatened species in Belgium, Germany, the Netherlands, France, and Austria. They are also protected in Croatia, Bulgaria, and Slovenia. ■

Black-bellied hamsters often store cereal grains, seeds, peas, and potatoes in their winter burrows. (Hans Dieter Brandl/FLPA—Images of Nature. Reproduced by permission.)

Egyptian spiny mouse (*Acomys cahirinus*)

EGYPTIAN SPINY MOUSE
Acomys cahirinus

Physical characteristics: Egyptian spiny mice have large ears; gray-brown to sandy spiny hairs covering its back; gray to white bellies; and scaly, hairless tails. Adults have a body length of 2.7 to 6.7 inches (7 to 17.0 centimeters); tail length of 1.9 to 4.7 inches (5 to 12 centimeters); and weight of 1 to 2.4 ounces (30 to 70 grams).

Geographic range: These mice are distributed through Africa and the Middle East.

Habitat: Egyptian spiny mice live in arid (dry) and semi-arid environments like deserts and savannas, often preferring to be around rocks. They live in burrows and are sometimes found in trees, but are considered to be terrestrial, ground-living, animals.

Diet: They eat mostly arthropods, along with snails, plant materials, grains, and grasses.

Behavior and reproduction: Egyptian spiny mice are fairly social animals, living in small groups with a dominant male who fights to maintain his control. They are good jumpers, and build simple nests. The gestation period is five to six weeks, with a litter of one to five pups. Young are well developed when born, having thin hair, open eyes (within a few days), and are able to breed almost immediately. Females help each other with the birthing process.

Egyptian spiny mice and people: People keep Egyptian spiny mice as pets.

Conservation status: Egyptian spiny mice are not threatened. ■

When threatened, the Egyptian spiny mouse expands its bristles to appear larger, hoping to scare off the intruder. (© E. R. Degginger/Photo Researchers, Inc. Reproduced by permission.)

Australian jumping mouse *(Notomys alexis)*

AUSTRALIAN JUMPING MOUSE
Notomys alexis

Physical characteristics: Australian jumping mice have light sandy brown to gray upperparts; white to light gray bellies; long tails with fine fur; large ears; narrow, large hind feet; and sebaceous (secretion) glands that are used for territorial marking. Adults have a body length of 3.9 to 5.9 inches (10 to 15 centimeters); tail length of 3.5 to 8.2 inches (9 to 21 centimeters); and weight of 0.7 to 1.7 ounces (20 to 50 grams).

Geographic range: They are found throughout central Australia.

Habitat: They inhabit arid desert environments; living around dunes and grasslands so that they can easily dig large, complicated burrows.

Diet: Their diet consists of berries and other vegetation. They can live without water as long as they receive enough moisture from their food.

Behavior and reproduction: Australian jumping mice are nocturnal, social creatures. As a group, they groom, huddle, walk over and crawl under each other, and sleep together. Their large hind feet allow them to jump higher than 3.2 feet (1 meter). When angry with another animal, they rush and leap at it, and punch it with their forelegs. They generally walk on all four limbs, but when necessary will leap with their hind legs. The gestation period is about one month. Females produce a litter with an average of three pups that are born naked and blind, but open their eyes within three weeks. They are weaned after five weeks and ready to reproduce within three months.

Australian jumping mice and people: People keep these animals as pets.

Conservation status: The Australian jumping mouse is not threatened. ■

The Australian jumping mouse's large hind feet allow it to jump higher than 3.2 feet (1 meter). (© Tom McHugh/Photo Researchers, Inc. Reproduced by permission.)

Hispid cotton rat *(Sigmodon hispidus)*

HISPID COTTON RAT
Sigmodon hispidus

Physical characteristics: Hispid cotton rats have a gray streaked coat with blackish or dark brownish hairs; pale to dark grayish underparts; dark tail; and five pairs of nipples, although some have four or six pairs. Adults have a total length of 8.8 to 14.4 inches (22.4 to 36.5 centimeters); tail length of 3.2 to 6.5 inches (8.1 to 16.6 centimeters); and weight of 3.5 to 8 ounces (100 to 225 grams).

Geographic range: They are found from southeast and south-central United States through the interior and eastern part of

Mexico, into Central America, and to northern Colombia and Venezuela.

Habitat: Hispid cotton rats usually live in grasslands.

Diet: Their diet consists mostly of grasses.

Behavior and reproduction: Hispid cotton rats are active during the day and night, and are able to swim. They breed throughout the year. The gestation period is about twenty-seven days. Litter size is from one to fifteen pups, with northern populations having larger litters. Young are well developed at birth; eyes open within thirty-six hours of birth; and are weaned in ten to fifteen days. Males are able to reproduce within sixty to ninety days, and females within ten to forty days.

Hispid cotton rats and people: Scientists observe hispid cotton rats to help them determine how environmentally healthy an area is.

Conservation status: The hispid cotton rat is not threatened, though two subspecies, populations that live in specific areas, are Near Threatened (likely will be threatened in the future). ■

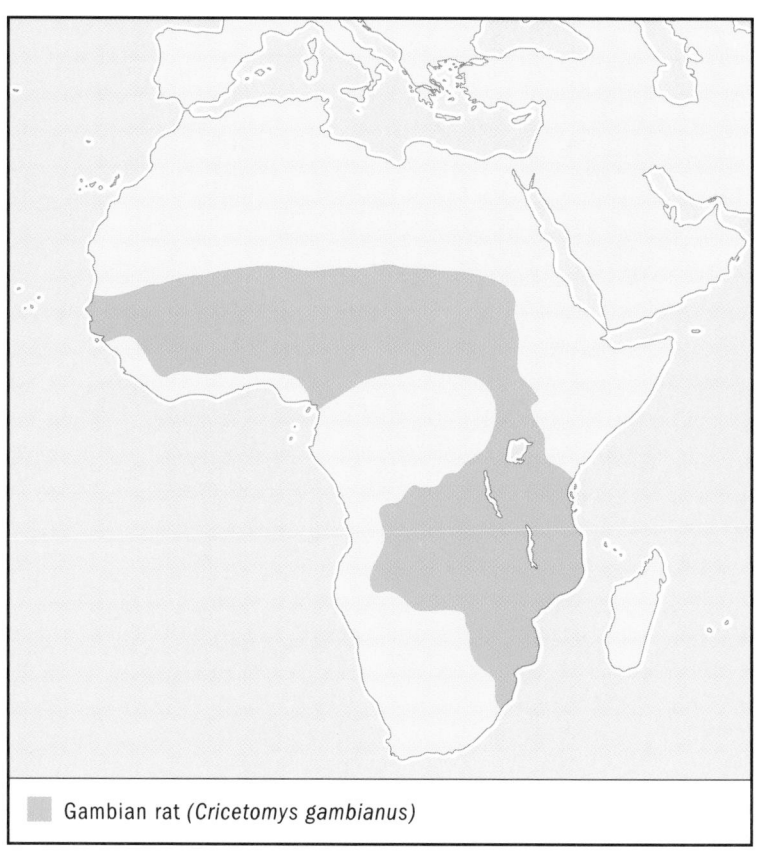

Gambian rat *(Cricetomys gambianus)*

GAMBIAN RAT
Cricetomys gambianus

Physical characteristics: Gambian rats are fairly large rodents with short fur that can range from soft to coarse. Some species are mottled, or splotched, with darker colors or may have an indistinct white line running across the shoulders. They have large ears; dark rings around the rather small eyes; a long and narrow head and face; cheek pouches to collect food and other materials; smooth incisor teeth; dark or grayish brown upperparts with red tinges; creamy underparts; and a long, scaly tail that is hairless and completely white for the last half of the length. They have good senses of smell and hearing, but have poor eyesight. Adults have a body length of 9.4 to 17.7 inches (24 to 45 centimeters); tail length of 14.3 to 18.1 inches (36.5 to

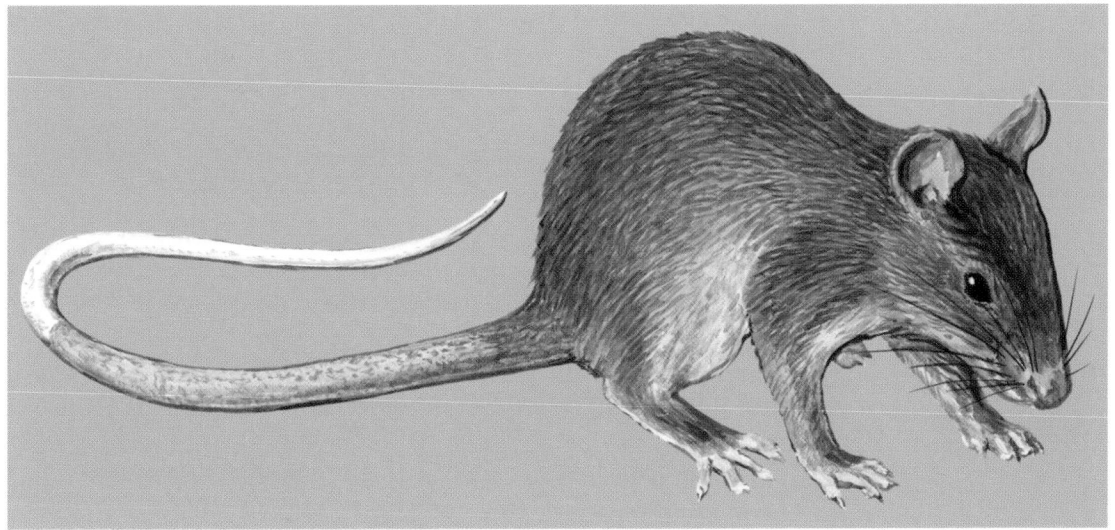

46.0 centimeters); male weight of about 6.1 pounds (2.8 kilograms); and female weight of about 3 pounds (1.4 kilograms).

Geographic range: Gambian rats are found in Africa, specifically from Senegal and Sierra Leone in the west to Sudan and Uganda in the east and as far south as Angola, Zambia, and northern South Africa.

Habitat: They inhabit forests, forest edges, thickets, and sometimes grasslands.

Diet: Their diet consists of insects, fruits (especially palm fruits and kernels), seeds, roots, nuts, leaves, snails, and crabs.

Behavior and reproduction: Gambian rats are mostly nocturnal although sometimes active during the day. They climb and swim well, and are usually seen alone. The rodents sometimes dig a simple burrow that has long passageways with side chambers for bedding and storage and is covered by dense vegetation. At other times, they use burrows of other animals, termite mounds, or natural crevices in rocks and hollow trees. Breeding occurs throughout the year. Up to ten litters per year are possible for females. The gestation period is twenty-seven to thirty-six days, with one to five pups born, although four pups in a litter is average. Young develop quickly and are able to breed as early as twenty weeks old.

Gambian rats and people: People buy and sell Gambian rats within the pet trade. These animals transmit diseases, such as monkeypox, to humans. Some people hunt them.

Female Gambian rats may have up to ten litters of pups each year, with an average of four pups per litter. (Illustration by Brian Cressman. Reproduced by permission.)

Conservation status: Gambian rats are listed as Rare in South Africa. Otherwise, they range from common to less common in their other ranges, and are not listed as threatened by the IUCN. ■

FOR MORE INFORMATION

Books:

Feldhemer, George A., Lee C. Drickamer, Stephen H. Vessey, and Joseph F. Merritt. *Mammalogy: Adaption, Diversity, and Ecology.* Boston: WCB McGraw-Hill, 1999.

Nowak, Ronald M. *Walker's Mammals of the World,* 6th ed. Baltimore and London: The Johns Hopkins University Press, 1999.

Vaughan, Terry A., James M. Ryan, and Nicholas J. Czaplewski. *Mammalogy,* 4th ed. Philadelphia: Saunders College Publishing, 2000.

Whitfield, Philip. *Macmillan Illustrated Animal Encyclopedia.* New York: Macmillan Publishing Company, 1984.

Wilson, Don E. and DeeAnn M. Reeder, eds. *Mammal Species of the World,* 2nd ed. Washington, D.C. and London: Smithsonian Institution Press, 1993.

SCALY-TAILED SQUIRRELS

Anomaluridae

Class: Mammalia

Order: Rodentia

Family: Anomaluridae

Number of species: 7 species

family

PHYSICAL CHARACTERISTICS

The scaly-tailed squirrels range in size from 7.3 to 18.5 inches (18.5 to 46 centimeters) along their head and bodies, with tail length measuring between 5.4 and 18.4 inches (13.8 to 45 centimeters). They generally weigh between 7 ounces and 4 pounds (200 to 1,800 grams). The family Anomaluridae (from words meaning "strange-tailed") look very much like regular squirrels (family Sciuridae) from the outside because they have adapted to similar environments, but major differences in their skulls, teeth, and other internal items show that they have no close relationship. Scaly-tailed squirrels, unlike regular tree squirrels, have a furred "gliding membrane" on each side of their bodies that stretches in a square shape between the front legs and the back legs and also between the hind legs and the tail. Only one genus, the mainly diurnal (active during the day) *Zenkerella*, lacks this membrane and cannot glide. The membrane is supported in front by a strut-like, rigid section of cartilage that extends from the elbow joint, rather than from the wrist, as in the true flying squirrels. They are the only gliding mammals in Africa. Scaly-tailed squirrels are so named because of the double rows of overlapping, spiky scales on the underside of the tails for one-third of its length along the base. When the animals land after a glide, the scales help to keep them from skidding on tree trunks, and also help them climb up trees. Their silky tails are bushy on top and have strongly colored tufts. They have strong digits for manipulating food and climbing, and very long whiskers and large ears for their mainly nocturnal activity. Their heads are large and placed

phylum

class

subclass

order

monotypic order

suborder

 **family**

forward on the face, providing excellent binocular vision for finding prey and good landing places.

GEOGRAPHIC RANGE

Scaly-tailed squirrels are native to the middle region of Africa, and live mainly south of the Sahara Desert in west, central, and east Africa. Countries in which they appear regularly are Sierra Leone, Kenya, Angola, Mozambique, Ghana, Liberia, Senegal, Congo, Cameroon, Gabon, the Central African Republic, and Ivory Coast.

HABITAT

Scaly-tailed squirrels prefer the open woodlands of east, central, and west Africa and the rainforests of west and central Africa.

DIET

Larger scaly-tailed squirrels eat bark and twigs from more than a dozen species of tree, but their favorites are miombo, velvet tamarind, ironwood, owala oil, and awoura. They occasionally also eat insects and gum (tree sap). The smaller squirrels eat almost nothing besides gum and insects.

BEHAVIOR AND REPRODUCTION

Because of the remoteness of their habitats and the animals' secretive nature, scientists know relatively little about the anomalurids, members of the Anomaluridae family. However, it has been observed that the scaly-tailed squirrels clear out small branches that obstruct their habitual gliding paths. In doing so, along with their method of pruning the tops of non-food trees to keep them from crowding out their favorite food trees, the squirrels perform important functions in their ecosystems. They dislike coming to the ground, and when forced to do so move in a clumsy, kangaroo-like fashion to the nearest tree. Their gliding membranes fold away neatly when not in use, and do not prevent the squirrels from quickly scurrying along tree branches like their familiar garden-variety counterparts.

Anomalurids compete with hornbill birds for dens, which they typically make in old, hollowed out trees up to 131 feet

(40 meters) high. They also battle eagles, which sometimes come in to snatch their young for prey. Females have litters of up to three pups, which are born with open eyes and thick fur. Their parents wean them from milk onto solid food by feeding the pups already chewed food from special cheek pouches. The squirrels communicate largely by scent, and use large glands in their groins to mark areas, but observers have heard them making a twittering noise as well. Field biologists believe that scaly-tailed squirrels may reach population densities of 500 individuals per 1.2 square miles (1 square kilometer). They often spend their days clinging to the side of a tree. The squirrels usually associate in pairs, but some species have been seen collected into large groups within a single den.

SCALY-TAILED SQUIRRELS AND PEOPLE

The mammals are sometimes accused of raiding oil palms for their nuts, but in general they have very little interaction with humans. Conservationists have worked to limit or stop the harvesting of the squirrels' food trees, many of which are valuable sources of high-quality commercial lumber.

CONSERVATION STATUS

Despite logging of their food trees and a general decline in habitat quality and quantity, scaly-tailed squirrel species are not considered threatened.

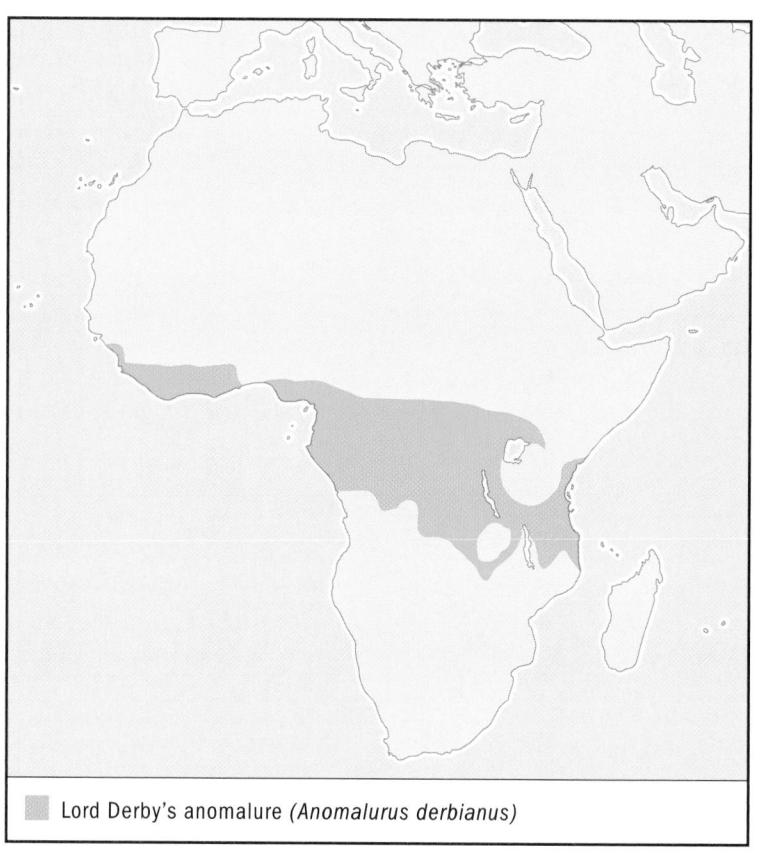

Lord Derby's anomalure (*Anomalurus derbianus*)

LORD DERBY'S ANOMALURE
Anomalurus derbianus

Physical characteristics: Although Lord Derby's anomalure's appearance varies across its range, this species is generally grey to a rich reddish brown with silver throughout. All of the 16 subspecies share the same facial pattern, however, of white cheeks, forehead, and snout with a black band over the nose, around the eyes, and on the back of the head. The fur on their heads is dense and soft, and the silky fur on their bodies can be up to 1 inch (25 millimeters) long. They also all have six pairs of scales underneath their tails. Their tails are shorter than their bodies, the last half being black. Lord Derby's anomalure has furless, pink ears.

Geographic range: This species is widely distributed in an area across central Africa, from Sierra Leone in the west to Kenya in the

Lord Derby's anomalures supplement their diet of tree bark with insects, tree sap, nuts, fruits, and flowers. (Illustration by Barbara Duperron. Reproduced by permission.)

east, and, less commonly, from Angola in the north to Mozambique in the south.

Habitat: This anomalure favors habitat in moist rainforests and seasonally dry woodlands from sea level to 7,875 feet (2,400 meters), although they are particularly attracted to areas that contain their favorite food trees. With regard to shelter, any tree will do for roosting as long as it is hollow in places. Roosting holes have been observed at both the tops and bottoms of trees, with entryways just large enough for anomalures to fit through. The dens are constructed so that temperature and humidity remain fairly consistent.

Diet: Like most of the larger anomalurids, Lord Derby's anomalure eats the bark of such trees as the miombo, velvet tamarind, ironwood, owala oil, and awoura, preferring the thickest portions of the main truck and large branches. The animals forage among several different trees, taking a thin strip from a tree one night and returning to take another strip during the next night's feeding, stopping when the removal site reaches about 6 inches (15 centimeters) wide to prevent permanent damage to the tree. Lord Derby's usually start a feeding site at natural wounds in a tree's bark caused by growth splits, elephant damage, or falling branches. Interestingly, the trees and this species have evolved together for so long that unlike most other trees, the rodents' food tree species can grow replacement bark.

The anomalures supplement their nutrient-poor bark diet with insects, tree sap, nuts, fruits, and flowers.

Behavior and reproduction: Although biologists have yet to study the social aspects of Lord Derby's anomalure behavior, they do know that the animals tend to share dens, and may crowd up to eight individuals into one roosting hole. They are mainly active at night, but seem to enjoy lying in the sun in the early morning and late afternoon. Using their gliding membrane to move across longer distances, they perform a final abrupt upturn to cause their flight to stall and allowing them to land safely. Biologists have measured the glide distances of Lord Derby's anomalure females at 1,770 feet (540 meters), but most are under 328 feet (100 meters). Males typically achieve even greater gliding distances and move through more territory. The Lord Derby's are fairly quiet animals, with vocalizations that include a variety of twitters and purrs along with growling and hissing when threatened or disturbed.

For Lord Derby's anomalures living in the rain forest, breeding occurs year round. For residents of the dry forests, breeding occurs seasonally. Pregnant females often move to a special nursery den, where they give birth to an unknown number of pups. Although the young are large, well formed, and able to move in a coordinated fashion soon after birth, they stay with the female parent until they are almost fully mature. After weaning, they receive chewed-up food from both parents. Observers have noted that mothers and pups will often glide among trees and chase each other playfully.

Lord Derby's anomalures and people: Although biologists have long sought to learn more about this secretive and easily frightened species, there are no records of any significant interactions between Lord Derby's anomalure and humans.

Conservation status: Despite their specialized diet and habitat requirements, Lord Derby's anomalure is not threatened. However, in Ghana, their population is on a conservation watch list due to habitat destruction and degradation. ■

FOR MORE INFORMATION

Books:

Kingdon, J. *The Kingdon Field Guide to African Mammals.* Princeton: Princeton University Press, 1997.

Nowak, Ronald M. "Family Anomaluridae: Scaly-tailed Squirrels." *Walker's Mammals of the World Online 5.1.* Baltimore: Johns Hopkins University Press, 1997. http://www.press.jhu.edu/books/walkers_mammals_of_the_world/rodentia/ (accessed on June 14, 2004).

Wilson, D. E., and D. M. Reader, eds. *Mammal Species of the World: A Taxonomic and Geographic Reference,* 2nd ed. Washington, DC: Smithsonian Institution Press, 1992.

Periodicals:

Dawson, M. R., et al. "Rodents of the Family Anomaluridae (Mammalia) from Southeast Asia." *Annals of Carnegie Museum* 72, no. 3 (2003): 203–213.

Julliot, C., et al. "Anomalures (Rodentia, Anomaluridae) in Central Gabon: Species Composition, Population Densities and Ecology." *Mammalia* 59 (1995): 441–443.

Web sites:

Fact Index. "Anomaluridae." http://www.fact-index.com (accessed on June 14, 2004).

SPRINGHARE
Pedetidae

Class: Mammalia

Order: Rodentia

Family: Pedetidae

One species: Springhare (*Yerbua capensis*)

phylum

class

subclass

order

monotypic order

suborder

▲ **family**

PHYSICAL CHARACTERISTICS

Springhares look like very small kangaroos. Their name actually means "jumping hare" in Afrikaans (one of the official languages of the Republic of South Africa). They have a body length of 13 to 17 inches (33 to 44 centimeters) when standing upright on their hind legs, a tail length of 14 to 19 inches (35 to 49 centimeters), and weigh 6 to 9 pounds (2 to 5 kilograms). Springhares have short front legs and long, powerful hind legs. Their front legs are one quarter of the length of their hind legs. Each front leg has five toes with long, sharp, curved claws that are used for digging. Each hind leg has four toes with claws that look like hoofs. The second toe from the outside is longer than the other toes. The heels, soles of their feet, and base of their toes do not have any hair covering them.

Springhares have short, blunt heads, big eyes, and long eyelashes. Their ears are narrow, have thin hairs on the upper half, are naked on the inside, and are about 3 inches (7 centimeters) long. At times, their ears have the tendency to droop to their sides. They also have a tragus (TRAY-gus; prominence in front of the ear's opening) that folds back and closes the opening of the ear to keep out sand when digging. Their necks are thin and muscular.

Long, soft, straight hairs cover springhares' bodies. Springhares are colored pink-brown to gray on their upper half with some black or white hairs in the fur. On the lower half, they are brown-white. This same color also spreads upward in front of their thighs and on the inside of their legs. Their tails are mostly tan with a thick, dark brown or black brush at the tip. The shading of their colors depends on the area where they live. For example, springhares from eastern South Africa have fur that is paler than those that live in the western areas of South Africa.

GEOGRAPHIC RANGE

Springhares can be found in Angola, Botswana, Congo, Kenya, Mozambique, Namibia, South Africa, Tanzania, Zambia, and Zimbabwe.

HABITAT

Springhares live in areas that have dry and sandy soil. They also live where there are cattle grazing and crop cultivation (areas where preparation for growing crops is occurring). They stay away from rocky ground and areas with a lot of trees, and live in grassland areas.

Springhares build burrows (also known as warrens) for shelter and protection in the grasslands. They will oftentimes build more than one warren, and they can be up to 32 inches (82 centimeters) deep and can cover up to 1,200 square feet (112 square meters). The burrows are usually created near the largest tree or a clump of bushes within their living area. When digging these burrows, they fold their ears back and seal their nose, so sand does not disturb them. It is easiest for the springhares to dig these burrows when the soil is wet during the rainy season. Sometimes during digging, they will stop, turn around, and push the soil they have collected back with their legs and chest. They then use their hind legs to kick this soil above the burrow to be redistributed on the ground. They sometimes cover the entrance of the burrow with soil from the inside. Springhares also create tunnels within their burrows that can be up to 51 yards (46 meters) long. Springhares also sometimes close down entrances to tunnels within their burrows by sealing them closed. Their burrows are formed in a circular shape and have many entry areas. There can be up to eleven entrances in a burrow. This makes it easier for springhares to escape if a predator, an animal that hunts it for food, gains access into their burrow.

DEFENSE AGAINST PREDATORS

Springhares have several lines of defense against predators. The first is early detection, which is aided by their wonderful senses of sight, sound, and smell. In the case that these senses do not alert them enough in advance, the second is their ability to quickly hop away with their powerful hind legs. Finally, their third line of defense is to viciously bite and kick, making use of the sharp claws on their hind feet.

Springhare *(Yerbua capensis)*

DIET

Springhares mostly eat grass stems, bulbs, and fleshy roots. When they live in crop-cultivated areas, they will eat corn, peanuts, barley, oats, and wheat. Sometimes, they eat plant stems. This can be seen especially in grazed areas where they eat the lower stems or roots after other animals have already eaten the upper grass layers. When they have a very difficult time finding food, they will eat beetles, locusts, or other insects. When springhares eat, they sit up and use their tails as support. They like to eat in darkness, so they do not usually stay out and feed when there is a full moon.

BEHAVIOR AND REPRODUCTION

When springhares sleep, they sit on their hind legs, with their front feet and head in between their thighs and their tail placed around their head and body. They sleep during the day, because they are nocturnal (active at night), although they can

occasionally be seen during the day. Their large eyes are signs that they are active during nighttime.

Springhares live alone or with another adult and young. They are not known for creating social units and usually do not communicate, with the exception of occasional low grunts. They can get along with one another in captivity, but aggression can also occur. When in the wild, they can also make male-female pairs.

Birds of prey, large carnivores, and humans are the main predators of springhares. Sometimes, when springhares first come out of their burrows at the beginning of the night, they leap into the air to try to scare off any predators that may be waiting for them. They cannot fight very well, but if they are very close to a predator, in an enclosed area, they will bite and kick fiercely with their hind feet, which have very sharp claws. However, it is more typical that they hop away from predators using their hind legs and head toward their burrow. Their great senses of sound, smell, and sight help them to stay away from predators. They also help them to notify other springhares of predators.

Springhares can be born at any time of the year. Females give birth in bare areas of their burrows, usually having only one offspring at a time, but twins do occur in rare cases. The average female springhare will have one young three times per year. At birth, springhares weigh around 9 to 11 ounces (256 to 312 grams). When they are seven weeks old, the young leave their mothers. They eat a lot of grasses at this point. They are then finished growing and go off to make their own burrows.

Springhares stand on their hind feet when in an upright posture and can travel using all four feet when they are eating or moving from place to place. When they jump, their tail becomes horizontal or curled upward. They can jump around 6 to 9 feet (1 to 3 meters) high and can also swerve sharply when they're chased by humans or other predators.

SPRINGHARES AND PEOPLE

Humans hunt springhares in areas where they cause damage to crops. The springhares cause problems by destroying seed and root systems in these areas. They can also be hunted as a source of food to humans, especially in South Africa. People may also kill them for their fur. One method they use to capture springhares, whether for fur or food, is to flood their burrows with water, so that the springhares must come out, and can be more easily captured. Another method is to chase them by foot, but it can be difficult to grab hold of them. Springhares may also be dangerous to humans since they can transmit diseases like the bubonic plague, rickettsiasis, babesiasis, theileriosis, and toxicosis paralysis through parasites they may carry.

CONSERVATION STATUS

The World Conservation Union (IUCN) lists springhares as Vulnerable, facing a high risk of extinction in the wild. This is due to the fact that their population is decreasing from poor habitat quality and hunting by humans.

FOR MORE INFORMATION

Books:

Alderton, David. *Rodents of the World.* New York: Facts on File, 1996.

Gould, Dr. Edwin, and Dr. George McKay, eds. *Encyclopedia of Mammals,* 2nd ed. San Diego, CA: Academic Press, 1998.

Nowak, Ronald M. "Springhare, or Springhaas." In *Walker's Mammals of the World,* 6th ed. Baltimore: The Johns Hopkins University Press, 1999.

Web sites:

Jackson, A. *"Pedetes capensis."* Animal Diversity Web. http://animal-diversity.ummz.umich.edu/site/accounts/information/Pedetes_capensis.html (accessed on May 21, 2004).

phylum

class

subclass

order

monotypic order

suborder

▲ **family**

PHYSICAL CHARACTERISTICS

Gundis are small rodents with soft, thick, and silky fur. Their fur helps to insulate their bodies from harm due to extreme sun exposure. They have large, blunt heads, flat skulls, and short, round ears. Their very round, large eyes help them to adjust quickly to bright sunlight when they come out of their rock shelters. They have a fringe of hair around the inner margin of their ears that protects the ears from sand that can be easily blown by the wind. Gundis have long vibrissae (stiff hairs that can be found near the nostrils or other parts of the face in many mammals). They also have short legs and short, furry tails. Their back feet are longer than their front feet, each foot having four digits (fingers or toes). On the hind feet, the two inner digits have stiff bristles that serve as a comb for the gundis' fur. The digits also have small, very sharp claws. Gundis have flexible ribcages, which help them squeeze into small spaces.

The color of gundis is anywhere from gray to yellow-red, the underparts usually having a whitish color. The rocks that they live among determine their overall color, because blending into their surroundings serves as protection. Overall, they have the appearance of guinea pigs. Their head and body length is 6 to 10 inches (15 to 25 centimeters). Their tail length is 0.3 to 2 inches (1 to 6 centimeters), and they can weight up to 6 ounces (171 grams), and the females are larger than the males.

GEOGRAPHIC RANGE

Gundis can be found in northern Africa.

HABITAT

Gundis live in rocky hills, cliffs, and mountains in deserts, sub-deserts, or on the edges of deserts. The rocks that make up their habitat can be of any age, but they cannot be extremely large. Gundis may even be found housed in building sites. Within these living areas, gundis find fissures (long, deep, and narrow openings or cracks), crevices, and caves to use for permanent or temporary shelter. They find ledges, flat rocks, and boulder tops to use for sunbathing. They prefer to live in areas where they can get exposure to the morning, as well as the evening sun. Gundis do not have adaptations for water conservation or temperature control, so they take advantage of the shade and wind in the areas where they live. This helps them to cool off during hot afternoons in the desert.

DIET

Gundis are herbivores (plant-eating animals) and mainly eat leaves, stalks, flowers, and plant seeds. They cannot gnaw well, so they mainly eat these softer foods. Food is usually somewhat difficult to find in their habitat, so they have to travel far to find it. Gundis do not store food or reserve fat in their bodies, so their search for nourishment is never-ending. They usually will take food back to their shelter so that they can safely eat.

BEHAVIOR AND REPRODUCTION

Gundis are diurnal (mainly active during daytime). They can run quickly when necessary, but they are usually slow, and also shy. When they move, their bodies are very close to the ground; their bellies almost touch the ground. They have rough friction pads on their feet that help them climb rocks and surfaces that are almost vertical. They come out of their shelters during the first light of the day, and they are active for up to five hours after this point. When the hottest part of the day arrives, they rest. Then, for the two to four hours before dusk, they become active again. However, they may not come out of their shelters when it is cold, wet, or windy. It can become very dangerous for gundis when it rains, because the water causes their fur to stick together and expose their skin, which makes them very cold very quickly. In order to retain heat in the winter, they pile on top of one another in their shelters. Their lives basically consist of foraging (wandering in search of food), sunbathing, playing, chasing, and exploring.

Gundis live in colonies, or groups. These colonies have different densities that are related to the food supply and terrain of the region being inhabited. Shelters of the gundis serve the purpose of keeping the heat from the day in the shelter during cold nights as well as staying cool during the day when the weather is hot. Gundis also have communal dunghills.

When gundis encounter predators, animals that hunt them for food, they become immobile, in order to make the predators believe that they are dead. They may also go under rocks in order to escape from predators. When they are excited or alarmed, they thump their feet against the ground. Their predators include snakes, lizards, foxes, jackals, and cats.

When female gundis give birth, there are usually one to three young in a litter. Female gundis typically only have one litter per year. Young are born with all their fur as well as their eyes open and feed on chewed leaves.

GUNDIS AND PEOPLE

Gundis are hunted as food by some North African tribes. They could possibly be harmful to crops and gardens, if there were any near their living areas.

CONSERVATION STATUS

The felou gundi is the only species that is listed as Vulnerable, facing a high risk of extinction, by the World Conservation Union (IUCN), due to a decrease in its range and habitat. The other species are not globally threatened, although they could be threatened locally by human disturbances.

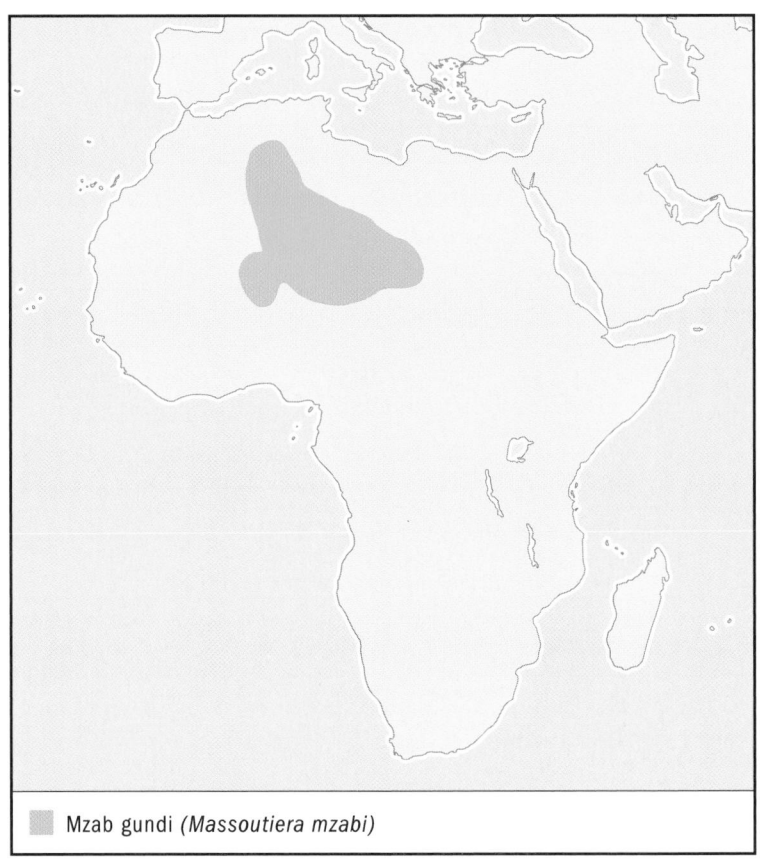

Mzab gundi (*Massoutiera mzabi*)

MZAB GUNDI
Massoutiera mzabi

Physical characteristics: Mzab gundis are yellow or brown in color with flat, round ears that are flattened against their heads and do not move. They have powerful limbs and bushy tails. They have rough, friction pads on their feet that help them climb rocks and almost vertical surfaces. These pads can also stand extreme heat. Bristles above their claws help them when they dig through sand and also when grooming themselves. They have long, thick fur to keep them warm during cold winters. The females weigh more than the males, adult males weighing around 6 ounces (171 grams), and adult females weighing around 6.7 ounces (190 grams). Their length, which includes their head and body, is 6 to 10 inches (15 to 26 centimeters). Their tail is about 1.4 inches (3.6 centimeters) long.

Geographic range: Mzab gundis live in the central Sahara Desert in Algeria, northern Niger, northwestern Chad, northeastern Mali, and southwestern Libya.

Habitat: Mzab gundis can be found in rock outcrops in mountainous areas above the Sahara Desert. They live in rock crevices and have many temporary shelters that they use.

Diet: Mzab gundis eat leaves, stems, flowers, and seeds. They sometimes drink water, but they also obtain it just from eating plants.

Mzab gundis are active for most of the day. When it is very hot, they rest in the shade, and if it is cold and wet, they stay inside their burrows. (Illustration by Bruce Worden. Reproduced by permission.)

Behavior and reproduction: Mzab gundis sleep during the night and forage in the early morning. They are active for most of the day, with the exception of when it becomes very hot, which is when they seek out shade. Their main activities are grooming and sunbathing. When they are grooming, a hind leg strokes the body while their other legs provide balance. They do not come out of their shelters when it is cold or wet. They communicate with chirps, but not very often. Even though males of the same and different groups can show aggressive behavior toward one another, Mzab gundis live in family groups that form close ties to one another. This can be seen especially in the fact that females will help out one another during pregnancy and when they are giving birth.

Young are usually born anywhere from March to June. Within an hour of their birth, young are roaming and sunbathing. They weigh around 0.7 ounces (20 grams) and have an adult weight within three months of being born.

If approached by a predator, Mzab gundis lie motionless on their side with their legs stretched out, their mouth half open, and their eyes wide open, so they look like they are dead. They will take flight after about two to three minutes of staying in this position.

Mzab gundis and people: Mzab gundis do not typically interact with people.

Conservation status: Mzab gundis are not globally threatened. ■

FOR MORE INFORMATION

Books:

Alderton, David. *Rodents of the World.* New York: Facts on File, 1996.

Delany, M.J. "Rodents." In *Reader's Digest Encyclopedia of Animals,* edited by Dr. Harold G. Cogger, et al. Sydney, Australia: Weldon Own Pty Limited, 1993.

Gould, Dr. Edwin, and McKay, Dr. George, eds. *Encyclopedia of Mammals,* 2nd ed. San Diego, CA: Academic Press, 1998.

Nowak, Ronald M. "Gundis." In *Walker's Mammals of the World,* 6th ed. Baltimore: The Johns Hopkins University Press, 1999.

Web sites:

Myers, P. "Ctenodactylidae." Animal Diversity Web. http://animal-diversity.ummz.umich.edu/site/accounts/information/Ctenodactylidae.html (accessed on May 22, 2004).

DORMICE

Myoxidae

Class: Mammalia

Order: Rodentia

Family: Myoxidae

Number of species: 26 species

PHYSICAL CHARACTERISTICS

Dormice look a lot like squirrels or chipmunks. Their fur is thick and soft and most species have long, bushy tails. Their tails help them to balance. Species are different sizes, but their average head and body length falls into the range of 1.6 to 8 inches (4.1 to 20.3 centimeters), their tail length ranges from 1.5 to 6.5 inches (3.8 to 16.5 centimeters), and they weigh from 0.5 to 7 ounces (15 to 200 grams). They are nocturnal, active at night, so they have large eyes and sensitive vibrissae, stiff hairs that can be found near the nostrils or other parts of the face in many mammals. They can also hear very well. These traits help them to function at night. Dormice also live in trees, so they have pads on the soles of their feet and strong, short curved claws on their four front toes and five hind toes so that they can grab onto the trees. Both their legs and toes are short. They can also hang upside down from branches by turning their hind feet backwards and grabbing onto the branches.

GEOGRAPHIC RANGE

Dormice are found in Europe, Africa, central and western Asia, and Japan.

HABITAT

Dormice can be found in deciduous forests, woodlands, grasslands, gardens, parks, rocky areas, or scrub areas. Within these areas, they create nests where they rest during the day. These nests are built off of the ground in holes in trees, rocky crevices, abandoned burrows, building attics, or in wedges of tree branches. The nests are ball-shaped, and are made out of leaves, grass, moss, lichen, shredded bark, other plant pieces, and saliva. They are lined with hair or feathers.

DIET

Dormice are omnivores, they eat plants and animals. Most of the time, they get their food from the trees in which they live. In the early spring and early summer, they eat buds and tree flowers. In the summer, they eat insects, small rodents, and bird eggs. In the late summer and fall, they eat fruit, berries, seeds, and nuts. They also eat snails and young birds. The specific type of food that they eat depends on their lifestyles and living areas, which is different from species to species. They also eat a lot during the fall in order to build up a layer of body fat to live on when they hibernate, go into a resting state during the winter season.

BEHAVIOR AND REPRODUCTION

Dormice usually live in small groups where half are younger dormice. Families hibernate together during winter. Hibernation occurs for about seven months. During this time period, their body temperature drops and their breathing and heartbeat slows down. They curl into a ball, with their tail covering their mouth so that they lose the least amount of water. They may wake up during this period in order to eat stored food, but this does not happen frequently. This extended resting time helps the dormice survive when there are low temperatures and little food to be found. Hibernation ends around April, when the weather gets warmer. At that time, they eat a lot of food and begin their mating season.

Dormice usually are not protective of their territory, but this changes during the mating season, when males become aggressive about their territory. Males use calls to attract the females. Males mate with more than one female during the mating season. The females can give birth from May to October. They are pregnant for three to four weeks. They can have anywhere from two to ten babies in a litter, although four babies is an average. The mother gives birth in her nest, in a tree hollow, on a branch, or maybe even underground in a shelter. When the young are born, they are pink, blind, and weigh around 0.07 ounces (2 grams). They grow gray hair by the time they are seven days old. When they are eighteen days old, they can see and hear and have brown hair. They are soon able to go out and find food with their mothers. When they are four to six weeks old, they are ready to go off and live on their own, but they may stay with their mothers through the next hibernation period. At the end of their first hibernation, the young are around a year old, and are ready to mate that spring. Dormice can live up to six years.

DORMICE AND PEOPLE

Due to the fact that dormice store food in their bodies in the form of fat, humans use dormice as a food source. They typically run into humans when they are trying to find areas in which to hibernate. They may even enter human homes for this very purpose. They can cause problems for humans when they eat the fruit in orchards.

CONSERVATION STATUS

More than half of dormice species are at risk. Dormice are threatened by loss of habitat and climate change, which changes their habitats and causes temperature shifts. The World Conservation Union (IUCN) lists four dormice species as Endangered, facing a very high risk of extinction; four as Vulnerable, facing a high risk of extinction; and five as Near Threatened, not currently threatened, but could become so.

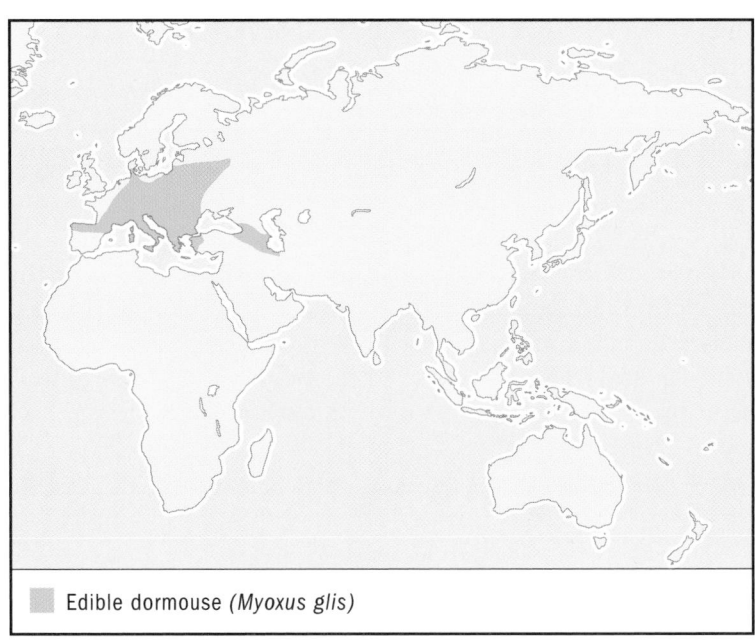

Edible dormouse (*Myoxus glis*)

EDIBLE DORMOUSE
Myoxus glis

Physical characteristics: Edible dormice are a silver-gray color with white or yellow undersides. They have black areas around their eyes. They look like squirrels. They have large, round ears, small eyes, and long, very bushy tails. They use the rough pads on their feet to climb trees. Their head and body length is 5 to 8 inches (13 to 20 centimeters), their tail length is 4 to 7 inches (10 to 18 centimeters), and their weight is 2.4 to 6.3 ounces (68 to 179 grams). They are the largest of all the dormice.

Geographic range: Edible dormice live in Europe, Iran, and Turkmenistan.

Habitat: Edible dormice can be found in deciduous and mixed forests, and fruit orchards. Within these areas, they build their nests in woodpecker holes, fake nest boxes, hollow trees, rocks, and barns. They use hairs and feathers to line their nests. If there is not enough food available in their living area, they will move elsewhere.

Diet: Edible dormice eat a lot. By the winter, their weight will be almost double the weight they were at the beginning of the summer. They will eat insects in the summer, since fruit and seeds are not ripe enough. Once fruit and seeds become suitable for eating, they will eat them, as well as nuts, acorns, berries, and buds. They are mostly herbivores, plant-eating, and only eat insects or small birds when they have no other choice.

Behavior and reproduction: Edible dormice can be very quick and can also jump more than 23 feet (7 meters) when going from tree to tree. The males are territorial and tough fighters during mating season, which goes from June until August. They will mark their territories by scent, so that other males know not to cross over into their areas. The males make a squeaking sound during mating season while they follow around the females, in hopes of attracting a mate. The females will only give birth once a year and the males help raise, clean, and protect the young. The families may stay with one another during the hibernation months. Edible dormice can make a variety of sounds, including clicks, whistles, and growling. These sounds can take on different meanings. If predators attack them, they can make their tails fall off as a form of defense—the predator keeps the tail, but the dormouse escapes.

Edible dormice eat mainly plant material, such as fruit and seeds. They eat insects in the summer, before the fruit and seeds are ripe. (© B. Brossette/ OKAPIA/Photo Researchers, Inc. Reproduced by permission.)

Edible dormice and people: Edible dormice can serve as food to people. In some areas, they are even considered to be a delicacy. They can also cause damage to humans when they destroy fruit or vine crops. They may also be captured for their fur.

Conservation status: Edible dormice are listed as Near Threatened by The World Conservation Union (IUCN), meaning that the species is not threatened now, but could be in the near future. ■

FOR MORE INFORMATION

Books:

Alderton, David. *Rodents of the World.* New York: Facts on File, Inc., 1996.

"Dormice" and "Fat Dormouse, or Edible Dormouse." In *Walker's Mammals of the World,* 6th ed. Vol. II. Baltimore: The Johns Hopkins University Press, 1999.

"Dormouse." In *National Geographic Book of Mammals.* Washington, DC: National Geographic Society, 1998.

"Edible Dormouse." In *Smithsonian Handbooks: Mammals.* New York: DK Publishing, 2002.

Macdonald, David, ed. *The Encyclopedia of Mammals.* Volume III. New York: Facts on File, Inc., 2001.

Web sites:

"Myoxus glis." Animal Diversity Web. http://animaldiversity.ummz. umich.edu/site/accounts/information/Myoxus_glis.html (accessed on June 12, 2004).

DASSIE RAT
Petromuridae

Class: Mammalia

Order: Rodentia

Family: Petromuridae

One species: Dassie rat (*Petromus typicus*)

PHYSICAL CHARACTERISTICS

Dassie rats look a lot like squirrels. Soft and silky hair covers their bodies, with the exception of the undersides, which are yellow and hairless. The hairs are joined together in groups of three or five. Their fur color is usually brown, gray, or buff, or a combination of those colors. These colors help them blend into the surrounding rocks in their habitat. This sort of camouflage helps keep birds from spotting them from above.

Dassie rats have blunt heads; big eyes; short, black, round ears; and long, black vibrissae, stiff hairs that can be found near the nostrils or other parts of the face in many mammals. The tail is shorter than the head and body length, and long hairs cover the end part of their tails. Their tails have soft joints, which allow the tail to break off at the base if a predator, animal that hunts it for food, grabs a dassie rat by the tail. The dassie rat can simply release its tail and escape, relatively unharmed.

Dassie rats' front feet have four toes with claws. The thumbs on the front feet are short. Their hind feet have five toes with short, curved claws. The hind feet also have thicker hairs that look like tiny combs and are probably used for grooming. The soles of their feet have round, naked pads that help them to move around in the rocky areas where they live. Their feet are narrow. The head and body length of males is 10.9 to 14.0 inches (27.9 to 36.0 centimeters) and the head and body length of females is 9.9 to 14.0 inches (25.3 to 35.8 centimeters). Males weigh 6.0 to 7.4 ounces (170 to 210 grams) while females weigh 8.8 to 9.2 ounces (250 to 261 grams). Their flexible ribs

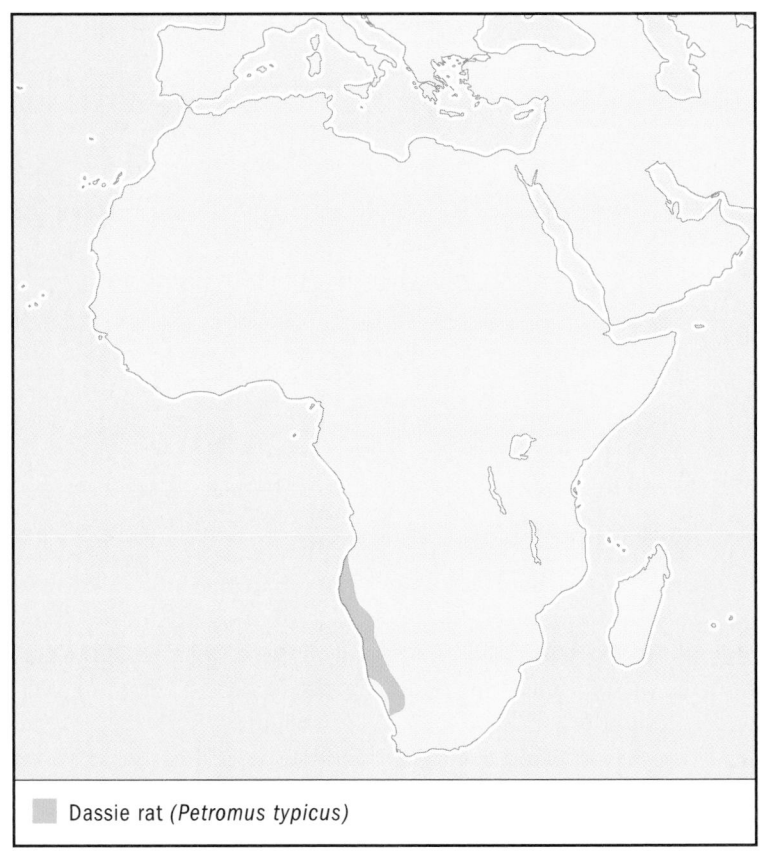

Dassie rat *(Petromus typicus)*

and flat skulls help them to flatten their bodies, and squeeze into small areas when necessary. This can be helpful when escaping from predators. The nipples on females are on their sides, rather on their undersides, so if they are squeezed into a small space, the young can still feed.

GEOGRAPHIC RANGE

Dassie rats can be found in the Southwest Arid Zone of Africa, from southwestern Angola to the central and western parts of Namibia to the northwestern Northern Cape Province in South Africa.

HABITAT

Dassie rats live in areas with a lot of rocks on hills or mountains. This environment allows them to find small areas between or under the rocks to crawl into in case of an attack by a predator. When examining living areas, dassie rats will choose an area with good shelter over an area with good plant life. The rocky shelters that they choose include lookout areas and sunbathing platforms. They make sure to choose shelters that have protecting rocks over the sunbathing platforms as a defense against birds of prey that may try to attack while they are sunbathing. In addition, feeding areas are near their shelters, so they do not have to travel long distances.

DIET

Dassie rats are herbivores, plant-eating animals. They eat leaves, berries, seeds, grasses, twigs, and shrubs. They look for this food on the ground or in bushes, and take it back to their shelters. They may use grasses and leaves to build a nest in the shelter. Dassie rats can regurgitate (re-GER-jih-tate), throw up partially digested food, into their mouths where they chew it again and then swallow it. They are also coprophagous (kuh-PRAH-fuh-gus), which means that they eat their own pellets, or dung, for additional nutrients. They do not usually drink water, but get all the water they need from their food instead.

BEHAVIOR AND REPRODUCTION

Dassie rats are active during the daytime, especially during the early morning and the late afternoon. They sunbathe under rocks that shelter them from possible attacks by birds. They often urinate in one spot, which makes the rocks at this spot become white due to stains from the urine. A dassie rat may live alone, with another dassie rat, or in a group. However, they only travel alone or with one other dassie rat.

When a predator attacks, dassie rats squeeze into a crack or other small area, quickly escape by jumping on rocks, or let out a warning whistling call to show that they are scared. Dassie rats are able to squeeze into very small cracks that most other animals would not be able to enter.

The dassie rat mating season is from November to December. Females give birth to one or two babies once a year, when the

Dassie rats can make their bodies almost flat, and squeeze into small crevices or cracks to escape predators. (Nigel Dennis/African Imagery.com. Reproduced by permission.)

raining season is just beginning. The young are born almost fully developed.

DASSIE RATS AND PEOPLE

Dassie rats do not have any special relationship with humans.

CONSERVATION STATUS

Dassie rats are not listed as threatened by The World Conservation Union (IUCN), but there is only a small population and they are not present in a large number of areas.

FOR MORE INFORMATION

Books:

Alderton, David. *Rodents of the World.* New York: Facts on File, Inc., 1996.

"Dassie Rat." In *Walker's Mammals of the World,* 6th ed. Vol. 2. Baltimore: The Johns Hopkins University Press, 1999.

Macdonald, David, ed. *The Encyclopedia of Mammals.* Vol. 3. New York: Facts on File, Inc., 2001.

Web sites:

Myers, Phil. "Family Petromuridae." Animal Diversity Web. http://animaldiversity.ummz.umich.edu/site/accounts/information/Petromuridae.html (accessed on June 12, 2004).

CANE RATS

Thryonomyidae

Class: Mammalia
Order: Rodentia
Family: Thryonomyidae
Number of species: 2 species

family

CHAPTER

PHYSICAL CHARACTERISTICS

The two species in the cane rat family, the greater cane rat and the lesser cane rat, are very similar in appearance, except for the fact that one is larger and heavier than the other. The second-largest rodents in their native continent of Africa after the South African porcupine, the cane rats range in length from 1.3 to 2.6 feet (40.9 to 79.3 centimeters) and in weight from 3.1 to 14.3 pounds (1.4 to 6.5 kilograms). Males are much larger and heavier than females. Cane rats are sturdy-looking animals, with solid, stocky bodies, short, brown, bristly, scaly tails, and small ears. Their speckled fur is sharp-ended and coarse, and can be any shade between grayish and yellowish brown. Cane rats have white lips, chins, and throats, with large, chisel-like incisor teeth that grow continuously. The upper teeth are grooved and bright orange. Their muzzles are squared and padded at the nose. These rodents have short, thick legs with heavily padded feet and straight, powerful claws with five digits in front and four in back. Their skin is very thin and tears easily, although it also heals quickly. Likewise, the tail will break off easily if the animal is caught by it. Sexually mature, those ready to mate, cane rats have orange-tinted fur in their genital areas. Cane rats do not seem to see well, but their senses of hearing and small are keen. Despite their heavy appearance, they are extremely fast and agile creatures.

GEOGRAPHIC RA\NGE

Both species are native to Africa, where they occupy habitats south of the Sahara Desert. They may be found everywhere

phylum
class
subclass
order
monotypic order
suborder
▲ **family**

A GENTLE GIANT

When threatened, cane rats thump their powerful rear feet on the ground to alert others while emitting a piercing whistling sound. Although its teeth are formidable, a frightened cane rat will virtually always run with great speed into dense vegetation and toward the nearest open water rather than turning to fight. If captured, the animals thrash frantically and are frequently injured. When enclosed in a box or crate, the rats often use their padded noses as battering rams to try to escape.

in west, central, and southern Africa all the way down to the eastern Cape in South Africa.

HABITAT

Although they look similar, the greater and lesser cane rats prefer different environments. The greater species is semi-aquatic and searches out marshes and reed beds near rivers and streams, while the lesser species looks for dry ground in moist savannas, or grasslands. Both animals are excellent swimmers and require tall grasses for hiding and foraging purposes.

DIET

Cane rats are herbivores, plant eaters, and eat a wide variety of grasses and other plant matter, as well as fruits, nuts, bark, and cultivated crops. Cane rats ferment their food in a special organ called the cecum (SEE-kum) to help digest it. They produce two kinds of feces: hard and soft pellets. Both are excreted, but the animals eat the soft pellets to extract any nutrients remaining in them.

BEHAVIOR AND REPRODUCTION

Cane rats earned their African nickname of "grass cutter" because of their method of eating: after using their powerful incisors to cut grasses at their base, the animals take the bunch of grass in their forefeet, sit upright on their haunches, and begin to feed the grass into their mouths slowly, cutting it up into small bits. When eating and when relaxed, they make soft grunting noises.

Primarily nocturnal, cane rats create and use narrow trails through the grass and reeds to move around their territories. Biologists think they live in groups of no more than twelve individuals. Males, who live with their young and a few mature females, do not tolerate the presence of other mature males, and aggressively defend their family groups. Males fight by pressing their padded noses together until one eases up on the pressure, at which point his opponent may swiftly swing his rump around to knock the weaker rat off balance.

Despite their well-developed claws, cane rats use burrowing only as a last resort for shelter and even then would rather use abandoned porcupine or aardvark burrows or holes in stream banks cause by erosion if dense vegetation for hiding is absent. Cane rats have been observed gnawing on rocks, pieces of tusk, and bones, presumably to sharpen their teeth.

The cane rats mate with multiple partners throughout the year, although primarily during the rainy season when more food is available. In captivity, pairs reproduce at any time of the year. Pregnant females create a special nursery nest, carving out a shallow depression in a sheltered area and using leaves and grass to line it. She gestates, is pregnant, for 137 to 172 days, and may have two litters of one to eight pups each year. The pups are born with open eyes and are completed furred. They nurse for about a month, but stay with the adults until they reach sexual maturity at five months of age, when males begin to show aggression toward each other.

CANE RATS AND PEOPLE

The meat of both cane rat species is highly prized as an excellent and good-tasting protein source in an often harsh environment. Organized hunts for the animals are frequently held. Some farmers have even started to domesticate "microherds" of them, and families sometimes rely on sale of their meat for income. In Ghana, the price of cane rat meat reportedly surpasses that of beef, sheep, and pork. Farmers are often angered by the rats' frequent raids on their crops, and encourage pythons to come into their fields to feed on the animals.

CONSERVATION STATUS

Abundant in all areas with suitable habitat, neither the lesser nor the greater cane rat is threatened.

Greater cane rat (*Thryonomys swinderianus*)

GREATER CANE RAT
Thryonomys swinderianus

Physical characteristics: The larger of the two cane rat species, the (male) greater cane rat ranges in length from 26.1 to 30.9 inches (67.0 to 79.2 centimeters) and in weight from 11 to 14.3 pounds (5 to 6.5 kilograms), although there are reports of these animals weighing as much as 19.8 pounds (9 kilograms). Females are generally smaller. Greater cane rats have powerful, stocky bodies, massive heads, and small, broad, fur-covered ears. Perhaps their most striking feature is their gigantic, bright-orange incisor teeth. The animals have thick, coarse, pointed hair over its body that varies in shades of brown on top and much lighter fur underneath, with orange-tinted fur in the genital areas of mature adults. The forefeet are smaller than the back feet, but both have large, well-formed claws. The forefeet have five digits, but the first and fifth are very small. There are reports of captive greater cane rats living for four years or more.

Geographic range: The greater cane rat is present in almost all countries west of the Sahara Desert except in areas of rainforest, dry scrubland, or desert. Their existence has been recorded in Gambia, Cameroon, the Central African Republic, Uganda, Sudan, Kenya, Tanzania, Malawi, Zambia, Mozambique, Angola, Namibia, Botswana, South Africa, and Zimbabwe.

Habitat: Greater cane rats favor low-lying, swampy places along streams and riverbanks where there are dense patches of reeds and tall grasses.

The greater cane rat is a good swimmer, and prefers to live in marshes and reed beds near rivers and streams. (© Yann Arthus-Bertrand/Corbis. Reproduced by permission.)

Diet: This species eats primarily the tender new shoots of elephant grass, pennisetum grass, kikuyu (kee-KUH-yuh), and buffalo or guinea grass, along with the plant roots and stems. They feed on bark, fruits, and nuts in more limited quantities. The greater cane rat also eagerly forages for vegetables in cultivated gardens and are voracious consumers of such crops as cane sugar, maize, pumpkins, sweet potatoes, millet, peanuts, sorghum, wheat, and cassava.

Behavior and reproduction: Mostly nocturnal, this polygamous (puh-LIH-guh-mus) cane rat lives alone or in small family groups with a dominant male, several adult females, and their young. They startle easily and run immediately for the closest water, using their excellent swimming, speed, and agility to outmaneuver predators. Females gestate for 152 to 156 days, giving birth to two to four pups on average, although the range is from one to six.

Greater cane rats and people: Like their smaller cousins, the greater cane rat is viewed by humans as both an important food source and a serious threat to cultivated crops.

Conservation status: These animals are abundant in all locations with habitat suitable for them, and not threatened. ■

FOR MORE INFORMATION

Books:

De Graff, G. *The Rodents of Southern Africa.* Durban and Pretoria: Butterworths, 1981.

Mills, M., et al. *The Complete Book of South African Mammals.* Cape Town: Struik Winchester, 1997.

National Research Council. *Microlivestock: Little-Known Small Animals with a Promising Economic Future.* Washington, DC: National Academic Press, 1991.

Nowak, Ronald M. "Cane Rats." In *Walker's Mammals of the World Online 5.1.* Baltimore: Johns Hopkins University Press, 1997. http://www.www.press.jhu.edu/books/walkers_mammals_of_the_world/rodentia (accessed on June 15, 2004).

Periodicals:

Van der Merwe, M. "Breeding Season and Breeding Potential of the Greater Cane Rat *Thryonomys swinderianus* in Captivity in South Africa." *South African Journal of Zoology* 34, no. 2 (1999): 69–73.

Web sites:

Animals Online. "Great Cane Rat *Thryonomys swinderianus:* Fact Sheet." http://www.animals-online.be (accessed on June 15, 2004).

AFRICAN MOLE-RATS
Bathyergidae

Class: Mammalia
Order: Rodentia
Family: Bathyergidae
Number of species: 14 species

PHYSICAL CHARACTERISTICS

African mole-rats are small to medium-sized rodents with streamlined bodies 3.2 to 11.0 inches (83 to 281 millimeters) in length and with a weight of 1.2 to 31.0 ounces (34 to 896 grams). African mole-rats bodies are covered in hair that is thick and short, except for one species. They have robust heads, small eyes, very small ears, and flattened pig-like noses. The stiff hairs are thicker on the front of the face and around the eyes. Their necks are muscular so there is not much change in size from their head to body and their limbs are short giving their bodies an overall cylindrical appearance. On the outer edges of their hind feet and on their short tail they also have stiff hairs, except for one species. They also have stiff hairs that are used for touching that are scattered all over their bodies. Under their loose skin they have long, strong muscles. The African mole-rats have large, ever growing, white incisors, sharp-edged teeth which are flat, in the front of the mouth used for cutting and tearing food.

GEOGRAPHIC RANGE

African mole-rats are found in sub-Saharan Africa.

HABITAT

African mole-rats inhabit dry regions such as savannas, or flat grasslands, and open woodlands. The rodents are not found in dense forests. They are usually found in areas with plants that provide an underground food source such as bulbs, tubers, and rootstalks. African mole-rats live in burrow systems consisting of a complicated network of foraging tunnels. The tunnels usually include a deeper nest complex with an area for relieving bodily waste, and usually one or more food storage areas. The surface opening is sealed except when dug-out soil is taken out.

DIET

They eat bulbs, tubers, and corms, the underground stem base of plants such as the crocus or gladiolus. Food is either eaten when it is found or brought back to a central storage area near the nest. Large food sources are often left to grow, and eaten on from time to time.

BEHAVIOR AND REPRODUCTION

African mole-rats are considered by experts to show the widest range in social structure of all mammals. They are solitary rodents, and spend much of their time underground. Almost all species dig by biting the soil with their large incisor teeth or in one genus (JEE-nus), a group of animals with similar characteristics, by loosening soil with strongly developed forefeet. Muscular lips with strong hairs keep soil out of the mouth. The loosened soil is pushed under their bodies with their forefeet and then collected and kicked behind them with their hind feet until it is kicked out of the surface opening.

Courtship and mating activities are short encounters between a male and female. Pups at about two months of age begin to make their own burrows. Colonies of social African mole-rats have divisions of labor for reproductive activities. A single female, the queen, and a few chosen males do the mating. Remaining members, who are related to the breeders, are helpers. They remain members of the colony unless environmental conditions allow them to go out on their own or if a breeder dies. If the breeding female dies, some of the oldest females in the colony become sexually active and often fight for the highest position of breeding female. The gestation period, the amount of time the offspring is in the womb, is forty-four to 100 days. Litter, a group of young animals born at the same time from the same mother, size is from less than four up to twenty-eight, depending on the species.

AFRICAN MOLE-RATS AND PEOPLE

African mole-rats are considered pests in farmlands and in urban developments. Their burrows often damage roads, airport runways, and other such structures. They can also chew through underground cables, irrigation pipes, and other human-made objects.

CONSERVATION STATUS

One species of African mole-rat is listed as Vulnerable, facing a high risk of extinction in the wild, and six species are listed as Data Deficient, meaning there is not enough information available to decide their status.

Damaraland mole-rat (*Cryptomys damarensis*)

DAMARALAND MOLE-RAT
Cryptomys damarensis

Physical characteristics: Damaraland mole-rats have either grayish yellow-brown or dark brown coat colors. In either case, they have a large white patch on the top of the head. Damaraland mole-rats have a flattened nose; very small eyes; two large incisor teeth on top and another set of large incisors on the bottom of the mouth; five thin claws on each foot; and a stubby tail. They weigh about 4.6 ounces (130 grams), with males a little larger than females. Weight varies depending on social status.

Geographic range: They are widely found in Namibia, most of Botswana, and extending into western Zimbabwe and northwestern South Africa.

Habitat: They inhabit dry regions with an average annual rainfall of under 15.6 inches (40 centimeters). They prefer red Kalahari desert arenosols, sandy soils featuring very weak or no soil development; loose deposits of rivers and streams; and sands.

Diet: They eat geophytes (JEE-oh-fites), plants with underground organs such as bulbs, tubers, and rootstalks. Large geophytes are eaten at the place they grow, while the smaller ones are carried back to a communal storage area. The animals dig together as a group in search for food.

The Damaraland mole-rat uses its incisors for digging. (Wendy Dennis/FLPA—Images of Nature. Reproduced by permission.)

Behavior and reproduction: Damaraland mole-rats are highly organized and social creatures. They use their incisor teeth for digging. These rodents live in colonies of up to forty animals. The colony consists of a single breeding female, her several male partners, and their non-breeding offspring. The breeding animals control the colony. Pups of breeders remain as non-breeding helpers. Breeding occurs throughout the year. The gestation, pregnancy, period is seventy-eight to ninety-two days. The litter size is one to five, but averages three. The breeding female can have up to four litters in one year. Breeders can live more than ten years.

Damaraland mole-rats and people: There is no known significance between people and Damaraland mole-rats.

Conservation status: Dameraland mole-rats are not threatened. ■

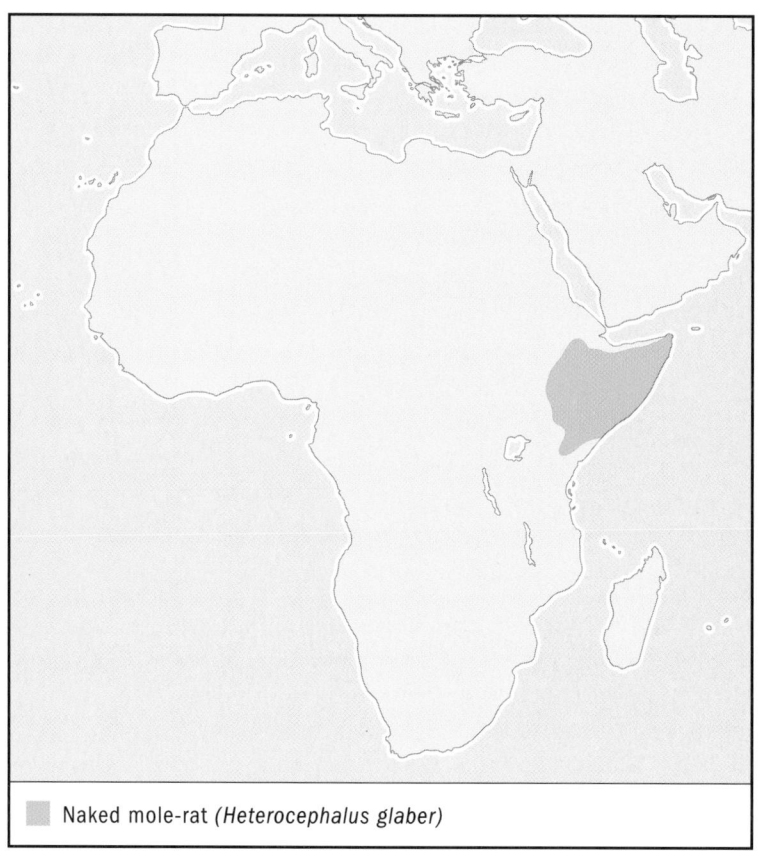

Naked mole-rat (*Heterocephalus glaber*)

NAKED MOLE-RAT
Heterocephalus glaber

Physical characteristics: Naked mole-rats, sometimes called sand puppies, are the smallest of the mole-rats. Even though they are called both moles and rats, they are much more closely related to porcupines, chinchillas, and guinea pigs. They are nearly hairless except for scattered sensory hairs. They lack the fur typically found on rodents have underdeveloped eyes and pinkish brown to pinkish gray wrinkled skin, long buck teeth, and long tails. Adults have an average length of 3 inches (7.6 centimeters), and an average weight of about 1.2 ounces (34 grams). Males and females look alike but size varies with social status; and dominant individuals can weigh up to 2.8 ounces (80 grams).

Geographic range: They are widely found in the regions of the Horn of Africa; that is, the east-central Africa area that includes Ethiopia, Somalia, and Kenya.

Habitat: Naked mole-rats inhabit dry regions with an average annual rainfall of under 15.6 inches (40 centimeters). They like fine sandy soils that become very hard in dry seasons.

Diet: Their diet consists of geophytes that are found through the coordinated foraging, searching for food, of colony members. They almost constantly dig tunnels in search of irregular food supplies and to escape snakes, their primary predator. The animals also eat feces, solid bodily waste; in fact, the breeding female and the weaning pups often beg for feces from colony members.

Behavior and reproduction: Naked mole-rats are highly social animals, living in complex underground colonies, which is unique among mammals, and much more common among insects, with 20 to 300 animals, but with an average of 75. They live almost their entire lives in the total darkness of underground burrows, living in the same home range for many years. The rodents have very underdeveloped eyes so,

Naked mole-rats live almost their entire lives in the total darkness of underground burrows, living in the same home range for many years. (© Gregory G. Dimijian, M.D./Photo Researchers, Inc. Reproduced by permission.)

instead, use highly accurate sensitivities to vibrations in the ground. They show a very highly developed division of labor that is centered on reproduction. One breeding female mates with several males, often one to three; all such animals are called the breeders. All other members are non-breeding worker and soldier animals that are offspring of the breeders and do all the jobs necessary within their territory in order to ensure the success of the group.

The breeding female stops non-breeding members from breeding with aggressive behaviors. Most non-breeders never leave the colony or breed. Odors separate friends from enemies, which is achieved by all members from rolling about in the burrow's toilet chamber, and coating their bodies with the familiar scent of the colony's feces and urine. Naked mole-rats will fiercely attack unfamiliar intruders, such as when another colony breaks into another colony's burrow system. Some breeding occurs outside the colony from animals that are highly sexed and attracted to animals from other colonies.

The breeding female has a distinctive elongated body and up to seven pairs of nipples. Her breeding occurs throughout the year. The gestation period is sixty-six to seventy-four days. The average litter size is one to twenty-eight, but the average size is twelve. Up to four litters are born each year. They live long lives, and females are able to reproduce into old age.

Naked mole-rats and people: There is no known significance between people and naked mole-rats.

Conservation status: Naked mole-rats are not threatened. ■

FOR MORE INFORMATION

Books:

Feldhemer, George A., Lee C. Drickamer, Stephen H. Vessey, and Joseph F. Merritt. *Mammalogy: Adaption, Diversity, and Ecology.* Boston: WCB McGraw-Hill, 1999.

Nowak, Ronald M. *Walker's Mammals of the World,* 6th ed. Vol. 2. Baltimore and London: The Johns Hopkins University Press, 1999.

Vaughan, Terry A., James M. Ryan, and Nicholas J. Czaplewski. *Mammalogy,* 4th ed. Philadelphia: Saunders College Publishing, 2000.

Whitfield, Philip. *Macmillan Illustrated Animal Encyclopedia.* New York: Macmillan Publishing Company, 1984.

Wilson, Don E., and DeeAnn M. Reeder, eds. *Mammal Species of the World,* 2nd ed. Washington, DC and London: Smithsonian Institution Press, 1993.

family

PHYSICAL CHARACTERISTICS

The Old World (living in Africa, Asia, and Europe) porcupines (called "quill pigs" in Latin) take their English name from the formidable spines, quills, and bristles that cover their sides, back, and tail. Their heads and bodies together range in length from between 13.8 to 36.6 inches (35 to 93 centimeters) and the animals usually weigh between 3.3 to 66.1 pounds (1.5 to 30 kilograms). The eleven species fall into three genera (JEN-uh-ruh; plural of genus): *Hystrix,* the Old World porcupines; *Trichys,* which are more slender mammals with flatter, shorter, and less-developed quills; and *Atherura,* which includes the brush-tailed porcupines. Most of the species have short tails, but others can have tails up to half of their head-body length. Eyes are usually small and can see only poorly, but the mammals' small ears are very keen. Nostrils are often S-shaped and contribute to a strong sense of smell.

Species in the *Hystrix* genus (JEE-nus) are stocky, somewhat lumbering animals with rounded, blunt heads; mobile, fleshy noses; split upper lips; and coats of thick flattened or cylindrical spines. The mammals stay on the ground at all times, never venturing into trees like their cousins, the New Age porcupines of North America. *Hystrix* alone among the porcupines has chambers in its skull that can be inflated, possibly to increase the ability to smell underground food sources. This slow-moving genus has short, thick front and back feet, with five digits on each foot, although the "thumb" on the front feet is much smaller than the other digits. Their claws are short and the pads on their feet are bare and smooth. The whole sole of

phylum

class

subclass

order

monotypic order

suborder

▲ **family**

the foot touches the ground when the animals run or swim. These porcupines have black or brown white-banded, barbless (no barb, or hook on the end) quills that can reach up to 7.9 inches (20 centimeters) in length. The longest spines are usually on the hindquarters and the shortest on the cheeks. Their short tail is tipped with many thin, open-ended quills that rattle loudly whenever the animal moves. If some quills detach during a fight, the area will grow back new ones.

In animals of the genus *Trichys,* spines are short, relatively flat, and not well developed. These more slender species, which look almost more like bristly weasels than porcupines, do not rattle their spines when they move or when threatened. The species of the genus *Atherura* are rat-like creatures with unusually long tails tipped with a tuft of bristles. The tail is easily broken. Their spines are also flattened, but stiletto-sharp quills on their backs and sides make them intimidating opponents. Webbed feet make them good swimmers, and they readily climb trees as well. All of the Hystricidae species are primarily nocturnal, hiding from predators during the day. Except for the genus *Trichys,* spines normally lie flat when the animals are relaxed, but can be raised instantly into a bristling, quivering mass when threatened. All of the Old World porcupines have large, chisel-shaped upper and lower cutting teeth (incisors) that grow continuously throughout their lives. They are reputed to be quite intelligent animals, as evidenced by their uncanny ability to avoid traps. They normally live about ten years in the wild, and average twenty years in captivity, which they seem to tolerate well.

GEOGRAPHIC RANGE

Old World porcupines tend to live in the warmer habitats of southern Europe, many islands of the East Indies, across southern Asia (particularly India and the Malay Archipelago), and through all of Africa.

HABITAT

Old World porcupines generally like to live in deep burrows, which they often dig themselves or appropriate after the former occupants leave. However, they will also live in caves, rotting logs, nooks in rock walls, and hollow trees.

DIET

Mostly herbivores, plant eaters, Old World porcupines eat numerous kinds of plant material and human-cultivated crops.

Some of their favorite foods are sweet potatoes, onions, bananas, grapes, corn, pineapple, cucumbers, and mangoes. They sometimes eat rotten meat (carrion) and chew up the bones as well, probably for calcium. They also chew on bark, branches, and tree trunks to keep their incisor teeth worn down to acceptable levels.

BEHAVIOR AND REPRODUCTION

Legendary for their ability to defend themselves, Old World porcupines (like their New World relatives) use their formidable spiny armor to fend off predators (mainly birds of prey, hyenas, pythons, large owls, leopards, and wild cats). Except for *Trichys* species, these shy, rather anxious creatures generally try to scare away an opponent first by clicking their teeth together, grunting and huffing, and stamping their hind feet, which rattles their quills to make an intimidating buzzing noise. If that tactic fails, the porcupines launch a lightning-fast backward or sideways charge toward the predator in an effort to puncture the offender's skin deeply with its quills.

The mating habits of porcupines are the subject of many jokes and much curiosity. The truth is close to the old punchline, "Very carefully." Old World porcupines engage in a complex courtship that occurs once (occasionally twice) a year from March to December. It involves a mating dance during which the male showers the female with urine. If she rejects her suitor, the female becomes very aggressive, stamping her feet and shaking her quills. If she approves of the male, he will stand still in front of her and then move toward and away from her many times while making certain sounds. The final phase of the courtship occurs when the female raises her hindquarters into the air and lowers her chest to the ground. The male approaches and mounts her with one paw on each of her sides, holding on loosely but not leaning on her at all. Their intercourse is accompanied by loud squeals, grunts, and whines.

The female will carry her young (gestate) for 93 to 112 days, and gives birth to one or two pups (sometimes up to four) in a grassy nest within the multichambered burrow. The 12-ounce

A MYTH DISPELLED

It is not true that porcupines can "throw" or project their quills in any way, but they do detach easily—sometimes just when the animals rattle them to try to scare away predators. The quills do not carry poison, although bacteria on the shafts often cause serious infections if they puncture deeply enough. Infections eventually kill many predators unlucky enough to tangle with a porcupine.

(340-gram) pups have fur when they are born and can move on their own immediately. They nurse for three or four months, but after just a week the pup's quills begin to form and they may leave the nest with their mother. Old World porcupines reach sexual maturity at anywhere from nine to 18 months.

OLD WORLD PORCUPINES AND PEOPLE

Porcupines are hunted in many countries for their meat, which is considered a delicacy, and for their quills, which many cultures use for decoration and religious symbols. Because of their fondness for human-grown crops, they are also hunted as a pest species. Often infested with fleas and ticks, porcupines carry the sometimes deadly bubonic (byoo-BON-ik) plague and rickettsiasis, a potentially serious bacterial infection.

CONSERVATION STATUS

Although many porcupine species are extremely adaptable to changing environmental conditions, some are threatened, according to the World Conservation Union (IUCN). The Malayan porcupine is listed as Vulnerable, facing a high risk of extinction in the wild; and the thick-spined and North African crested porcupines are Near Threatened, not currently threatened, but could become so.

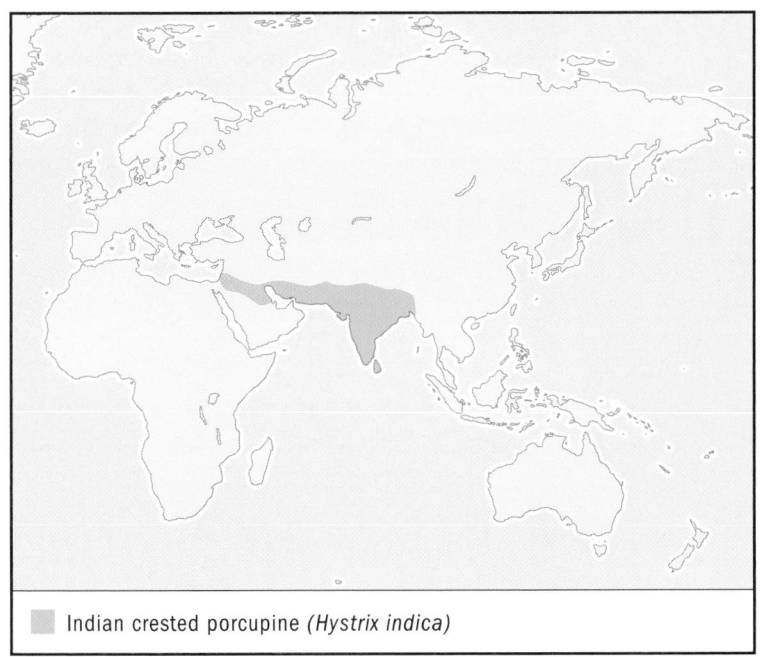

Indian crested porcupine *(Hystrix indica)*

INDIAN CRESTED PORCUPINE
Hystrix indica

Physical characteristics: The Indian crested porcupine is known among the other *Hystrix* species for its ability to produce an especially loud rattle with its quills. It ranges in head-to-rump length from 27.6 to 35.4 inches (70 to 90 centimeters) and is the largest of the African porcupines, ranging from 24.3 to 39.7 pounds (11 to 18 kilograms). This species has a short, high head that features a prominent mane of quills on its head and neck that can be up to 16 inches (40 centimeters) long and which the animal can raise into a tall, threatening crest immediately. Its sides and back are covered with thick, cylindrical spines and its tail is layered with white, shorter quills. Each of the porcupine's feet is broad and has a thick, well-developed claw for digging burrows and finding food.

Geographic range: This porcupine is endemic throughout southwest and central Asia, including India, Bhutan, Nepal, Bangladesh, and Sri Lanka, and in some parts of the Middle East, such as Iran, Israel, and Saudi Arabia.

An Indian crested porcupine with relaxed quills. The porcupine can quickly raise the quills on its head and neck into a tall crest when it's threatened. (© S. Nagendra/Photo Researchers, Inc. Reproduced by permission.)

Habitat: This species prefers to live on rock-strewn hillsides to as high as 7,875 feet (2,400 meters), but can adapt to just about any environment. They also make homes in scrublands where trees are sparse and in grasslands and forests. Like most of the porcupine species, the Indian crested shelters in caves, crevices, or burrows they or other animals have dug. When used for a period of time, their burrows become quite complex, with multiple entrances, chambers, and exits.

Diet: Like its cousins, the Indian crested porcupine eats human-grown crops of almost all kinds, in addition to wild vegetation, carrion, small bugs and mammals, and bones or antlers. Except when parents are teaching their young to forage, the search for food is usually solitary. They seems to prefer wandering along roads or tracks, and have been observed traveling more than nine miles in a single nighttime foraging trip.

Behavior and reproduction: Females of this species carry their young for an average of 112 days before giving birth, usually in February or March, in a grass-lined nest to a litter of one to four pups. Most females have only one litter per breeding season. Adults form monogamous (muh-NAH-guh-mus) pairs and both care for the young during the three-and-a-half–month nursing period. Up to fifteen members of a family group will share one burrow.

Indian crested porcupine and people: This porcupine species is hunted as a source of food in many cultures, and its voracious appetite for human-grown crops makes it a major threat to agriculture. Its extensive burrowing is damaging in gardens and other landscaped areas, and run-ins with the porcupines can cause serious illness and injuries to domestic animals and humans.

Conservation status: The Indian crested porcupine is common throughout its range. Its ability to adapt to multiple habitats and environmental changes make it a hardy species. Hunting of the creatures, however, has all but eliminated them from areas heavily populated by humans. ■

South African porcupine *(Hystrix africaeaustralis)*

SOUTH AFRICAN PORCUPINE
Hystrix africaeaustralis

Physical characteristics: The South African porcupine is the biggest rodent in its native region, ranging in head-to-rump length from 2.3 to 2.8 feet (71 to 84 centimeters) and weighing from 39.7 to 66.1 pounds (18 to 30 kilograms). Females tend to weigh slightly more than males. Even among animals known for their sharp senses of smell and hearing, this species has exceptionally keen senses. Their bodies are stocky, with sharp quills up to 11.8 inches (30 centimeters) long emerging from among the course, black hair that covers them. Their spines, as in the other species, are even longer, reaching up to 19.7 inches (50 centimeters). The animals can voluntarily erect the crest of spines and quills on their backs and napes, which are colored in black and white bars. The quills on the tips of their tails are

South African porcupines eat bulbs and tubers, and many aboveground plants. Here one feeds on gemsbok cucumbers. (Clem Haagner/Bruce Coleman Inc. Reproduced by permission.)

hollow at the ends, which cause them to make a startling whizzing sound when shaken. The South African porcupine has long whiskers and air-filled cavities in the facial area of its skull, while its nasal bones are larger than normal for a creature of its size. All of these are probably adaptations to help the porcupine find food more easily. The creatures walk with an alternating gait, as a dog or cat would. They can swim and climb trees well, and often live twelve to fifteen years even in the wild.

Geographic range: This porcupine is found only African countries south of the Sahara, not including the southwestern coastal desert.

Habitat: This species seeks out habitat with rocky outcroppings and hillsides, but may be found at elevations up to 11,480 feet (3,500 meters) where vegetation is abundant. It requires shelter during the day, and uses caves or other animals' abandoned holes for that purpose.

Diet: The South African porcupine uses its powerful claws to dig up tubers, roots, and bulbs of many kinds. They especially like such cultivated crops as sugar cane, pineapples, bamboo, melons, cocoa and oil palms, and corn, but also occasionally eat carrion and gnaw on bark and bones. This species has special microorganisms in its front large intestine and appendix that help digest tough plant fibers.

Behavior and reproduction: The animals dig out cavernous, extensive dens that can reach up to 65.6 feet (20 meters) in depth, with a 6.6-foot (2-meter) deep central living chamber. As many as six family members may live together in the den, and they sometimes use it for defensive purposes by running into an entrance and erecting its spines to make it difficult (if not impossible) for predators to pull them out.

Reaching sexual maturity at between eight and eighteen months, the South African porcupine is a devoted parent that cares for its young over the long term. Females are "in heat" (estrus) for thirty-five days, during which they mate with their chosen partner. This species usually has two litters a year, during the wettest months between March and April. Females gestate for 93 to 105 days, then give birth to one to four pups in the family's grass-lined nesting chamber. Although they can eat solid food from birth, the pups nurse for about 100 days. The female cannot conceive another litter for three to five months after her season's first litter is weaned, stops feeding on breast milk.

South African porcupine and people: This species is hunted for its meat in many locations where people consider it a delicacy, while the porcupine's destructive and voracious feeding habits make them the enemy of many farmers, gardeners, and landscapers.

Conservation status: The South African porcupine is not threatened anywhere in its range, although humans and large cats sometimes reduce populations significantly for a short time. ■

FOR MORE INFORMATION

Books:

Alderton, David. *Rodents of the World.* New York: Facts on File, 1996.

Gould, Edwin, and George McKay, eds. *Encyclopedia of Mammals,* 2nd ed. San Diego: Academic Press, 1998.

Nowak, Ronald M. *Walker's Mammals of the World,* 6th ed. Vol. 2. Baltimore and London: Johns Hopkins University Press, 1999.

Vaughn, Terry A. et al. *Mammology,* 4th ed. Philadelphia: Saunders College Publishing, 2000.

Web sites:

"The Porcupine." African Wildlife Foundation. http://www.awf.org/wildlives (accessed on June 22, 2004).

"*Hystrix indica.*" Discovery.com. http://animal.discovery.com (accessed on June 22, 2004).

"*Hystrix africaeaustralis.*" Fernkloof Nature Reserve. http://fernkloof.com (accessed on June 22, 2004).

"Seh Porcupine-*Hystrix indica.*" Haryana (India) State Online. http://haryana-online.com (accessed on June 22, 2004).

"Hystricidae." The Free Dictionary. http://encyclopedia.freedictionary.com (accessed on June 22, 2004).

"Hystricidae." Animal Diversity Web. http://animaldiversity.ummz.umich.edu (accessed on June 22, 2004).

NEW WORLD PORCUPINES
Erethizontidae

Class: Mammalia
Order: Rodentia
Family: Erethizontidae
Number of species: 19 species

phylum
class
subclass
order
monotypic order
suborder
▲ **family**

PHYSICAL CHARACTERISTICS

New World porcupines are some of the largest North American rodents. They are stocky animals with many sharp quills, modified guard hairs, and spines that in most species are hidden beneath long fur but are visible in others. Quills lie facing downward and spines cover most of their upper bodies and tail, except for a few species that have no spines. The animals have a prehensile, able to grasp by wrapping around, tail that can reach about one-fourth to over one-half its length. Its head consists of a blunt muzzle, small rounded eyes that are nearly hidden by hair, and small rounded ears. Its body has humped shoulders, short bowed legs, and long curved claws. Adults are 15.5 to 51.0 inches (40 to 130 centimeters) long and weigh between 6.5 and 22.0 pounds (3 to 10 kilograms).

GEOGRAPHIC RANGE

New World porcupines are found in North, Central, and South America, from Canada and Alaska to Argentina.

HABITAT

These porcupines live primarily in trees throughout rainforests and deciduous and coniferous woods, except for one species that lives in deserts and a few others that are found in plantations and other cultivated areas.

DIET

New World porcupines eat fruits, seeds, leaves, and bark.

BEHAVIOR AND REPRODUCTION

New World porcupines are assumed to be nocturnal, active at night, and arboreal, living in trees, spending their days sleeping in trees or in private ground places. They spend most of their time alone, but during winter months, several animals often share a winter den. Their winter territory averages 12 acres (5 hectares), while the larger summer territory reaches a maximum of 35 acres (14 hectares). Although not territorial, they defend feeding grounds during winters. They can spear their quills into attackers with spines that are detached. When faced with a predator, an animal that hunts and eats other animals, they erect their quills so they stick out in many directions and chatter their teeth. New World porcupines either remain stationary in a defensive position, or may charge the predator by quickly whipping out with their quill-laden tail.

Most of the time New World porcupines do not communicate with each other. Females do touch their young with their nose, giving them gentle grunts and whines. During the mating season, porcupines become noisy with various grunts, moans, screams, and barks. It is believed that females are either pregnant or lactating, producing milk, for most of their lives. The gestation period, the time period the offspring are in the womb, lasts about 200 days. When gestation is over the female mates again. Females nurse, feed on mother's milk, their newborns for eight to twelve weeks. A litter, young animals born together from the same mother, is usually only one young, which is born with fur and soft quills that harden quickly. The young reach adult size in about one year, and become sexually mature (able to mate) in one-and-a-half to two-and-a-half years. Their average lifespan is fifteen years.

NEW WORLD PORCUPINES AND PEOPLE

Some New World porcupines are hunted by people. The quills of some species are used in artwork.

CONSERVATION STATUS

New World porcupines are not threatened.

North American porcupine *(Erethizon dorsatum)*

NORTH AMERICAN PORCUPINE
Erethizon dorsatum

Physical characteristics: North American porcupines have stiff, dark-brown or black hair on their back along with scattered white barbed quills at the head, rear of body, and on the tail. They may have more than 30,000 barbed quills, many of which have a yellow-white base with a dark tip. Their face is a dark brown, with a woolly belly that does not have quills. Their undersides are covered with stiff, dark hairs. North American porcupines have a short, thick tail that contains quills above and stiff bristles below and large, naked feet. Their large incisor teeth are deep orange. Adults have a length of about 39 inches (1 meter) with the tail being one-fifth to one-third of the total length. Body weight is less than 26 pounds (12 kilograms), but a large male can be up to 33 pounds (15 kilograms). Juveniles

have a nearly all-black head, back, and tail. Their quills are short but sharp. Females have two pairs of mammae (MAM-ee), milk-secreting organ of female mammals.

Geographic range: North American porcupines range throughout Canada, except the far north-central regions, and down into the northeastern and north-central part of the United States and almost all of the western United States except the most southern regions. They also extend into the northern edge of central Mexico.

Habitat: North American porcupines are found in mixed hardwood and softwood forested areas, tundra, and occasionally in open areas and even deserts as long as plenty of water sources are around. They prefer rocky areas, ridges, and slopes.

Diet: North American porcupines are herbivores, animals that eat plant material, such as fruits, grains, and seeds. They feed on foliage for much the year and on inner bark of pine and oak trees in winter. They also eat seeds, fruits, nuts, berries, and plant stems, buds, twigs, leaves, roots, and flowers. Their chisel-like teeth scrape away the tough outer bark, and then slice off pieces of inner bark to eat. North American porcupines eat alone, except for mothers and their young. They feed at night, but sometimes during the day, especially if the weather has been bad.

Behavior and reproduction: North American porcupines are mostly arboreal and nocturnal animals. They are good at climbing trees, although their slow movements seem awkward, and are good swimmers. They use hollow trees and logs, or gaps beneath rocks for their winter dens. The animals normally live alone, but will share a winter den when few good locations are available. They are not territorial, but will defend a feeding site if resources are few. During the breeding season, females produce bodily odors to show males they are ready to mate. Several males fight over the right to mate with one female. One of their courtship rituals is for the male to spray the female with urine. When females are ready, they will dance with their chosen male, rising on their hind feet, embracing while whining and grunting loudly, and pushing one another playfully to the ground. Their main predators include mountain lions, lynx, fishers, coyotes, bobcats, red foxes, wolves, wolverines, and great horned owls. During winter months they stay close to their den but go further out during summer months.

They are polygynous (puh-LIH-juh-nus), having more than one mate. Mating occurs only once a year, in the late summer and early autumn, and only during an eight to twelve hour period when the female is receptive. Females give birth to one but sometimes to two young. The gestation period is about seven months. Young weigh about 1.0 to 1.1 pounds (450 to 490 grams) at birth, and are born with both spines and fur. They double their weight within the first two weeks. They usually feed on their mother's milk for only a short period then begin to feed on vegetation shortly after birth. They soon become entirely independent of the mother. Young males move in and out of the mother's range for months or years, while young females leave the range permanently. They become sexually mature at about one-and-a-half years and most can live to about fifteen years of age.

North American porcupines and people: Native Americans used their quills for artwork and as a type of currency. North American porcupines were also hunted for food. They are often considered as pests when they gnaw through valuable wood and trees.

Conservation status: North American porcupines are not threatened. ■

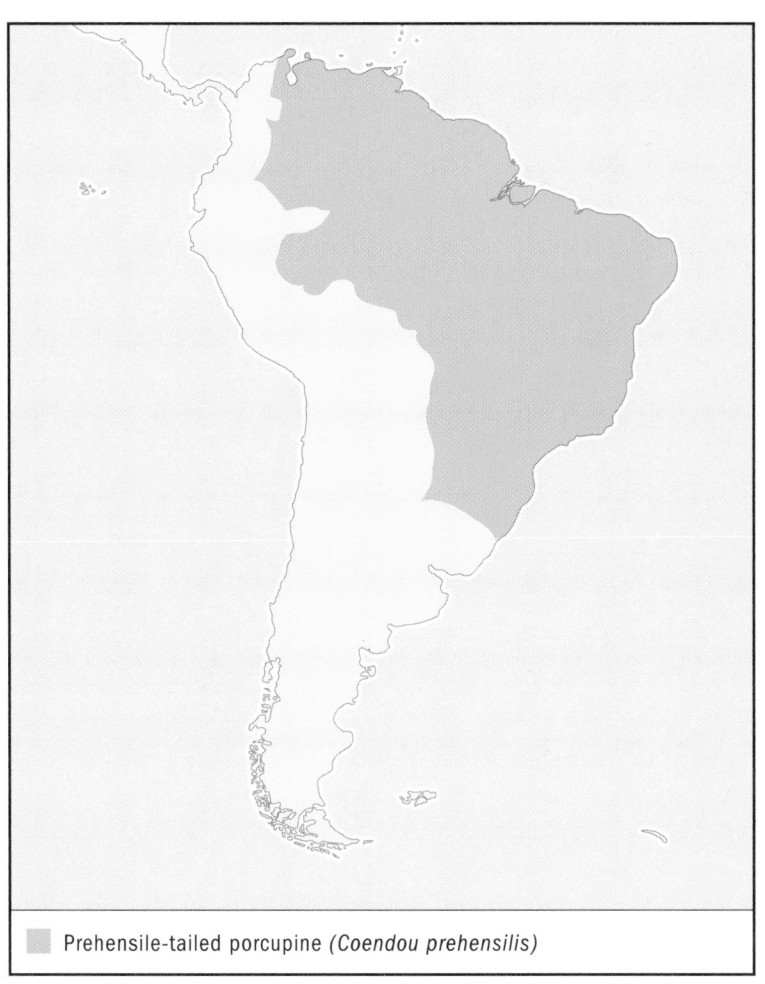

Prehensile-tailed porcupine (*Coendou prehensilis*)

PREHENSILE-TAILED PORCUPINE
Coendou prehensilis

Physical characteristics: Prehensile-tailed porcupines have a grayish to yellowish brown body with short, thick spines that are whitish or yellowish and mixed with darker hair. Their face is whitish and undersides are gray. Their padded feet have four long-clawed toes. The tail is small, long, black, and prehensile with a curled tip. The last one-third of the tail does not contain spines on its upper surface, which helps it to wrap around thin branches. Juveniles have an orangish brown to brown body with longer fur that sometimes hides its spines. Adults are 3 to 4 feet (0.9 to 1.2 meters) long with half of

the length being its tail. They weigh between 9 and 12 pounds (4.0 and 5.5 kilograms).

Geographic range: They are found in eastern South America from eastern Venezuela and Trinidad to northeastern Argentina and Uruguay.

Habitat: The animals inhabit vine-covered rainforests and jungles, but can also be found in agricultural areas, gardens, and drier forests near water sources.

Diet: Prehensile-tailed porcupines are herbivores, eating mostly fruits, seeds, stems, leaves, roots, small twigs and shoots, and bark. They usually eat during the late part of the day.

Behavior and reproduction: Prehensile-tailed porcupines are shy, nocturnal porcupines that are solitary, alone, or live in pairs or gather in groups occasionally. They spend most of their time high in tree branches; going from tree to tree by climbing down one tree, walking across the ground, and climbing up another tree. The animals move slowly, but can move fast when they must. They are good climbers, mostly due to their long, prehensile tail and padded, clawed feet. Prehensile-tailed porcupines sleep during the day, usually within a clump of vegetation in the forest's canopy. When threatened by a predator, they are not aggressive but will defend themselves if attacked. Prehensile-tailed porcupines often roll into a ball and raise their quills. Sometimes they attack the predator by quickly moving toward the intruder with spines erect. They will also stomp feet, shake spines, and make threatening snarls and grunts. They communicate with each through long moaning sounds.

During breeding periods, a male will spray urine onto a female and may also spray newborns. Females reproduce about every seven months. They often give birth during the rainy season, but it is not clear if this is always the case. The gestation period is 195 to 210 days. After giving birth usually to one young, the female will almost immediately mate again. Newborns are covered with red hairs and small spines, which harden shortly after birth. Young are weaned, no longer fed its mother's milk, after three months. Adulthood is reached in about eleven months and sexual maturity in about nineteen months.

Prehensile-tailed porcupines and people: People occasionally hunt prehensile-tailed porcupines for food. They are sometimes considered an agricultural pest.

Conservation status: Prehensile-tailed porcupines are not threatened. ■

FOR MORE INFORMATION

Books:

Feldhemer, George A., Lee C. Drickamer, Stephen H. Vessey, and Joseph F. Merritt. *Mammalogy: Adaption, Diversity, and Ecology.* Boston: WCB McGraw-Hill, 1999.

Nowak, Ronald M. *Walker's Mammals of the World,* 6th ed. Vol. 2. Baltimore and London: The Johns Hopkins University Press, 1999.

Vaughan, Terry A., James M. Ryan, and Nicholas J. Czaplewski. *Mammalogy,* 4th ed. Philadelphia: Saunders College Publishing, 2000.

Whitfield, Philip. *Macmillan Illustrated Animal Encyclopedia.* New York: Macmillan Publishing Company, 1984.

Wilson, Don E., and DeeAnn M. Reeder, eds. *Mammal Species of the World,* 2nd ed. Washington, DC and London: Smithsonian Institution Press, 1993.

Class: Mammalia

Order: Rodentia

Family: Chinchillidae

Number of species: 6 species

CHAPTER

phylum

class

subclass

order

monotypic order

suborder

 **family**

PHYSICAL CHARACTERISTICS

Known for their luxuriously thick fur, these cuddly-looking, rabbit-like animals range in head-and-body length from 11.8 to 23.6 inches (30 to 60 centimeters) and can weigh from 1.1 to 19.8 pounds (0.5 to 9 kilograms). Females are usually larger than males. The animals' fur, which vary in color from brown to bluish gray to pearly white, have a uniform, soft underfur. The chinchillas and mountain viscacha have especially fine, silky fur, as well as special bristles on their back feet to groom themselves. As many as sixty hairs can grow out of one hair follicle. All the species have bushy tails. Viscachas are generally larger than chinchillas, while chinchillas have much larger ears and longer tails relative to their size. All of the species have broad, large heads, thick necks, and strong feet and rear legs. With its distinctive black-and-white facial pattern, the plains viscacha is unique among the family. Depending on their native environment, some of the animals are adapted to jumping, while others have evolved to burrow. The pads of their feet are hairless, and front feet are usually shorter than the back feet, which are long and bony. The four digits on their front feet are dexterous and useful in manipulating food. Their cheek teeth grow continuously and must be worn down regularly. The pupils of their eyes are cat-like, with vertical slits.

GEOGRAPHIC RANGE

This family of mammals occurs only in western and southern South America, but their largest populations are in southern Peru, Argentina, Bolivia, and northern Chile to the foothills of the Andes Mountains in Patagonia (Argentina).

HABITAT

While most of the viscacha species tend to remain at elevations below 1,640 feet (500 meters), the mountain viscacha and chinchillas colonize areas from 13,120 to 16,400 feet (4,000 to 5,000 meters). The plains viscacha lives in grasslands with sparse vegetation, but all the other species seek out rocky areas where they can dig their burrows and hide from numerous predators.

DIET

Chinchillids (members of the Chinchillidae family) are mainly herbivores, plant eaters, and live on seeds and grass, although those species endemic at higher elevations also eat mosses and lichens. All species occasionally eat insects as well.

BEHAVIOR AND REPRODUCTION

The mountain viscacha and all the chinchillas eat, sunbathe, and groom while sitting erect on their hindquarters. The plains viscacha and all the chinchillas look for food at sunset and throughout the night, but the mountain viscacha is alert and active by day and hides by night. All of these animals live in colonies of some sort, but some are more tightly knit and structured than others. For instance, the plains viscacha is compelled to use a communal burrow system, and the colony is dominated by a strong male and an assistant he chooses from the fifteen to thirty members of the family group. On the other hand, chinchillas and mountain viscachas have a more relaxed social structure in which the colony is more spread out and can consist of from four up to 300 animals, with different burrows housing individual family groups. As colonial animals, there is always at least one individual on guard to watch for predators and other dangers. The mountain viscacha has a warning call that sounds like a high whistle, whereas the plains viscachas have a more varied palette of sounds, including a characteristic "uh-huh" sound, numerous whines, and their own species-specific warning calls. All six species have been observed taking dust baths and engaging in play chases, and all but the plains viscacha are amazingly agile as they jump among rocky outcroppings.

Female chinchillids are very aggressive to other females and even many males, with much growling, teeth chattering, and urinating, although there are rarely serious fights in the wild. They have unusually long gestation periods for rodents of their size, carrying their young 90 to 154 days before giving birth to one to six pups. The average female, which reaches sexual maturity (able to mate) at from eight to fifteen months, can produce one to three litters every year. Pups are born with open eyes and are fully furred, and their mothers nurse them for six to eight weeks. This species usually has more than one mating partner during the breeding season.

LONG LIVE THE CHINCHILLA

Many chinchilla species live up to ten years in the wild and sometimes over twenty in captivity. Some have even been known to start families at fifteen years old, having been sexually mature since eight months of age.

VISCACHAS, CHINCHILLAS AND PEOPLE

All species in this family, but especially the chinchillas, have been intensively harvested and farmed commercially for their valuable fur as well as for their meat. Their pelts are still the most expensive in the world. Plains viscachas are considered a pest and are destroyed in large numbers in many areas because their foraging leaves large swaths of bare ground (ten of them are rumored to eat as much as a sheep daily) and their burrows cause many cows and horses to break legs when they accidentally step into them.

CONSERVATION STATUS

Due to overharvesting, the long-tailed chinchilla is listed as Vulnerable, facing a high risk of extinction, by the World Conservation Union (IUCN), while the short-tailed chinchilla is Critically Endangered, facing an extremely high risk of extinction. The animals are now protected by law in their native habitats, although this is of limited benefit due to their remote habitats. Conservation groups have attempted to reintroduce chinchillas to Andean habitats, but with no success so far.

Long-tailed chinchilla (*Chinchilla lanigera*)

LONG-TAILED CHINCHILLA
Chinchilla lanigera

Physical characteristics: As its English name indicates, the long-tailed chinchilla has an unusually long and bushy tail, averaging 5.6 inches (141 millimeters). The animals weigh about one pound (0.5 kilogram) and measure about 14.4 inches (365 millimeters) from nose to rump. Females can be much larger than males. This chinchilla has gray and black fur on its back and sides, with lighter fur on its belly. Every hair on its body has a black tip.

Geographic range: Also known as the Chilean chinchilla, it lives only in the mountainous regions of northern Chile.

Habitat: This species lives in semiarid, rocky, and sparsely vegetated areas between 9,840 and 16,400 feet (3,000 to 5,000 feet).

Diet: The long-tailed chinchilla eats mainly grass and seeds of any available plants, but sometime eats insects and bird eggs as well.

Behavior and reproduction: Biologists report that female long-tailed chinchillas are generally monogamous, meaning that they have only one mate. They carry their young for an average of 111 days, usually delivering two pups. Most will have two litters a year. Mating seasons are from May to November in the Southern Hemisphere and from November to May in the Northern Hemisphere.

This species is active mostly at dusk and at night. Females are the dominant species in the colonies, which can reach up to 300 individuals, and show high levels of aggression with much vocalization. Long-tailed chinchillas are famous for their feats of agility as they leap about their rocky homes. Captive-bred chinchillas are very shy and bond easily with their owners.

Long-tailed chinchillas and people: Even among mammals prized by humans for their pelts, the long-tailed chinchilla is especially sought after. Coats made of their fur have sold for more than $100,000. Many of the animals are cross-bred with other species in captivity for this purpose.

Conservation status: The IUCN has listed this species as Vulnerable. With the last sighting of the animal in 1953, it is virtually unknown in the wild. Before laws had been put in place to protect the species, seven million pelts (individual furs) had been exported to buyers in other countries. They are also threatened by habitat destruction—specifically the burning and harvesting of the algarobilla shrub. ■

FOR MORE INFORMATION

Books:

Burton, J. *The Collins Guide to the Rare Mammals of the World.* Lexington, MA: The Stephen Greene Press, 1987.

Nowak, Ronald M. "Chinchillas." In *Walker's Mammals of the World Online 5.1.* Baltimore: Johns Hopkins University Press, 1997. http://www.press.jhu.edu/books/walkers_mammals_of_the_world/rodentia (accessed on June 23, 2004).

Redford, K. H. *Mammals of the Neotropics: The Southern Cone.* Vol. 2. Chicago: University of Chicago Press, 1992.

Periodicals:

Jimenez, J. "The Extirpation and Current Status of Wild Chinchillas, *Chinchilla lanigera* and *C. brevicaudata.*" *Biological Conservation* 77 (1995): 1–6.

Web sites:

"Long-tailed Chinchilla; *Chinchilla lanigera.*" ARKive Images of Life on Earth. http://www.arkive.org (accessed on June 23, 2004).

"*Chinchilla lanigera.*" Animal Diversity Web. http://animaldiversity.ummz.umich.edu (accessed on June 23, 2004).

Class: Mammalia

Order: Rodentia

Family: Dinomyidae

One species: Pacarana (*Dinomys branickii*)

family

CHAPTER

phylum

class

subclass

order

monotypic order

suborder

▲ **family**

PHYSICAL CHARACTERISTICS

Also known as Branick's giant rat after the Polish count who first described the species in 1873, the pacarana is the sole member of the Dinomyidae ("terrible mouse") family. The name pacarana comes from a Tupi Indian term meaning "false pig." Full-grown pacaranas weigh between 22 and 33 pounds (10 to 15 kilograms), and from nose to rump measure from 28 to 31 inches (730 to 790 millimeters). Their tails are usually 7.5 inches (190 millimeters) long. Sturdy and compactly built, their heads are broad and large in proportion to their bodies. They have short but extremely powerful limbs with four digits and formidable claws on each. Pacaranas have a thick coat of coarse, grayish brown or blackish hair with rows of white spots on the back half of the body. The animal has bushy, white whiskers on either side of its blunt snout and a deeply split upper lip. It is the third-largest rodent on Earth, after the capybara and the beaver, and some people say it looks like a gigantic guinea pig or spineless porcupine.

GEOGRAPHIC RANGE

A South American rodent, pacaranas' sparse populations may be found in the mountainous areas of a band running through western Venezuela, western Colombia, central Ecuador, Peru, part of western Brazil, and into northwestern Bolivia.

HABITAT

In Peru, this species occupies suitable habitat from 800 to 6,600 feet in elevation (240 to 2,000 meters), but in Venezuela they

PACARANAS IN SAN DIEGO?

Although their ancestors' native land of Colombia is thousands of miles away, a thriving colony of pacaranas has been established at the San Diego Zoo. The animals can live for at least thirteen years in captivity, and are easily trained to perform in shows.

occur up to 7,870 feet (2,400 meters). Pacaranas live in montane forests and rainforest valleys of the Andes Mountains. They prefer to live in cracks in rock walls or outcroppings, but caves are also attractive habitats.

DIET

Pacaranas are mainly vegetarian and especially favor palm berries and other fruits as well as the stems and leaves of tender young plants.

BEHAVIOR AND REPRODUCTION

Because most pacarana behavior has been studied among captive animals, biologists know little about how these animals act in the wild. However, we do know that they are active mostly at night, when they spend most of their time in solitary searches for food. They occasionally climb trees to get to food sources, but spend most of their time on the ground, sitting up on their haunches to manipulate food with their forelimbs. They do not seem to dig, despite their sturdy claws. Although their Latin name indicates a placid nature and slow-moving ways, pacaranas are well equipped to defend themselves and have a strong will to do so. They can be surprisingly vicious in attacks on interlopers and predators, animals that hunt them for food, alike, including pet dogs and other pacaranas. They can climb well and walk on two feet occasionally for various purposes. Adults often live alone, but have also been observed cohabiting in pairs and family groups. Their communication with each other is fairly sophisticated and features seven different sounds, including singing, hissing, tooth chattering, stamping their front feet, and whining.

Pacaranas make a sound like crying to attract mating partners, and then engage in an elaborate courtship ritual during the breeding season in about November through January. The ritual has been described as a mixture of dancing and wrestling, with much sniffing, growling, and whimpering as a male and female stand on their hind legs to grapple with each other and interlock their front cutting teeth. Head-tossing is common prior to the male mounting the female, which he does after approaching her with dramatically trembling legs. Females

Pacarana *(Dinomys branickii)*

gestate, or experience pregnancy, for about 222 to 283 days and can be quite aggressive during the pregnancy. Scientists have never observed pacaranas building nests. Litter sizes are usually one or two pups, each of which weighs about 32 ounces (900 grams). Young can move around independently almost immediately and are born with eyes open and fully furred.

PACARANAS AND PEOPLE

Many native South Americans hunt pacaranas as a food source.

CONSERVATION STATUS

The IUCN has classified the pacarana as Endangered, facing a very high risk of extinction. Its normally low population

The pacarana is a slow-moving, nocturnal herbivore found in the Andes Mountains. (Francisco Erize/Bruce Coleman Inc. Reproduced by permission.)

levels, which in past years led scientists to believe the animals were extinct, are especially vulnerable to human predation and to habitat loss from human activities.

FOR MORE INFORMATION

Books:

Anderson, Sydney. *Simon and Schuster's Guide to Mammals.* New York: Fireside, 1984.

Burton, John A. *Rare Mammals of the World.* Lexington, MA: Stephen Greene Press, 1987.

McKenna, Malcolm C. *The Classification of Mammals.* New York: Columbia University Press, 2000.

Nature Encyclopedia: An A to Z Guide to Life on Earth. Oxford, U.K.: Oxford University Press, 2001.

Periodicals:

White, T. G. "*Dinomys branickii.*" *Mammalian Species* 410 (1992).

Web sites:

"Animal Info-Pacarana." Animal Info-Information on Endangered Mammals. http://animalinfo.org (accessed on June 23, 2004).

"Comparative Placentation." University of California, San Diego Medical School. http://medicine.ucsd.edu/cpa/pac.html (accessed on June 23, 2004).

"*Dinomys branickii.*" Animal Diversity Web. http://animaldiversity.ummz.umich.edu (accessed on June 23, 2004).

CAVIES AND MARAS
Caviidae

Class: Mammalia
Order: Rodentia
Family: Caviidae
Number of species: 17 species

family

CHAPTER

PHYSICAL CHARACTERISTICS

Cavies and maras, also called cavids (members of the family Caviidae), range in size from 8 to 30 inches (20 to 75 centimeters) and have a vestigial, no longer functional, tail. They generally have plump, robust bodies with large heads, and short limbs and ears. Their fur in the wild is short and coarse. Cavids have high-crowned jaw teeth that grow continuously. The size and shape of cavids range from small, tailless, short-legged cavies with body lengths of 5.9 to 15.7 inches (15 to 40 centimeters) and weights of 7.0 to 21.1 ounces (200 to 600 grams) to the larger, rabbit-like salt-desert cavies and maras with shorter tails and, slender limbs, that are 17.7 to 29.5 inches (45 to 75 centimeters) in length and weighs 2.2 to 35.2 pounds (1 to 16 kilograms). Cavies have four clawed front toes and three clawed rear toes. The rock cavy has padded feet and claw-like toes that help it climb rocks and trees. Cavies have flat-crowned teeth that are always growing.

GEOGRAPHIC RANGE

Cavies are found over most of South America, except Chile and some areas of the Amazon River basin. Maras inhabit southern Bolivia, Peru, and Argentina.

HABITAT

Cavies and maras are found in a variety of habitat, depending on the species. These include marshes, tropical floodplains, rocky mountain meadows, grassland, desert, and areas with lots

NAME GAME

Guinea pigs are neither pigs nor from the African country of Guinea. So how did they get their common name? One theory is that when they were first introduced into Great Britain in the 1500s, they were the closest animal to a pig that could be bought for a guinea, an old British coin. Another is that the sounds they make reminded people of pigs, and since they were shipped to Europe via Guinea, people thought they originated from there.

of trees and bushes near water, grasslands, and cultivated lands. They are generally not found in dense jungle or rainforests.

DIET

Cavies and maras are herbivores, meaning they eat only plants, including grasses and cacti (KACK-tie, or KACK-tee), and plant material, such as seeds, flowers, and fruits.

BEHAVIOR AND REPRODUCTION

Cavies and maras are diurnal, meaning they sleep at night and are active during the day, or crepuscular (kri-PUS-kyuh-lur), meaning they are active at twilight. They do not hibernate and live in burrows they dig or were dug by other animals. They are generally very social, living in pairs or groups. Cavies and maras have a variety of mating regimens, including hierarchical promiscuity (HI-uh-raar-kick-al prah-miss-KYOO-it-ee), which is frequent sexual intercourse based upon ranking or status in the group; polygamy (puh-LIH-guh-mee), where they have multiple mates in a single breeding season; and monogamy (muh-NAH-guh-mee), which is having sexual relations with a single partner during the breeding season. They breed year round and produce multiple litters per year. Cavids have a gestation period, pregnancy, of fifty to seventy days. The number of offspring per litter is usually one to three but can be up to seven. Maras and salt-desert cavies have seasonal breeding patterns and have litters of one or two young.

CAVIES, MARAS AND PEOPLE

Cavies, commonly known as guinea pigs, have been domesticated, tamed, and used as pets for three thousand years. Scientists also use them extensively as laboratory animals. They are raised for food in areas of Ecuador, Peru, and Bolivia. Guinea pigs are believed to have been used by the ancient Incas in religious sacrifices. Small cavies are considered to be pests by farmers in agricultural areas. Larger cavies are hunted for food and their pelts, or fur.

CONSERVATION STATUS

No cavy species are currently listed as endangered by the World Conservation Union (IUCN). Maras, sometimes called Patagonian hares, are listed as Near Threatened, not currently threatened, but could become so, by the IUCN.

FAMILY TREE FEUD

Taxonomists, scientists who classify living things, have always placed cavies and maras in the order of rodents (Rodentia) because they most resemble rats and mice. However, newer research into the genes of cavies and maras indicate they are not related at all to rodents. Instead, some scientists suggest that their genes, the basic units capable of transmitting characteristics from one generation to the next, more closely resemble those of primates.

Rock cavy (*Kerodon rupestris*)

ROCK CAVY
Kerodon rupestris

Physical characteristics: Rock cavies are about the same size or slightly larger than the common guinea pig, 11.8 to 15.7 inches (30 to 40 centimeters) long and weigh 31.7 to 35.2 ounces (900 to 1,000 grams). They have long, slender legs with well-developed, blunt nails on their padded feet and one claw used for grooming. The upper body fur is generally gray with irregular black and white patches. The lower body fur is yellow and brown while the throat fur is white. The face has a muzzle shape with a longer, blunter snout, similar to that of a dog.

Geographic range: Rock cavies are found in eastern Brazil from the state of Piaui to northern Minas Gerais.

Habitat: The species prefers dry areas with rocky outcroppings near mountains and hills.

Diet: Rock cavies are herbivores, meaning they eat only plants and plant material. Their diet primarily consists of tender leaves and shoots of plants.

Behavior and reproduction: Rock cavies received their name because they are excellent rock climbers. They are generally most active late in the day. Males claim one or several rock piles as their territory, which they will defend. Each male has a number of female mates and each group has a hierarchy, a structured order of rank. The gestation period is about seventy-five days. Rock cavies reach sexual maturity, the age when they can produce offspring, at two months. Females produce several litters per year from July to March, each with one or two young. Individuals make several vocal sounds, including a slow whistle when they leave their rock piles to search for food, and an alarm whistle. The average lifespan is six to eight years.

Rock cavies and people: Rock cavies are easily tamed and make suitable pets. Brazilians who live in the rock cavy habitat area use the mammal as food and medicine.

Conservation status: Rock cavies are not listed as threatened by the IUCN. ∎

Mara (*Dolichotis patagonum*)

MARA
Dolichotis patagonum

Physical characteristics: Maras, also called Patagonian maras or Patagonian hares, have a head and body length of 27.6 to 30 inches (69 to 75 centimeters) and a tail length of 1.6 to 2 inches (4 to 5 centimeters). They weigh form 17.6 to 35.2 pounds (8 to 16 kilograms). Their body shape looks like that of a long-legged rodent. The hind legs are slightly larger than the front legs, making them fast runners. The front feet have four toes and the back feet three toes with sharp claws. The fur of maras is grayish brown on the upper body and cream or white on the lower body. The rump has a large white patch of fur.

Geographic range: Maras are found in central and southern Argentina.

Habitat: Maras prefer milder foothill regions where there is coarse grass and scattered shrubs. They also are found in forested canyons and open grasslands.

Diet: Maras are herbivores. Their diet includes a variety of vegetation, such as leaves, grass, herbs, fruits, cactus, and seeds. In captivity, they eat primarily hay, leaves, vegetables, and oats.

Behavior and reproduction: Maras are diurnal and they live in groups of up to forty. They use a variety of movements, including walking, hopping like a rabbit, galloping like a horse, and stotting, which is bouncing on all four legs at once. They are very fast runners, capable of reaching 27.9 miles per hour (45 kilometers per hour). They make several vocal sounds, including a "wheet" when they want contact with another mara, and a grunt they use to threaten others. Maras are monogamous, meaning they have a sexual relationship with only one mate, for several years. Females give birth to three or four litters a year, each consisting of one to three offspring. Females reach sexual maturity at eight months. Gestation is 93 to 100 days. The average lifespan of the Pantagonian mara is five to seven years in the wild and up to ten years in captivity.

Maras and people: Maras are hunted in the wild for food and their skin. They are also tamed and used as pets.

Conservation status: Maras are listed as Near Threatened by the IUCN. Their numbers appear to be declining in the wild, due primarily to destruction of their habitat by humans.   ■

FOR MORE INFORMATION

Books:

Harris, Graham. *A Guide to the Birds and Mammals of Coastal Patagonia.* Princeton, NJ: Princeton University Press, 1998.

Macdonald, David. *The New Encyclopedia of Mammals.* Oxford, U.K.: Oxford University Press, 2001.

Nowak, Ronald M. *Walker's Mammals of the World,* 6th ed. Baltimore: Johns Hopkins University Press, 1999.

Siino, Betsy Sikora. *The Essential Guinea Pig.* Hoboken, NJ: Howell Book House, 1998.

Waters, Jo. *The Wild Side of Pet Guinea Pigs.* Chicago: Heinemann Library, 2004.

Periodicals:

Kolar, Patricia. "The *C. porcellus:* (a.k.a.) Pocket Pet." *Hopscotch* (August–September 2002): 46–48.

Kostel, Ken. "Guinea-zilla." *Science World* (December 8, 2003): 6–7.

Morales, Edmundo. "The Guinea Pig in the Andean Economy: From Household Animal to Market Commodity." *Latin American Research Review* (Summer 1994): 129–143.

Rowe, D. L., and R. L. Honeycutt. "Phylogenetic Relationships, Ecological Correlates, and Molecular Evolution Within the Cavioidea (Mammalia, Rodentia)."*Molecular Biology and Evolution* 19 (2002): 263–277.

Web sites:

"*Dolichotis patagonum.*" Animal Diversity Web. http://animaldiversity.ummz.umich.edu/site/accounts/information/Dolichotis_patagonum.html (accessed on May 4, 2004)

"Family Caviidae." Animal Diversity Web. http://animaldiversity.ummz.umich.edu/site/accounts/information/Caviidae.html (accessed on May 4, 2004)

CAPYBARA

Hydrochaeridae

Class: Mammalia

Order: Rodentia

Family: Hydrochaeridae

One species: Capybara
(*Hydrochaeris hydrochaeris*)

CHAPTER

PHYSICAL CHARACTERISTICS

Capybaras are the world's largest rodents. They resemble guinea pigs but are much larger. They have large, broad heads with short, rounded ears and eyes placed far back on the head. Their snout is heavy and blunt with a large upper lip and big nostrils. Their neck and legs are short. Adults weigh between 110 and 173.8 pounds (50 to 79 kilograms) and have a head and body length of 39.4 to 51.2 inches (100 to 130 centimeters).

Capybaras have four toes on their front legs and three on their back legs, all with short and strong claws. Their feet are partially webbed, making them good swimmers. Their front legs are shorter than the hind legs.

Their bodies are covered with short, coarse fur ranging in color from reddish brown to grey on the upper body and light yellow to brown on the lower body. Adult males have a bare, raised area at the top of their snouts that contains a scent gland that is used to mark their territories. The tail is short and not functional. Female capybaras are usually larger than males.

GEOGRAPHIC RANGE

Capybaras are found on the eastern side of the Canal Zone in Panama, and on the east side of the Andes Mountains in South America, including Peru, Colombia, Venezuela, French Guiana, Guyana, Uruguay, Paraguay, Bolivia, Ecuador, Brazil, and northeastern Argentina.

phylum

class

subclass

order

monotypic order

suborder

▲ **family**

HABITAT

Capybaras live in areas of dense trees and plants near rivers, streams, lakes, ponds, marshes, and swamps. There are four areas in South America where there are large concentrations of capybaras: the llanos (plains) in Venezuela, the Pantanal wetlands in western Brazil, the Taim lowlands in southern Brazil, and Marajó Island, at the mouth of the Amazon River in northeastern Brazil.

DIET

Capybaras are herbivores, meaning they are plant-eaters. Much of their time is spent grazing and foraging for food, which consists primarily of protein-rich grasses. An adult eats 6 to 8 pounds (2.7 to 3.6 kilograms) of grasses a day. They also eat water plants, fruits, and vegetables, including wild melons and squashes.

Since grasses are difficult for most mammals to digest, the capybara's digestive system has adapted to make it easier. One of these adaptations is a large fermentation chamber in the intestines called the cecum (SEE-kum). Capybaras also engage in coprophagy (kuh-PRAH-fuh-gee), which means they eat some of their own feces. These softer feces are rich in nutrients.

BEHAVIOR AND REPRODUCTION

Capybaras are social, living in groups of six to twenty animals, although groups of one hundred or more have been reported. The group has a dominant male, several adult females, their offspring, and several submissive adult males. The group is usually composed of family members and outsiders are rarely accepted. There is a social hierarchy in the group as a whole and within female members. The dominant male aggressively and sometimes viciously enforces this hierarchy.

In the wild, capybaras are usually active in the early morning and twilight. During the heat of the day, they rest intermittently in shallow beds in the ground or shaded areas of shallow water. In areas where there are higher concentrations of people, the capybara has become nocturnal, meaning it is most active at night.

Capybara (*Hydrochaeris hydrochaeris*)

When a capybara becomes startled or alarmed on land, it will run with a gallop much like that of a horse. If it feels it is in immediate danger, it will seek safety in water where it can stay submerged for about five minutes. With its partially webbed feet, the capybara is an extremely capable swimmer and diver. It can swim while submerged or with its eyes, nostrils, and ears just above the water's surface, much like a hippopotamus. It can also hide among water plants, with just its nostrils above the water line. Capybaras can make several vocal sounds, including a low-pitched clicking noise when it is content; long, sharp whistles; short grunts; and a purr to indicate submissiveness. When a capybara spots a predator or feels it is in imminent danger, it will bark. Nearby capybaras will stand motionless at alert. If the caller continues to bark, they will race into the nearest water and gather closely in a group, with their young in the center for protection.

Capybaras are somewhat territorial and the home territory of a herd or group averages about 200 acres (80 hectares). The

Newborns capybaras can see soon after birth and eat grass after one week. Young capybaras stay together in a group and females will allow infants other than their own to nurse. (Erwin and Peggy Bauer/Bruce Coleman Inc. Reproduced by permission.)

size of the range varies, depending on the season. Home ranges of groups often overlap. A group tends to get larger during the dry season and smaller in the wet season when groups tend to break into smaller groups as more marshes and wetlands are available. There are core areas within a group's range that it will protect for its exclusive use.

Mating occurs throughout the year but is highest in April and May. Females usually have one litter per year although two litters are not uncommon if conditions are favorable. The female gestation period, the time they carry their young in the womb, is 104 to 156 days. Litter size ranges from one to eight, with five being the average. Newborns can see soon after birth and can eat grass after one week. Young capybaras stay together in a group and females will allow infants other than their own to nurse. Both males and females reach puberty, the age of sexual maturity, at about fifteen months of age. The average lifespan in the wild is eight to ten years. In captivity, several capybaras have lived for more than twelve years.

Capybaras have several natural predators, animals that hunt them for food, in the wild, including jaguars, anacondas (large water snakes), and caiman (KAY-mun), a large reptile similar to alligators and crocodiles. Young capybaras are eaten by foxes, vultures, and wild dogs.

CAPYBARAS AND PEOPLE

Capybaras are hunted in the wild by humans for their meat and skin, which is used to make wallets and purses. They are also raised on ranches, much like cattle, for their commercial value. Their meat when cooked is said to taste similar to pork or chicken but with a slight fishy flavor. Its fat is used in the manufacture of pharmaceuticals (medicinal drugs). Capybaras are considered agricultural pests in some areas because they raid crops of fruits, vegetables, and sugar cane.

CONSERVATION STATUS

The capybara is not currently threatened, according to the IUCN. Hunting and exterminations by humans have caused populations to decline in some areas, particularly Venezuela and Peru, while they remain stable in others. However, some conservationists say the overall numbers are in decline.

FOR MORE INFORMATION

Books:

Alho, C. J. R., Z. M. Campos, and H. C. Gonçalves. "Ecology, Social Behavior, and Management of the Capybara *(Hydrochaeris hydrochaeris)* in the Pantanal of Brazil." In *Advances in Neotropical Mammalogy,* edited by K. H. Redford and J. F. Eisenberg. Gainesville, FL: Sandhill Crane Press, 1989.

Herrera, E. "Reproductive Strategies of Female Capybaras: Dry-Season Gestation." In *The Behaviour and Ecology of Riparian Mammals,* edited by N. Dunstone and M. L. Gorman. Cambridge, U.K.: Cambridge University Press, 1998.

Macdonald, David. *The New Encyclopedia of Mammals.* Oxford, U.K.: Oxford University Press, 2001.

Nowak, Ronald M. *Walker's Mammals of the World,* 6th ed. Baltimore: Johns Hopkins University Press, 1999.

Periodicals:

Johnson, Owain. "World's Largest Rodent Risks Extinction." *United Press International* (September 20, 2002.)

Jones, Bart. "In Venezuela, Rodent Has Cuisine Status." *The Atlanta Journal-Constitution* (August 18, 1999): D12.

Rowe, D., and R. Honeycutt. "Ecological Correlates, Molecular Evolution, and Phylogenetic Relationships within the Rodent Superfamily Cavioidea." *Molecular Biology and Evolution* 19, no. 3. (2002): 263–277.

Thomas, Z., et al. "On the Occurrence of the Capybara , *Hydrochaerus hydrochaeris* (Linnaeus, 1776) in the Dry *Chaco* of Paraguay (Mammalia: Rodentia: Hydrochaerus.)" *Faunistische Abbandlungen Dresden* 22, no. 2 (2002): 423–429.

Web sites:

Ciszek, D., and C. Winters. *"Hydrochoerus hydrochaeris."* Animal Diversity Web. http://animaldiversity.ummz.umich.edu/site/accounts/information/Hydrochaeris_hydrochaeris.html (accessed on July 12, 2004).

AGOUTIS

Dasyproctidae

Class: Mammalia
Order: Rodentia
Family: Dasyproctidae
Number of species: 12 species

family
CHAPTER

PHYSICAL CHARACTERISTICS

Agoutis are medium sized rodents, about the size of a rabbit, with long, thin legs and a squirrel-like face. Their bodies are slender in the front and bulkier in the rear. There are two genera (JEN-uh-rah; plural of genus, a group of related animals): *Dasyprocta* and *Myoprocta*. Agoutis have a head and body length of 12.6 to 25.2 inches (32 to 64 centimeters) and weigh 1.3 to 8.8 pounds (0.6 to four kilograms). They have a large head, plump body, and glossy fur. Their faces have prominent noses with whiskers, large eyes, and small ears positioned high on their head.

The tail on *Dasyprocta* species is a barely visible nub, while the tail on *Myoprocta* species is longer and readily visible. There is a wide range of colors within agoutis. In most species, the fur on their lower bodies is usually white, yellow, or buff. Their upper body fur ranges from pale orange, several shades of brown, to black. Several species have faint stripes. Their hind legs have three toes and are longer than their front legs, which have four toes. All toes have sharp, hoof-like claws.

GEOGRAPHIC RANGE

Agoutis are found from southern Mexico to southern Bolivia and northern Argentina. Their range includes Brazil, Belize, Colombia, Costa Rica, Cuba, Ecuador, Guatemala, Honduras, Nicaragua, Panama, Peru, Paraguay, El Salvador, and Venezuela. They have also been introduced into the Cayman Islands.

SOWING THE SEEDS

The agouti is an important component in the health and regeneration of the rainforests. When food is plentiful, they will bury seeds of fruit and other forest trees to eat later when food is scarce. This helps distribute seeds of a wide variety of tropical trees, including *Virola nobilis*, a giant canopy tree of the rainforest. They often follow groups of monkeys and eat fruit the monkeys drop from trees.

HABITAT

Agoutis are found throughout the forests of Central and South America, usually in areas with heavy brush, and near streams, rivers, ponds, and marshy areas. They generally graze in open areas and grassland.

DIET

Agoutis are primarily herbivores, meaning they are plant-eaters, although they will occasionally eat seafood. Their diet consists primarily of fruit. They also eat tender leaf plants, seeds, wild vegetables, freshwater crabs, and fungi. They have extremely hard teeth, which they use to crack open nuts, including the tough Brazil nut.

BEHAVIOR AND REPRODUCTION

The agouti is diurnal, meaning it is most active during the day. Agoutis are fast and agile. Their movements include walking, trotting, galloping, and they can jump up to 6.6 feet (2 meters) from a stationary position. They live mostly on the ground, making nests inside hollow logs or under aboveground tree roots. They also make burrows under stream banks.

Agoutis have a remarkable sense of direction and are able to find nuts or fruits easily, even months after they have buried them. In the wild, the agoutis' main predators are jaguars, ocelots, snakes, birds of prey, cats, dogs, and humans. In the wild, agoutis have a lifespan of thirteen to twenty years.

Agoutis are monogamous (muh-NAH-guh-mus), meaning they mate with only one partner during a period of time, and mate for life. They are able to breed throughout the year but especially when there is an abundance of fruit. Agoutis reach puberty, the age of sexual maturity, at six months. The female agouti has one or two litters per year, each consisting of one to four babies. Her gestation period, the time she carries her young in the womb, is 104 to 120 days.

AGOUTIS AND PEOPLE

Agoutis are hunted for their meat and skin. They are important seed dispersers in the tropical forests of South America. They can also be tamed as pets.

CONSERVATION STATUS

Two species, the Ruatan Island agouti and the Coiban agouti are listed as Endangered, facing a very high risk of extinction, by the IUCN. Azara's agouti is listed as Vulnerable, facing a high risk of extinction, by the IUCN. No other species are considered currently threatened by the IUCN.

Central American agouti (*Dasyprocta punctata*)

CENTRAL AMERICAN AGOUTI
Dasyprocta punctata

Physical characteristics: The Central American agouti has a head and body length of 12.6 to 25.2 inches (30 to 64 centimeters) and weighs 1.3 to 8.8 pounds (0.6 to 4 kilograms), about the size of a small cat. The body is slender. It has short ears, four toes on its front feet and three on its back feet, all with sharp hoof-like claws.

Its fur is coarse and glossy and it increases in length from the front to the rear of the body. Fur color ranges from pale yellow and orange to several shades of brown. The fur on the rump is usually a contrasting darker color. Central American agoutis in eastern Panama and Costa Rica have dark brown fur on their front, orange fur on

their middle back, and a cream-colored rump. Some Central American agouti have faint stripes.

The Central American agouti lives in lowland rainforest in Central and South America. (© Gregory G. Dimijian/Photo Researchers, Inc. Reproduced by permission.)

Geographic range: Central American agoutis are found from the states of Tabasco and Chiapas in southern Mexico to southern Bolivia and northern Argentina. Their range includes Brazil, Belize, Colombia, Costa Rica, Cuba, Ecuador, Guatemala, Honduras, Nicaragua, Panama, Peru, Paraguay, El Salvador, and Venezuela. They have also been introduced into the Cayman Islands.

Habitat: The Central American agouti prefers to live in rainforests, thick bushes, savannas, and in areas farmers have cultivated for crops. In Peru, they are concentrated around the Amazon River in the surrounding dense, low lying tropical rainforests, and in higher rainforests up to about 6,600 feet (2,000 meters) in elevation.

Central American agoutis prefer to be near water and are frequently found along the banks of rivers, streams, and lakes. They usually build dens where they sleep in hollow logs, among rock outcroppings, and under above-ground tree roots.

Diet: Central American agoutis are primarily herbivores, meaning they eat plants, although they occasionally eat seafood. Their diet consists primarily of fruit, which they are able to hear falling to the ground from far away. They also eat tender leaf plants, wild vegetables, freshwater crabs, fungi, and insects. When feeding, the Central American agouti sits on its hind legs and holds the food in its front paws, much like a common squirrel. It turns the fruit around several times, peeling it with its teeth.

Behavior and reproduction: A pair of Central American agoutis claims a territory of about 2.5 to 5 acres (1 to 2 hectares), an area containing fruit trees and a water supply. When other agoutis enter the territory, the male drives them off, fighting occasionally becoming vicious and causing serious wounds.

This agouti species is diurnal, meaning they are most active during the day. They are fast and agile. Their movements include walking, trotting, galloping, and they can jump up to 6.6 feet (2 meters) from a stationary position. When in danger, the Central American agouti stands motionless with one front paw raised. They spend much of their time grooming to remove parasites, such as ticks and mites.

Central American agoutis have a courtship ritual in which the male sprays the female with his urine several times, causing the female to jump around in frenzy, before mating. The female has one or two litters a year, each usually with two young although she can have three or four. Her gestation period, the time they carry their young in the womb, is 104 to 120 days.

Central American agoutis and people: Central American agoutis are hunted extensively for their meat and skin. They are important seed dispersers in the tropical forests of South America. They are also easily tamed as pets.

Conservation status: The Central American agouti is not listed by the IUCN. ■

FOR MORE INFORMATION

Books:

Bernard, Hans Ulrich. *Insight Guide: Amazon Wildlife,* 4th ed. London: Insight Guides, 2002.

Eisenberg, J. F., and K. H. Redford. *Mammals of the Neotropics.* Vol. 3, *The Central Tropics: Ecuador, Peru, Bolivia, Brazil.* Chicago: University of Chicago Press, 1999.

Macdonald, David. *The New Encyclopedia of Mammals.* Oxford, U.K.: Oxford University Press, 2001.

Nowak, Ronald M. *Walker's Mammals of the World,* 6th ed. Baltimore: Johns Hopkins University Press, 1999.

Periodicals:

Asquith, N. M., et al. "The Fruits the Agouti Ate: *Hymenaea courabil* Seed Fate When Its Disperser is Absent." *Journal of Tropical Ecology* 15 (1999): 229–235.

Lambeth, Ellen. "The Tree, the Bee, and the Agouti." *Ranger Rick* (March 2000): 26.

Lee, T. E. Jr., et al. "The Natural History of the Roatán Island Agouti *(Dasyprocta ruatanica)*, a Study of Behavior, Diet, and Description of Habitat." *The Texas Journal of Science* 52 (2000): 159–164.

Taylor, David. "The Agouti's Nutty Friend." *International Wildlife* (March–April 2000).

Web sites:

Myers, Phil. "Dasyproctidae." Animal Diversity Web. http://animaldiversity.ummz.umich.edu/site/accounts/information/Dasyproctidae.html (accessed on July 12, 2004).

PACAS
Agoutidae

Class: Mammalia
Order: Rodentia
Family: Agoutidae
Number of species: 2 species

phylum

class

subclass

order

monotypic order

suborder

▲ **family**

PHYSICAL CHARACTERISTICS

There are two species of paca: *Agouti paca*, commonly known as the paca, and *Agouti taczanowskii*, commonly known as the mountain paca. Though the genus name *Agouti* may be confusing, pacas and agoutis (family Dasyproctidae) are not in the same family. Pacas are among the largest of all rodents, with a head and body length of 20 to 30.5 inches (50 to 77.4 centimeters) and weight of 13.2 to 31 pounds (6 to 14 kilograms.) Their tail length is 5 to 9 inches (13 to 23 centimeters).

The paca resembles the mountain paca in most features, except the paca is slightly larger, has thinner and harsher fur, shorter nostrils, larger eyes, and thicker claws.

In both species, the upper body fur varies from reddish brown to dark chocolate or smoke-gray. There is a pattern of white or pale yellow irregular spots on the sides, arranged in rows of two to seven. The average number of rows is four. One or two upper rows are shorter and limited to the rear half of the body. Two or more middle rows run from the neck to the rump.

GEOGRAPHIC RANGE

Pacas are found from southern Mexico to northern Argentina. Their range includes Belize, Bolivia, Brazil, Colombia, Costa Rica, Cuba, Ecuador, El Salvador, French Guiana, Guatemala, Guyana, Honduras, Nicaragua, Panama, Paraguay, Peru, Suriname, and Venezuela.

HABITAT

Pacas primarily live in tropical rainforests but are also found in a wide variety of forest habitats, including mangrove swamps, deciduous and semi-deciduous forest, dense upland scrub, and narrow growth along river banks.

DIET

Both species of paca eat mainly fruit but their diet changes throughout its range and based on the seasons. Other foods include roots, seeds, leaves, buds, and flowers. In the wild, pacas are herbivores, meaning they eat only plants. In captivity, they are omnivores, meaning they eat both plants and flesh. Pacas in zoos eat fruits, vegetables, raw meat, lizards, and insects.

BEHAVIOR AND REPRODUCTION

Pacas are nocturnal, meaning that they are most active at night, and solitary animals. In the wild, they have sometimes been seen active in the early morning and late afternoon. During the day, they sleep in a den dug under tree roots or rock outcroppings, or in hollows in trees, usually along riverbanks or hillsides. The den usually has several entrances or exits concealed by leaves.

Pacas are capable swimmers and when they feel threatened, take to the water where they can remain submerged for up to fifteen minutes. They have an acute sense of smell and hearing. They walk along fixed trails, but should a trail become disturbed by humans or other animals, they will abandon it.

Pacas breed year-round. Females are sexually mature, able to mate, at nine months, while males are sexually mature at one year. The gestation, or pregnancy, period is 114 to 119 days. Females have one or two litters of young a year, each usually with one baby but in rare instances, two babies.

PACAS AND PEOPLE

Pacas are hunted by humans for their meat and are often killed by farmers who see them as agricultural pests. However, pacas are important dispersers of seeds from the *Attalea oleifera* palm tree in the Brazilian Atlantic Forest, and *Virola surinamensis*, a commercial timber tree.

NAME CHANGE

In the 1700s, the scientific name for the paca was *Cuniculus brisson* and in the twentieth century it was called *Odobenus brisson*. In the early twentieth century, it was known by the common name of coelogenys. The paca is called conejo pintado in Panama, tepezcuintle in Costa Rica, guardatinajas in Mexico, hee in Suriname, and lapa in Venezuela. Paca is the common name in Brazil and Argentina.

CONSERVATION STATUS

Pacas and mountain pacas are not listed as threatened by the IUCN. However, several wildlife surveys show their numbers in the wild are dwindling, due to extensive hunting and habitat destruction by humans.

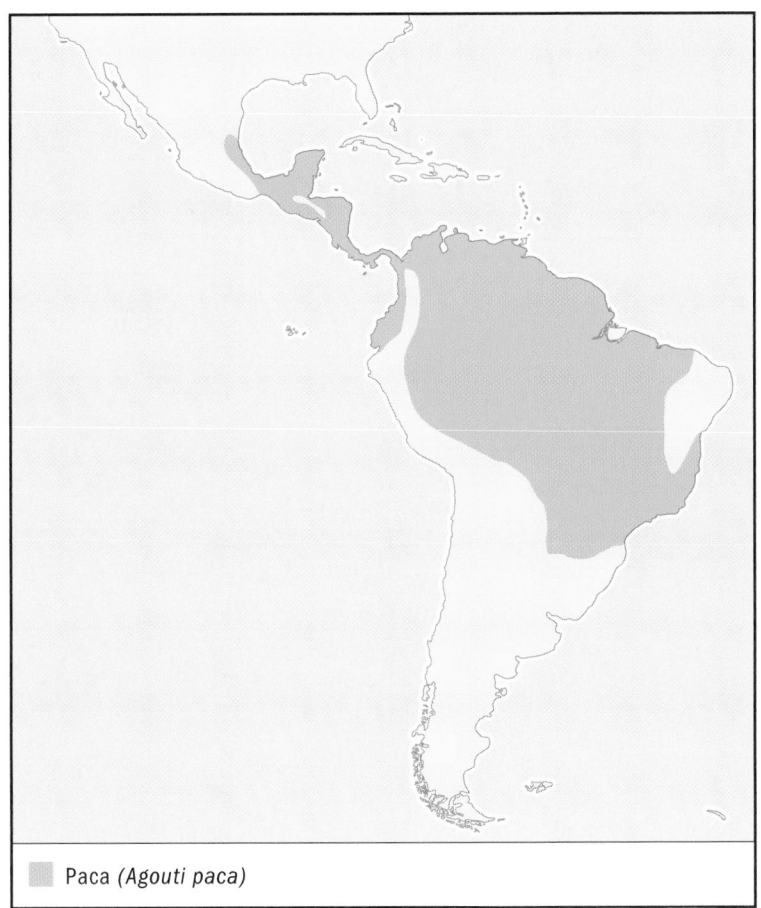

Paca *(Agouti paca)*

PACA
Agouti paca

Physical characteristics: The paca has a head and body length of 20 to 20.5 inches (50 to 77.4 centimeters) and a weight of 13 to 31 pounds (6 to 14 kilograms). They have course, slick, glossy fur that is gray, red, black, or brown on the upper body and white on the lower body. They may also have four horizontal rows of cream, gray, or white spots or marks on their sides. Pacas have four toes on their front paws and five on their back feet. They also have a somewhat arched back.

Geographic range: Pacas live in east-central Mexico to Paraguay, including Belize, Brazil, Colombia, Costa Rica, El Salvador, French

Pacas eat fruit, but do not climb trees. They count on tree-climbing animals such as monkeys to drop fruit from trees, which the pacas eat on the ground. (Frans Lanting/Minden Pictures. Reproduced by permission.)

Guiana, Guatemala, Guyana, Honduras, Nicaragua, Panama, Suriname, and Venezuela.

Habitat: Pacas live primarily in rainforests near rivers and streams. They can also be found in seasonally dry areas, swamps, and deciduous forests bordering water sources.

Diet: Pacas are herbivores that feed on leaves, stems, roots, seeds, and fruit, especially avocados and mangos. Pacas do not climb trees so they depend on tree-climbing animals such as monkeys, to drop fruit from trees.

Behavior and reproduction: Pacas are nocturnal, meaning they are most active at night. During the day, they sleep in a den dug under tree roots or rock outcroppings, usually along riverbanks or hillsides. The den usually has several entrances and exits concealed by leaves. Pacas are capable swimmers and take to the water when they feel threatened. They have an acute sense of smell and hearing.

The paca is monogamous and territorial, with a mated pair sharing a territory, which can be up to 8.6 acres (3.5 hectares). However, their territories are not exclusive and may overlap with other pairs of pacas.

Female pacas usually have one litter of babies a year but can have two or three. A litter contains one or two babies. Their gestation period, the time they carry their young in the womb, is 114 to 119 days.

Pacas and people: Pacas are hunted by humans for their meat. They are often killed by farmers who see them as pests.

Conservation status: Pacas are not listed as threatened by the IUCN. ■

FOR MORE INFORMATION

Books:

Domestication and Husbandry of the Paca (Agouti paca) *(FAO Conservation Guide: 26).* United Nations, NY: Food and Agriculture Organization of the United Nations (FAO), 1995.

Eisenberg, J. F., and K. H. Redford. *Mammals of the Neotropics.* Vol. 3, *The Central Tropics: Ecuador, Peru, Bolivia, Brazil.* Chicago: University of Chicago Press, 1999.

Macdonald, David. *The New Encyclopedia of Mammals.* Oxford, U.K.: Oxford University Press, 2001.

Nowak, Ronald M. *Walker's Mammals of the World,* 6th ed. Baltimore: Johns Hopkins University Press, 1999.

Periodicals:

Laska, M., et al. "Food Preferences and Nutrient Composition in Captive Pacas, *Agouti paca* (Rodentia, Dasyproctidae)." *Mammalian Biology* (January 2003): 31–41.

Pérez, Elizabeth M. *"Agouti paca." Mammalian Species* (December 1992): 1–7.

Pimentel, Domingos S., and Marcelo Tabarelli. "Seed Dispersal of the Palm *Attalea oleifera* in a Remnant of the Brazilian Atlantic Forest." *Biotropica* (March 2004): 74–84.

Ramirez–Pulido, Jose, et al. "New Records of *Agouti paca* (Linnaeus) from the Mexican State of Puebla." *The Texas Journal of Science* (August 2001): 285.

Web sites:

Fox, David L. *"Agouti paca."* Animal Diversity Web. http://animaldiversity.ummz.umich.edu/site/accounts/information/Agouti_paca.html (accessed on July 12, 2004).

TUCO-TUCOS
Ctenomyidae

Class: Mammalia
Order: Rodentia
Family: Ctenomyidae
Number of species: 58 species

PHYSICAL CHARACTERISTICS

Tuco-tucos are small to medium-sized rodents with heavily built bodies, strong and large heads, and short, powerful legs. Their general appearance is that of the pocket gopher (Geomyidae), found in North America. The head and body length is 8.6 to 16.9 inches (22 to 53 centimeters) and they weigh from 3.5 ounces to 2.4 pounds (100 grams to 1.1 kilograms). Their skin is loose on their bodies, making it easier for them to turn around in their narrow burrows. They have tiny ears and short, stiff, hairless tails. The front paws of tuco-tucos are longer than the hind legs.

They have very distinct bright orange incisors, the two long, flat, sharp teeth at the front of the mouth, that are wide and powerful. Their fur is thick and long. It varies in color between species, including different shades of cream, red, brown, gray and black. The upper body fur is generally darker than the lower body fur.

GEOGRAPHIC RANGE

Central and southern South America, including Argentina, Bolivia, Brazil, Chile, Paraguay, Peru, and Uruguay.

HABITAT

Tuco-tucos range from the tropics to the sub-Antarctic regions at the tip of South America. They seem to prefer coastal areas, grassland, rainforest, deciduous forest, the large treeless semi-arid grassy plains called steppes, and meadows. They are found from sea level up to 13,120 feet (4,000 meters) in the Andes Mountains.

Most species live in a very small geographic area, including the Bolburn's tuco-tuco and the silky tuco-tuco that inhabit extreme southwestern Argentina. There are only several species that have a wider geographic range, such as the collared tuco-tuco, which lives in Argentina, Brazil, and Uruguay, and the highland tuco-tuco, found in Argentina, Bolivia, Chile, and Peru.

DIET

All species of tuco-tucos are believed to be herbivores, meaning they are plant-eaters. Their primary food sources are roots, grasses, herbs, and shrubs.

BEHAVIOR AND REPRODUCTION

Tuco-tucos are extremely solitary animals and are found in pairs only when mating. The one known exception is the social tuco-tuco, found in Argentina, which lives in colonies. They are diurnal, meaning they are most active during the day, and polyrhythmic, meaning they alternate between short periods of activity and resting throughout the day.

Tuco-tucos build burrows that are an intricate system of connecting tunnels and small caverns. The main tunnel is about 46.2 feet (14 meters) long, about 2 to 2.8 inches (5 to 7 centimeters) wide, and 12 inches (30 centimeters) below the surface. The burrow usually contains a grass-lined chamber for nesting, and several chambers for storing food. At least two species, the talas tuco-tuco and collared tuco-tuco, keep the temperature of their borrows at 68 to 71.6°F (20 to 22°C) by blocking and unblocking their burrow entrances based on sun and wind.

Tuco-tucos use sounds, smells, and touch to communicate with each other. The name "tuco-tuco" is an attempt by native South Americans to express in words the sound that several species of tuco-tuco make when they are giving a warning to animals that invade their territory. The actual sound is more like "tloc-tloc." Tuco-tucos have several other sounds including a deep rumbling noise made by the male when courting a female.

GOOD DIGGERS

Tuco-tucos are natural diggers. They prefer soil that is sandy or loamy, meaning it is a fertile mixture of clay, sand, silt, and other organic matter. They live in burrows that they dig. These burrows are very long and usually have several branching tunnels, along with many entrances and exits, usually concealed with plant material or plugged with rocks. Within these tunnels, they dig chambers for nesting and storing food. Tuco-tucos dig with their incisors, the two long, flat, sharp teeth at the front of their mouths, and kick the dirt out of the tunnel with their strong hind legs.

Tuco-tucos have one or two mating periods each year where the female produces a litter of babies. The gestation period, the time they carry their young in the womb, varies from species to species but generally is 100 to 120 days. Litter sizes vary from one to seven babies, called pups. Males and females reach are sexually mature, able to mate, at about eight months. The average lifespan of a tuco-tuco in the wild is about three years.

TUCO-TUCOS AND PEOPLE

Tuco-tucos are hunted for their meat by several native South American groups, including the Tehuelches and Onas. Farmers who consider them an agricultural pest because they eat crops often kill them. They can also cause problems for horseback riders when their burrows cave in under the weight of the horses, causing broken legs to the horses and often injury to the riders when they fall.

CONSERVATION STATUS

The Magellanic tuco-tuco is listed as Vulnerable, facing a high risk of extinction, by the IUCN due to declining habitat. In southern Patagonia, an area of Argentina between the Andes Mountains and the south Atlantic Ocean, extensive grazing by sheep on grasses and plants eaten by the highland tuco-tuco and other agricultural activities, have caused the animal to become rare and endangered. Three species are listed as Near Threatened, at risk of becoming threatened, by the IUCN: mottled tuco-tuco, Natterer's tuco-tuco, and social tuco-tuco. No other species are listed as threatened by the IUCN.

Pearson's tuco-tuco (*Ctenomys pearsoni*)

PEARSON'S TUCO-TUCO
Ctenomys pearsoni

Physical characteristics: The head and body length for Pearson's tuco-tuco is 7.5 inches (19 centimeters) and they weigh about 7 ounces (200 grams). They have brown-red fur with a white band of fur under the neck and white patches on the sides of the neck.

Geographic range: Pearson's tuco-tucos live in Peru, Chile, southwest Uruguay, and Entre Rios province in Argentina.

Habitat: These tuco-tucos prefer coastal sand dunes and grassland.

Pearson's tuco-tuco leaves its burrow only to find food and to mate. It defends its burrow against intruders. (Illustration by Joseph E. Trumpey. Reproduced by permission.)

Diet: Pearson's tuco-tuco are herbivores. Their diet consists primarily of grasses, herbs, shrubs, and roots.

Behavior and reproduction: The Pearson's tuco-tuco is solitary and individuals come together only to mate. The animal is territorial, meaning it is protective of an area it considers home and claims exclusively for itself. It will aggressively defend its territory and burrow from other tuco-tucos. It leaves its burrow only to find food and to mate. It has several vocalizations, including a sound to warn intruders away from its territory. It also has an excellent sense of hearing and can detect a human moving from about 165 feet (50 meters) away.

The mating season for Pearson's tuco-tuco in Peru is during the dry season and the babies are born in the wet season, when there is an abundance of plants. Female Pearson's tuco-tucos have one litter of babies per year. The number of babies ranges from two to four. They are believed to be polygamous, meaning they take more than one mate during the breeding season.

Pearson's tuco-tuco and people: They are rarely hunted and because they are so solitary, they have no known significance to humans.

Conservation status: Pearson's tuco-tuco is not listed as threatened by the IUCN. ∎

FOR MORE INFORMATION

Books:

Macdonald, David. *The New Encyclopedia of Mammals.* Oxford, U.K.: Oxford University Press, 2001.

Nowak, Ronald M. *Walker's Mammals of the World,* 6th ed. Baltimore: Johns Hopkins University Press, 1999.

Redford, Kent H., and John F. Eisenberg. *Mammals of the Neotropics: The Southern Cone, Chile, Argentina, Uruguay, Paraguay.* Chicago: University of Chicago Press, 1992.

Wilson, Don E., and DeeAnn M. Reeder. *Mammal Species of the World— A Taxonomic and Geographic Reference,* 2nd ed. Washington, DC: Smithsonian Institution Press, 1993.

Periodicals:

"Social Tuco-tucos Develop More Variety." *Science News* (August 26, 2000): 143.

El Jundi, Tarik A. R. J., and Thales R. O. De Freitas. "Genetic and Demographic Structure in a Population of *Ctenomys lami* (Rodentia-Ctenomyidae)." *Hereditas* (February 2004): 18–23.

Lacey, Eileen A., and John R. Wieczorek. "Ecology of Sociality in Rodents: A *Ctenomyid* Perspective." *Journal of Mammalogy* (November 2003): 1198–1211.

Lessa, Enrique P., and Joseph A. Cook. "The Molecular Phylogenetics of Tuco-Tucos (Genus *Ctenomys*, Rodentia: Octodontidae) Suggests an Early Burst of Speciation." *Molecular Phylogenetics and Evolution* (February 1998): 88–99.

Schwartz, Lisa E., and Eileen A. Lacey. "Olfactory Discrimination of Gender by Colonial Tuco-Tucos (*Ctenomys sociabilis.*)" *Mammalian Biology* (January 2003): 53–60.

Web sites:

Myers, P. "Ctenomyidae." Animal Diversity Web. http://animaldiversity.ummz.umich.edu/site/accounts/information/Ctenomyidae.html (accessed on July 12, 2004).

family

CHAPTER

phylum
class
subclass
order
monotypic order
suborder
▲ family

PHYSICAL CHARACTERISTICS

Octodonts are similar in appearance and size to gerbils and rats. They have stocky bodies, large heads, pointed noses, and medium-sized rounded ears. Octodonts have rear legs that are slightly shorter than their front legs. They have four clawed toes on their front paws and five on their back paws.

Octodonts have a head and body length of 5 to 8.7 inches (125 to 221 millimeters) and a tail length of 1.5 to seven inches (40 to 180 millimeters). Their weight ranges from 2.8 to 10.6 ounces (80 to 300 grams). They have long, dense, silky fur that is yellow, brown, or gray on their upper bodies and white or cream on their underside. One exception is the coruro, which is almost entirely black.

GEOGRAPHIC RANGE

Octodonts are found in southwest Peru, Chile, Argentina, and southwest Bolivia.

HABITAT

The octodont habitat ranges from coastal scrub brush to barren rocky outcroppings in mountains. They are found in desert, deciduous forest, grassland, and foothills.

DIET

Octodonts are herbivores, meaning they eat only plants. All but one species eat mainly at night. The degu feeds during the early morning and early evening. Most species eat a diet of grass, leaves, herbs, bark, and seeds. The coruro feeds mostly on underground portions of plants.

BEHAVIOR AND REPRODUCTION

All but one species of octodont are nocturnal, meaning they are most active at night. Degus are diurnal, meaning they are most active during daylight hours.

Octodonts are extremely talented and organized diggers. They build burrows consisting of many branched tunnels and multiple entrances. When digging a burrow, the adults form a chain that speeds up the activity. Most octodonts, such as degus, coruros, and rock rats exhibit a complex system of social behavior, living in colonies of five to ten adults and their young. They groom each other, lay bunched together when sleeping, and the females nurse each other's babies. Other species of octodonts are solitary.

The mating system for octodonts is not well understood although in several species it appears to involve courtship rituals. Most species, including the degu and coruro, usually breed twice a year. Females reach puberty, the age of sexual maturity at which they can bear offspring, at six months. The gestation period, the amount of time the young are carried in their mother's womb, is seventy-seven to 105 days. Litters usually consist of four to nine babies.

OCTODONTS AND PEOPLE

Most octodonts have little interaction with humans. Degus are used for laboratory research. They are also sold as pets in the United States. In the wild, degus and coruros are often killed by farmers who consider them agricultural pests, blaming them for destroying grain fields, orchards, and vineyards.

CONSERVATION STATUS

The Mocha Island degu is listed by the World Conservation Union (IUCN) as Vulnerable, facing a high risk of extinction, due to their small distribution area. The plains viscacha rat is listed as Vulnerable due to a loss of at least 20 percent of its population within ten years. Other species are not listed by IUCN.

TALE OF THE DEGU TAIL

Never try to catch or pick up a degu by its tail. As a defense against predators in the wild, the end of the tail will come off when it is pulled, allowing the degu to make an escape. However, it results in a bloody injury and can become infected. Usually, part or all of the remaining tail will either dry up and fall off or the degu will chew it off. The lost part never grows back.

Degu (*Octodon degus*)

DEGU
Octodon degus

Physical characteristics: Degus, also called trumpet-tailed rats, are similar in body size and appearance to gerbils, except for the fact that their faces share more of a resemblance with squirrels. They have chubby, round bodies, large heads and short necks. The head and body length of degus are from 9.8 to 12.2 inches (25 to 31 centimeters, with a tail length of 2.9 to 5.1 inches (7.5 to 13.0 centimeters. They weigh 6 to 10.5 ounces (170 to 300 grams).

They have long whiskers and relatively long tails that have very little hair, except for a tuft of fur at the tip. The degus' rear legs are slightly shorter than their front legs. They have four clawed toes on their front paws and five on their back paws. Degus have yellow or brown fur mixed with some black on their upper bodies, and white fur on their underside. Their teeth are bright orange.

Geographic range: In Chile, from the coastal areas of the west slopes of the Andes Mountains to about 9,000 feet (2,700 meters).

Habitat: Degus live in the brush, shrubs, and grassy plains of grasslands and deciduous forests.

Diet: Degus are herbivores, meaning they eat only plants. They eat mainly during the early morning and early evening. Their diet consists mainly of grass, leaves, herbs, bark, and seeds.

Degus eat mostly plants, and search for their food in the early morning and early evening. (© Fletcher & Baylis/Photo Researchers, Inc. Reproduced by permission.)

Behavior and reproduction: Degus are extremely social and live in groups of five to ten adults and their young. They groom each other, lay bunched together when sleeping, and the females nurse each other's babies. A degu group builds burrows consisting of many branched tunnels and multiple entrances. When digging a burrow, the adults form a chain that speeds up the activity.

Degus are diurnal. In the wild, they live about one to three years. In captivity, their average lifespan is five to nine years, with some reportedly living up to thirteen years.

Degus usually breed twice a year. Females are sexually mature, able to bear offspring, at six months. Litters usually consist of four to nine babies.

Degus and people: Degus are used for laboratory research. They are also sold as pets in the United States. In the wild, degus are often killed by farmers who consider them to be agricultural pests, blaming them for destroying grain fields, orchards, and vineyards.

Conservation status: Degus are not listed as threatened by the IUCN. ■

FOR MORE INFORMATION

Books:

Boruchowitz, David. *The Guide to Owning a Degu.* Champaign, IL: TFH Publications, 2002.

Griffiths-Irwin, Diane, and Julie Davis. *How to Care for Your Degu.* Champaign, IL: TFH Publications, 2001.

Macdonald, David. *The New Encyclopedia of Mammals.* Oxford, U.K.: Oxford University Press, 2001.

Nowak, Ronald M. *Walker's Mammals of the World,* 6th ed. Baltimore: Johns Hopkins University Press, 1999.

Vanderlip, Sharon (DVM), and Michele Earle-Bridges. *Degus.* Hauppauge, NY: Barrons Educational Series, 2001.

Periodicals:

Bacigalupe, Leonardo D., et al. "Activity and Space Use by Degus: A Trade-Off Between Thermal Conditions and Food Availability?" *Journal of Mammalogy* (February 2003): 331–318.

Begall, Sabine, et al. "Activity Patterns in a Subterranean Social Rodent, *Spalacopus cyanus* (Octodontidae)." *Journal of Mammalogy* (February 2002): 153–158.

Begall, Sabine, and Milton H. Gallardo. "*Spalacopus cyanus* (Rodentia: Octodontidae): An Extremist in Tunnel Constructing and Food Storing Among Subterranean Mammals." *Journal of Zoology* (May 2000): 53–60.

Gallardo, M. H., and F. Mondaca. "The Systematics of *Aconaemys* (Rodentia, Octodontidae) and the Distribution of *A. sagei* in Chile." *Mammalian Biology* (April 2002): 105–112.

Kenagy, G. J., et al. "Microstructure of Summer Activity Bouts of Degus in a Thermally Heterogeneous Habitat." *Journal of Mammalogy* (April 2004): 260–267.

Torres-Mura, Juan C., and Luis C. Contreras. "*Spalacopus cyanus.*" *Mammalian Species*(December 4, 1998): 1–5.

Woods, Charles A., and David K. Boraker. "*Octodon degus.*" *Mammalian Species* (November 21, 1975): 1–5.

Web sites:

Cloyd, Emily. "*Octodon degus.*" Animal Diversity Web. http://animaldiversity.ummz.umich.edu/site/accounts/information/Octodon_degus.html (accessed on July 12, 2004).

Myers, Phil. "Family Octodontidae." Animal Diversity Web. http://animaldiversity.ummz.umich.edu/site/accounts/information/Octodontidae.html (accessed on July 12, 2004).

CHINCHILLA RATS

Abrocomidae

Class: Mammalia

Order: Rodentia

Family: Abrocomidae

Number of species: 4 species

family
CHAPTER

PHYSICAL CHARACTERISTICS

Chinchilla rats have large, round ears, large eyes, and an elongated head. They have short legs with four toes on the front feet and five toes on the back feet. The head and body length of the chinchilla rat is 6 to 10 inches (15 to 25 centimeters with a tail length of 2.4 to 7.2 inches (6 to 18 centimeters). They weigh from 7.1 to 10.6 ounces (200 to 300 grams).

The fur of the chinchilla rat is thick and soft. Fur coloring is silver-gray or gray-brown on the upper body and light brown, cream, white, or yellow on its underside.

GEOGRAPHIC RANGE

They are found from coastal areas to the Andes Mountains in southern Peru, northern Chile, northwest Argentina, and central Bolivia.

HABITAT

Chinchilla rats live in rock crevices and elaborate burrows under rocks or at the base of shrubs.

DIET

Chinchilla rats are herbivores, meaning they eat only plants. The feed at night on seeds, fruits, and nuts.

BEHAVIOR AND REPRODUCTION

There is very little scientific information on the behavior of chinchilla rats, due to their small population. Only a handful of research has been done on the small rodents. What is known

phylum

class

subclass

order

monotypic order

suborder

▲ **family**

ROCK CLIMBERS

Chinchilla rats love to climb and are extremely talented. Although they spend most of their time on or under the ground, they do climb rock outcroppings, plants, and trees. Sometimes they live within crevices of rocky cliffs. Often they will build sidewalls inside their rocky dens up to 10 feet (3 meters) high. They use a construction material made of their own feces and urine. When dry, the mixture is almost as hard as rock.

has usually been gained by observing the behavior of only a few of each species.

Chinchilla rats live inside burrows in colonies of up to six individuals. Colonies are usually close together, sometimes as little as 59 feet (18 meters) apart. Little is known about the reproductive behavior of chinchilla rats. They usually mate in January or February. The gestation period, the length of time the female carries the babies in her womb, is 115 to 118 days. Litters are usually one or two babies.

There are four species: Bennett's chinchilla rat, which lives in the coastal foothills and high plains of the Andes Mountains in Chile; Bolivian chinchilla rat, which is found in central Bolivia; ashy chinchilla rat, found in the high plains of the Andes in Bolivia, Chile, and Peru; and *Cuscomys ashaninki*, which does not have a common name, found in Peru.

Cuscomys ashaninki was discovered in 1999 when a single dead body was found. As a result, there is virtually no information available on this species. The skeletal remains of another species, *Cuscomys oblativa*, have been found in Peru but the species is believed to be extinct.

Bennett's chinchilla rat sometimes shares burrows with similar-sized degus. A Bennett's chinchilla rat in captivity lived two years and four months. Their lifespan in the wild is believed to be one to two years.

CHINCHILLA RATS AND PEOPLE

Chinchilla rats are sometimes hunted by humans for their fur, which is sold at local fur markets and has a low value. It is sometimes sold to tourists as real chinchilla fur. They were hunted extensively for their fur in the early twentieth century and all species were nearly extinct by the 1920s when several South American countries passed laws to protect them.

CONSERVATION STATUS

The Bolivian chinchilla rat is listed as Vulnerable, facing a high risk of extinction in the wild, due to its population being confined to a small area. The other chinchilla rats are not listed as threatened by the IUCN.

Ashy chinchilla rat *(Abrocoma cinerea)*

ASHY CHINCHILLA RAT
Abrocoma cinerea

Physical characteristics: The head and body length of the ashy chinchilla rat is 6 to 10 inches (15 to 25 centimeters) with a tail length of 2.4 to 7.2 inches (6 to 18 centimeters). They weigh from 7.1 to 10.6 ounces (200 to 300 grams). They have large, round ears, large eyes, and an elongated head. They have short legs with four toes on the front feet and five toes on the back feet. The fur of the ashy chinchilla rat is thick and soft. Fur coloring is silver-gray on the upper body and cream, white, or yellow on its underside.

The ashy chinchilla rat communicates through grunts and squeaks. (Hernan Torres. Reproduced by permission.)

Geographic range: Ashy chinchilla rats live in the Altiplano, a high plateau area of the Andes Mountains, from southern Bolivia and Peru to central Chile.

Habitat: They are found in rocky regions of 12,000 to 16,400 feet (3,700 to 5,000 meters). They usually live in burrows under rocks or at the base of shrubs.

Diet: Ashy chinchilla rats are herbivores, meaning they eat only plants. They feed at night on seeds, fruits, and nuts.

Behavior and reproduction: Ashy chinchilla rats live in burrows in colonies of up to six individuals. Colonies are usually close together, sometimes as little as 59 feet (18 meters) apart. Little is known about the reproductive behavior of ashy chinchilla rats. They usually mate in January or February. The gestation period, the length of time the female carries the babies in her womb, is 115 to 118 days. Litters are usually one or two babies.

This species of chinchilla rat makes several vocal sounds, including a grunt when it is fighting or about to fight, a squeak when it is frightened, and a low gurgle when being groomed by one of its colony members.

Ashy chinchilla rats and people: Ashy chinchilla rats are sometimes hunted by humans for their fur, which is sold at local fur markets and has a low value. It is sometimes sold to tourists as real chinchilla fur.

Conservation status: The ashy chinchilla rat is not listed as threatened by IUCN. However, its population is believed to be low and in decline due to hunting and habitat destruction by humans. ■

FOR MORE INFORMATION

Books:

Macdonald, David. *The New Encyclopedia of Mammals.* Oxford, U.K.: Oxford University Press, 2001.

Nowak, Ronald M. *Walker's Mammals of the World,* 6th ed. Baltimore: Johns Hopkins University Press, 1999.

Wilson, Don E., and DeeAnn M. Reeder. *Mammal Species of the World—A Taxonomic and Geographic Reference,* 2nd ed. Washington, DC: Smithsonian Institution Press, 1993.

Periodicals:

Braun, Janet K., and Michael A. Mares. "Systematics of the *Abrocoma cinerea* Species Complex (Rodentia: Abrocomidae), with a Description of a New Species of *Abrocoma*." *Journal of Mammalogy* (February 2002): 1–19.

Huchon, Dorothée, and Emmanuel J. P. Douzery. "From the Old World to the New World: A Molecular Chronicle of the Phylogeny and Biogeography of *Hystricognath.* Rodents." *Molecular Phylogenetics and Evolution* (August 2001): 238–251.

Meserve, Peter, et al. "Role of Biotic Interactions in a Small Mammal Assemblage in Semiarid Chile." *Ecology* (January 1996): 133–148.

Meserve, Peter L., et al. "Thirteen Years of Shifting Top-Down and Bottom-Up Control." *BioScience* (July 2003): 633–646.

Web sites:

Myers, Phil. "Family Abrocomidae." Animal Diversity Web. http://animaldiversity.ummz.umich.edu/site/accounts/information/Abrocomidae.html (accessed on July 12, 2004).

Nash, Natalee. "*Abrocoma cinerea*." Animal Diversity Web. http://animaldiversity.ummz.umich.edu/site/accounts/information/Abrocoma_cinerea.html (accessed on July 12, 2004).

SPINY RATS
Echimyidae

Class: Mammalia

Order: Rodentia

Family: Echimyidae

Number of species: 78 species

phylum

class

subclass

order

monotypic order

suborder

▲ **family**

PHYSICAL CHARACTERISTICS

The physical characteristics of spiny rats vary greatly from species to species, from rat-sized to the size of a small cat. Their head and body length is from 4.13 to 18.9 inches (10.5 to 48 centimeters) and a tail length of 0.2 to 16.6 inches (0.5 to 42 centimeters). They weigh from 0.46 to 2.9 pounds (210 to 1,300 grams). In appearance, most species of spiny rat are rat-like, with pointed noses, although several species have blunt noses and resemble squirrels. Their front feet have four toes while their hind feet have five.

Spiny rats got their name because most species have spiny or bristly fur, most noticeably on their backs and rumps. The spiny qualities vary between species: the armored rat has well-developed spines, spiny rats, or casiragua, have broad and stiff hair, and the punaré has soft fur with no hint of spines.

Fur color also varies greatly between species, with upper body fur being gray or various shades of brown, and white or cream on their undersides. Several species, including the toro and the white-faced arboreal spiny rat have black-and-white or white faces.

GEOGRAPHIC RANGE

Spiny rats are found throughout southern Central America and northern and central South America, from southern Honduras to northern Argentina and Chile.

HABITAT

Spiny rats live in a wide variety of habitats, from species that live exclusively in treetops, to forest floor dwellers to those that live underground in complex burrow systems. Many species live near the coast, rivers, or streams. The rato de Taquara lives exclusively in bamboo thickets along stream and river banks. They are found in both old growth and new-growth forests, but are most abundant in forests of intermediate age where there are large numbers of fruit trees, such as palm and fig. Spiny rats are often the most abundant animal in their geographic range.

DIET

Spiny rats are mostly herbivores, meaning they eat only plants, although some species eat insects. Their diet includes fruits, nuts, grass, and sugar cane. Several species, including rato de Taquara, eat only bamboo shoots and leaves.

BEHAVIOR AND REPRODUCTION

Spiny rats are nocturnal, meaning they are mostly active at night. Most die if they are exposed to heat or dryness. Depending on the species, they live either individually, in small groups, or like the broad-headed spiny rat, in large colonies. The average lifespan is two to four years in the wild.

They are generally territorial, meaning they are protective of an area they consider home and claim exclusively for themselves. Males and females have separate territories. Males defend their burrows against other males but females are less aggressive and their territories frequently overlap. Territories are usually small, from 1.2 to 14.8 acres (0.5 to 6 hectares) and can vary greatly between the seasons.

Spiny rats play a critical role in the health of the rainforest of Central and South America by dispersing the seeds from a wide variety of trees and other forest plants through their excretions. They are also an important source of food for predators such as ocelots, owls, boa constrictors, anacondas, and jaguars.

Little is known about the breeding habits of many species. In general, spiny rats breed throughout the year and females can give birth to four to six litters a year. The litter size ranges from one to seven babies, with the average being two to four.

A RAT'S TAIL

As a defensive feature against predators, spiny rats have a tail that easily breaks off. If grasped by the tail, it will break off between the fourth and fifth vertebrae. The rat can then escape to its burrow. There is little blood loss and the break does not appear to harm the rats. However, this way of escape can only be used once since the tail does not grow back. A survey of spiny rats in central Panama found that 15 to 20 percent of all adult spiny rats did not have tails.

Gestation period, the time the female carries the young in her womb, varies but is generally sixty to seventy days. In the punaré, a species of spiny rat, the females produce two or three litters per year and gestation period is from ninety-five to ninety-eight days.

SPINY RATS AND PEOPLE

Several species are hunted and eaten by humans, some are killed by farmers who consider them agricultural pests, and several species are used as laboratory animals.

CONSERVATION STATUS

The IUCN lists three species of spiny rats as Extinct, or died out; one species as Critically Endangered, facing an extremely high risk of extinction; five species as Vulnerable, facing a high risk of extinction in the wild; and nine species are Near Threatened, not currently threatened, but could become so. The remaining species are not listed as threatened by the World Conservation Union (IUCN).

Spiny rat (*Proechimys semispinosus*)

SPINY RAT
Proechimys semispinosus

Physical characteristics: The spiny rat is about the size of a common house rat, except with a larger head and smaller ears. Head and body length is 6.4 to 12 inches (16.0 to 30.0 centimeters) and a tail length of 4.4 to 12.8 inches (11.2 to 32.5 centimeters). They weigh from 10.5 to 17.5 ounces (300 to 500 grams). Their fur is orange-brown on the upper body and white underneath.

Geographic range: The spiny rat is found in Colombia, Costa Rica, Ecuador, Honduras, Nicaragua, and Panama.

Habitat: The spiny rat lives in rainforest, usually in dense underbrush and near rivers and streams.

Diet: They are mostly herbivores, feeding primarily on fallen fruit but sometimes on fungi.

Behavior and reproduction: The spiny rat is nocturnal, meaning it is mostly active at night. It sleeps, nests, and stores food in burrows dug by other animals, rock crevices, or hollows in trees or logs. It does not dig its own burrow. The male defends its burrow against other males. The lifespan of the spiny rat is two to four years.

The species breeds throughout the year and the females may have three to six litters per year. The gestation period, the time the female carries a litter in her womb, is sixty-three to sixty-six days, with the number of babies ranging from one to five. They reach sexual maturity at six to seven months.

Spiny rats and people: Spiny rats are trapped and eaten by local people.

Conservation status: The IUCN does not consider the spiny rat to be threatened. ■

FOR MORE INFORMATION

Books:

Leite, Yuri L. R. *Evolution and Systematics of the Atlantic Tree Rats, Genus* Phyllonrys *(Rodentia, Echimyidae).* Berkeley, CA: University of California Press, 2003.

Macdonald, David. *The New Encyclopedia of Mammals.* Oxford, U.K.:

Oxford University Press, 2001.

Nowak, Ronald M. *Walker's Mammals of the World,* 6th ed. Baltimore: Johns Hopkins University Press, 1999.

Wilson, Don E., and DeeAnn M. Reeder. *Mammal Species of the World— A Taxonomic and Geographic Reference,* 2nd ed. Washington, DC: Smithsonian Institution Press, 1993.

Periodicals:

Adler, Gregory H. "Impacts of Resources on Populations of a Tropical Forest Rodent." *Ecology* (January 1998): 242–255.

Lambert, Thomas D., and Gregory H. Adler. "Microhabitat Use by a Tropical Forest Rodent, *Proechimys semispinosus,* in Central Panama." *Journal of Mammalogy* (February 2000): 70–76.

Lara, Marcia C., and Patton, James L. "Evolutionary Diversification of Spiny Rats (Genus *Trinomys,* Rodentia: Echimyidae) in the Atlantic Forest of Brazil." *Zoological Journal of the Linnean Society* (December 2000): 661–686.

Marcomini, Monique, and Elisabeth Spinelli de Oliveira. "Activity Pattern of Echimyid Rodent Species from the Brazilian Caatinga in Captivity." *Biological Rhythm Research* (April 2003): 157–166.

Matacq, Marjorie D, et al. "Population Genetic Structure of Two Ecologically Distinct Amazonian Spiny Rats: Separating History and Current Ecology." *Evolution* (July 2000): 1423–1432.

Morato, Manaf P., et al. "Profile of Wild Neotropical Spiny Rats (*Trinomys,* Echimyidae) in Two Behavioral Tests." *Physiology and Behavior* (July 2003): 129–133.

Web sites:

Myers, Phil. "Family Echimyidae." Animal Diversity Web. http://animaldiversity.ummz.umich.edu/site/accounts/information/Echimyidae.html (accessed on July 12, 2004).

HUTIAS

Capromyidae

Class: Mammalia

Order: Rodentia

Family: Capromyidae

Number of species: 14 living
species

phylum

class

subclass

order

monotypic order

suborder

▲ **family**

PHYSICAL CHARACTERISTICS

Hutias are medium to large, stocky rodents with broad, round heads. They have small eyes and short, rounded ears. Their head and body length is 14 to 32 inches (36 to 80 centimeters) and their tail length is 1.4 to 17 inches (3.5 to 43.1 centimeters). They weigh 1.1 to 18.7 pounds (0.5 to 8.5 kilograms). Their stomachs are divided into three compartments, making it one of the most complex stomachs in all rodents.

Hutias have short legs and five toes on each foot. Each toe has a strong, usually curved, claw. Their fur is generally thick and coarse and the color is usually various shades of black, brown, or gray, with the underside fur being slightly lighter.

GEOGRAPHIC RANGE

Hutias are found exclusively in the Caribbean, particularly Cuba, the Bahamas, Jamaica, Haiti, and the Dominican Republic.

HABITAT

Hutias usually live in forests, plantations, scrublands, marshy areas, and mountainous, rocky areas of rainforest. Brown's hutia, also known as the Jamaican hutia, usually lives on exposed areas of limestone in the interior of Jamaica. They build their nests in rock crevices or tunnels. The largest populations of hutia are in Cuba, including the Cuban hutia, black-tailed hutia, and prehensile-tailed hutia.

DIET

Some hutias, such as the eared hutia, are omnivores, meaning that they eat both plants and flesh, but eat mostly plants. Their diet includes leaves, fruit, and bark, and occasionally lizards, and small animals. Some species, such as Brown's hutia, are herbivores, meaning that they eat only plants.

BEHAVIOR AND REPRODUCTION

While very shy towards humans, hutias are usually extremely social with each other. They engage in various activities as a group, including foraging for food and grooming. They generally live in social groups and do not seem to be territorial.

Some hutias are terrestrial, meaning they live mainly on the ground, while other species of hutia are primarily arboreal, meaning they live mostly in treetops. Most species are diurnal, meaning they are mostly active during the day. Brown's hutia is nocturnal, meaning it is most active at night.

Hutias breed year-round and have one to three litters of babies a year. Females have a gestation period, the length of time they carry their young in the womb, of 110 to 150 days. Females have one to six babies per litter with an average litter size of one or two. The mothers nurse their young until they are about five months old, and the young are able to reproduce at ten months. The average lifespan is eight to eleven years.

HUTIAS AND PEOPLE

Some species of hutia are widely hunted by humans for their meat, such as Brown's hutia in Jamaica, despite its threatened status. In some areas of Cuba hutias are abundant and considered an agricultural pest by farmers. There is growing concern among conservationists that more species will become extinct soon due to human activities. Brown's hutia is continuing to drop in population despite its protected status under Jamaica's Wildlife Protection Act of 1945, which is rarely enforced.

BACK FROM THE DEAD

The Bahamian hutia was once common throughout the Bahamas until the first European settlers arrived in the 1600s. Their numbers then started to drop due to hunting and destruction of its habitat and it was believed extinct by the 1800s. In 1966, however, a survey expedition discovered hundreds of Bahamian hutias living on the small remote uninhabited island of East Plana Cay. The mammal became a protected species in 1968 and by the start of the twenty-first century, numbered about 10,000. It has been introduced to several nearby small, uninhabited islands where it is thriving. It is listed by IUCN as Vulnerable due to its limited geographic range.

CONSERVATION STATUS

The World Conservation Union (IUCN) lists five species that have recently become Extinct, died out; six species that are Critically Endangered, facing an extremely high risk of extinction; and four species that are Vulnerable, facing a high risk of extinction.

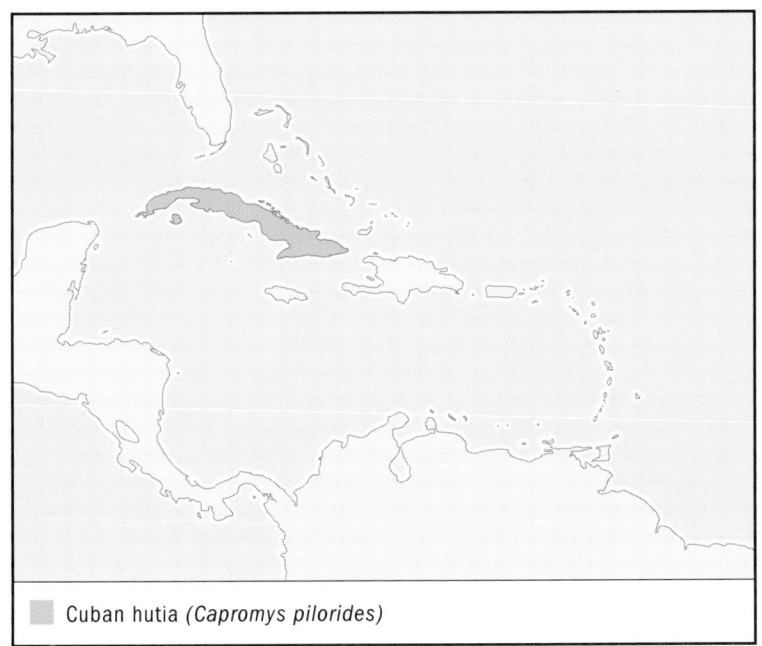

Cuban hutia (*Capromys pilorides*)

CUBAN HUTIA
Capromys pilorides

Physical characteristics: Cuban hutias, also known as Desmarest's hutias, are the largest species of hutia. They have a head and body length of 18 to 35 inches (46 to 90 centimeters), a tail length of 6 to 12 inches (15.2 to 30 centimeters) and a weight of 6.6 to 18.7 pounds (3 to 8.5 kilograms). They have short, stocky legs and "waddle" when they move. Their feet are broad and each foot has five toes with prominent claws.

They have thick, coarse fur and on the upper body, which can be various shades of black, gray, brown, red, yellow, and cream. Their underside fur is usually softer and a lighter shade.

Geographic range: These hutias live on mainland Cuba and its surrounding islands.

Habitat: Their habitat includes tropical rainforest, mangrove forests, marshy areas, scrubland, and the mountains of eastern Cuba.

The Cuban hutia uses its strong claws to climb trees. (Frank W. Lane/FLPA—Images of Nature. Reproduced by permission.)

Diet: Cuban hutias are omnivores, meaning they eat both plants and flesh, but eat mostly plants. Their diet includes leaves, fruit, bark, lizards, and small animals.

Behavior and reproduction: Cuban hutias are shy and usually live in pairs, although pairs have often been observed living in larger, loosely-associated groups. They are extremely social among others of their species. They are primarily arboreal, meaning they live mostly in treetops, and diurnal, meaning they are most active during the day. One of the Cuban hutias' main types of social behavior is a combination of grooming and play wrestling between a pair.

Cuban hutias breed all year but births peak in June. Females have a gestation period, the length of time they carry their young in the womb, of 110 to 140 days. Females have one to six babies per litter with the average litter size of two or three offspring. The mothers nurse their young until they are about five months old and reach sexual maturity at ten months. The average lifespan is eight to eleven years.

Cuban hutias and people: Cuban hutias are hunted by humans for their meat. In some areas of Cuba they are in such abundance that they are considered an agricultural pest by farmers.

Conservation status: The Cuban hutia is not currently threatened. While the Cuban hutia is abundant in many areas of the island-nation, their population has decreased drastically in the mountains of eastern Cuba. ■

FOR MORE INFORMATION

Books:

Macdonald, David. *The New Encyclopedia of Mammals.* Oxford, U.K.: Oxford University Press, 2001.

National Research Council. "Hutia." In *Microlivestock: Little-Known Small Animals with a Promising Economic Future.* Washington, DC: National Academies Press, 1991. Online at http://books.nap.edu/books/030904295X/html/251.html (accessed on July 12, 2004).

Nowak, Ronald M. *Walker's Mammals of the World,* 6th ed. Baltimore: Johns Hopkins University Press, 1999.

Periodicals:

Huchon, Dorothée, and Emmanuel J. P. Douzery. "From the Old World to the New World: A Molecular Chronicle of the Phylogeny and Biogeography of Hystricognath Rodents." *Molecular Phylogenetics and Evolution* (August 2001): 238–251.

Nedbal, Michael A., et al. "Molecular Systematics of Hystricognath Rodents: Evidence from the Mitochondrial 125 rRNA Gene." *Molecular Phylogenetics and Evolution* (September 1994): 206–220.

Web sites:

Myers, Phil. "Family Capromyidae." Animal Diversity Web. http://animaldiversity.ummz.umich.edu/site/accounts/information/Capromyidae.html (accessed on July 12, 2004).

Reis, Brianna. *"Capromys pilorides."* Animal Diversity Web. http://animaldiversity.ummz.umich.edu/site/accounts/information/Capromys_pilorides.html (accessed on July 12, 2004).

Raffo, Erica. *"Geocapromys_brownii."* Animal Diversity Web. http://animaldiversity.ummz.umich.edu/site/accounts/information/Geocapromys_brownii.html (accessed on July 12, 2004).

CHAPTER

PHYSICAL CHARACTERISTICS

The coypu, sometimes called the South American beaver or nutria, looks like a muskrat, only larger. It has a stout body that is highly arched and a large, somewhat triangular head. It has small eyes and ears on the upper part of its head. Coypus have a head and body length of 1.4 to 2.1 feet (43 to 63.6 centimeters), and a tail length of 0.8 to 1.4 feet (25.5 to 42.5 centimeters. They weigh from 11 to 37 pounds (5 to 17 kilograms).

They have short, hairless legs with the hind feet longer than the front feet. Each hind foot has five toes, four of which are connected by webbing. The fifth toe is used for grooming. The front feet have four long, flexible toes without webbing, and a non-functioning thumb. Their tails are long, round, and hairless. One of the coypu's most distinguishing features is its large, wide, bright orange incisors, the flat, sharp-edged teeth at the front of the mouth used for gnawing and cutting and tearing food. They can close their lips behind the incisors, allowing them to gnaw while underwater. Their ears, nose, and nostrils are located near the top of the head so they are above water when the coypu is swimming.

Coypus have two types of hair; soft, dense under fur, and outer fur of long, course, bristly hair, called guard hair. The undercoat is dark gray and the outer coat is various shades of red, brown and yellow. The stomach fur is soft and dense and usually a pale yellow. The fur on the chin and around the nose is usually white.

Coypu *(Myocastor coypus)*

GEOGRAPHIC RANGE

The coypu is native to southern South America, from the middle of Bolivia and southern Brazil to Tierra del Fuego at the southern tip of the continent, including Argentina, Chile, Paraguay, and Uruguay. It has been introduced into North America, Europe, northern Asia, east Africa, and the Middle East where there are populations in the wild. In the United States, it is found in fifteen states coast to coast but particularly in Louisiana, Florida, Oregon, and Maryland. In Canada, it is found in British Columbia, Ontario, and Quebec. It is found throughout continental Europe, including France, Germany, Scandinavia, Austria, Russia, and Poland. Other non-native populations include those in Israel, Zimbabwe, and Japan.

HABITAT

Coypus adapt well to a wide range of habitats, including rainforest, deciduous forest, coniferous forest, scrub forest,

Coypus are not native to the United States, but were brought to Louisiana to raise for fur. A number escaped, and now breed in the wild. (© YVA Momatiuk and John Eastcott/Photo Researchers, Inc. Reproduced by permission.)

grassland, wetland such as swamps and marshes, and the banks or shores of lakes, ponds, rivers, and streams.

DIET

South American coypus are omnivores, meaning they eat both plants and flesh, although they eat mostly plant material. Coypus in other parts of the world are herbivores, meaning they eat only plants. Their diet consists of a wide variety of plants and plant material, including aquatic plants such as rushes, arrowhead, smartweed, reeds, cattail, bullwhip, alligator weed, and duckweed. They also eat plant leaves, stems, roots, bark, clover, and cultivated crops such as sugarcane, sugar beets, and soybeans. On occasion, coypus in South America will eat insects, mussels, snails, mollusks, and earthworms.

BEHAVIOR AND REPRODUCTION

Coypus are extremely passive and rarely aggressive. They are shy and fearful; the slightest disturbance will send them scurrying to the shelter of water, burrow, or other hiding places.

Depending on their habitat, coypus are nocturnal, meaning they are most active at night, or crepuscular (kri-PUS-kyuh-lur), meaning they are most active at dawn and twilight.

Coypus are semi-aquatic, meaning they live both on land and in water. On land, they walk with slow, clumsy, awkward movements but if threatened, they can run fast and jump short distances. They are excellent swimmers and can remain submerged in water for more than ten minutes. Coypus can close their nostrils and lips behind their incisors while cutting vegetation under the water. The coypu is social and territorial, meaning it is protective of an area it considers home and claims exclusively for itself and its mate or family group. They live in groups of two to thirteen individuals, usually related female adults, their offspring, and one adult male. Young adult males usually live alone. Males and females have separate territories. The average home range is 6.1 acres (2.47 hectares) for females and 13.8 acres (5.68 hectares) for males.

Coypus sleep and nest in burrows, which range from a single, short tunnel, to multiple tunnels with small nesting chambers. Tunnels are often 50 feet (15 meters) or more in length. Above ground, they make raised beds of vegetation where they feed and groom.

Breeding occurs year-round and females have two or three litters per year. The gestation period, the time the females carry their young in the womb, is 127 to 139 days. The average litter size is six babies although it can range from one to thirteen. Coypus born in the summer reach sexual maturity at three to four months of age. For those born in the fall, it is reached at six or seven months of age. The average lifespan is less than one year in the wild. In a few cases under ideal conditions, coypus have lived for three to six years in the wild. However, in captivity, they can live for ten years.

In the wild, coypus have many predators, including large snakes like the anaconda and boa constrictor, large cats such as ocelots and jaguars, red wolves, crocodiles, and otters.

WANTED: DEAD OR ALIVE

In 1938, about 20 coypus were imported into Louisiana from Argentina to be bred for their fur. But many escaped captivity and adapted well to the warm, wet climate and swampy habitat, breeding voraciously. They spread quickly to nearby states. As of 2004, there were an estimated twenty million coypus in the Louisiana. In 1998, it is estimated coypus destroyed 100,000 acres of swamp and marshland, posing a serious threat to many native species of birds, mammals, and amphibians. To combat the threat to the environment, the Louisiana Department of Wildlife and Fisheries received a $10 million, five-year federal grant to help eradicate, remove, coypus from the state. In 2002, the state began paying hunters $4 for each coypu they brought into state wildlife offices. Most are brought in dead but wildlife workers kill any that are trapped and brought in alive. In the first two weeks of the program, 9,000 coypus were killed. The goal is to kill 400,000 per year.

COYPUS AND PEOPLE

The fur of coypus is valued for its soft, velvety texture and people in South America, North America, Europe, and Japan eat the meat. Much of the meat and fur from South American comes from captive coypu breeding farms while in the United States it comes from coypus hunted in the wild, especially in Louisiana and Maryland.

In the 1930s, coypus were introduced into southeast England and the population there quickly grew. Coypus were blamed for destroying native marsh plants along riverbanks and raiding cultivated crops. Their burrows were also believed to weaken and damage river and stream banks. In the 1980s, the British government began an intensive campaign to eradicate (remove completely) coypus from England and in 1989, the government officially declared the program a total success with the killing of the last coypu.

There are eradication efforts underway in the United States, Japan, and France.

CONSERVATION STATUS

Coypus are not currently threatened, according to the World Conservation Union (IUCN). Their numbers are declining along many rivers and lakes in Argentina due to hunting and trapping by humans. The eradication efforts in the United States, France, and Japan are likely to significantly reduce populations in those areas.

FOR MORE INFORMATION

Books:

Eisenberg, John F., and Kent H. Redford. *Mammals of the Neotropics: The Central Neotropics: Ecuador, Peru, Bolivia, Brazil.* Chicago: University of Chicago Press, 2000.

Eisenberg, John F., and Kent H. Redford. *Mammals of the Neotropics: The Southern Cone: Chile, Argentina, Uruguay, Paraguay.* Chicago: University of Chicago Press, 1992.

Macdonald, David. *The New Encyclopedia of Mammals.* Oxford, U.K.: Oxford University Press, 2001.

National Research Council. "Coypu." In *Microlivestock: Little-Known Small Animals with a Promising Economic Future.* Washington, DC:

National Academies Press, 1991. Online at http://books.nap.edu/books/030904295X/html/217.html (accessed on July 12, 2004).

Nowak, Ronald M. *Walker's Mammals of the World,* 6th ed. Baltimore: Johns Hopkins University Press, 1999.

Periodicals:

"Coypu Invasion." *Sea-River Newsletters* (October 27, 2003): 118.

Felipe, A. E., et al. "Characterization of the Estrous Cycle of the *Myocastor coypus* (Coypu) by Means of Exfoliative Colpocytology." *Journal of Mastozoologia Neotropical* (July–December 2001): 129–137.

Guichón, M. Laura, et al. "Social Behavior and Group Formation in the Coypu (*Myocastor coypus*) in the Argentinean Pampas." *Journal of Mammalogy* (February 2003): 254–262.

Kamerick, Megan. "Nutria Bounty Lures Hunters into Effort to Save Land." *New Orleans CityBusiness* (December 23, 2002).

Nickens, Edward T. "Exotic Species: Trying to Show the Door to a Marsh Munching Immigrant from South America."*National Wildlife* (December–January 1999): 14.

Woods, Charles A., et al. "*Myocastor coypus.*" *Mammalian Species* (June 5, 1992): 1–8.

Web sites:

D'Elia, Guillermo. "*Myocastor coypus.*" Animal Diversity Web. http://animaldiversity.ummz.umich.edu/site/accounts/information/Myocastor_coypus.html (accessed on July 12, 2004).

order

PHYSICAL CHARACTERISTICS

Lagomorphs are small to medium-sized mammals categorized into two families: Leporidae (rabbits and hares) and Ochotonidae (pikas [PEE-kuhz]). Rabbits and hares have long hind legs adapted for running at fast speeds over open ground. Pikas are small mammals with large, round ears and resemble guinea pigs in size and appearance. Adult rabbits and hares have a body length of 10 to 28 inches (25.4 to 71.1 centimeters) and weigh 14 ounces to 15.3 pounds (400 to 7,000 grams). They have short, furry tails and ear sizes vary greatly and generally are shorter in rabbits and longer in hares. The main exceptions are the rabbit breeds known as lops, which have long, floppy ears. Females are generally larger than males. Hares generally are larger than rabbits and have black-tipped ears.

Rabbits and hares usually have thick, soft fur that comes in a wide spectrum of colors, shades, and combinations, including black, white, brown, beige, tan, blue, orange, red, pink, cream, lilac, silver, and lavender.

Pikas are small, compact mammals with short front and rear legs. They range in length from 5 to 12 inches (125 to 300 millimeters) and weigh 3.5 to 7 ounces (100 to 200 grams). Pikas lack a noticeable tail. They have long, soft fur that is usually gray or brown.

Lagomorphs have eyes set high on their head, looking sideways, giving them a wide field of vision. They have weak but flexible necks, allowing them to turn their heads with a wide range of motion. Lagomorphs have a single opening to pass both urine and feces. They also have a specialized part of their large intestine, called the cecum (SEE-kum), which acts as a fermentation chamber and aids in digestion of grasses.

GEOGRAPHIC RANGE

Lagomorphs are found on every continent except Antarctica. They are native to every continent they are found on, except Australia where they were introduced.

HABITAT

Pikas are found in two distinct habitats. Some live among rocks and rocky areas. Others live in meadows, steppes (semi-arid, grass-covered plains), shrubs and desert. Hares live in arctic tundra, steppes, wetlands, forests, and deserts. Rabbits live in pine and deciduous forests, desert, mountainous areas, scrubland, tropical rainforest, near rivers and streams, rocky outcroppings, grasslands, and areas of dense brush or other low-lying vegetation.

DIET

Lagomorphs are herbivores, meaning they are plant-eaters, with a primary diet of grasses and herbs but also will feed on fruit, seeds, leaves, shoots, and bark.

BEHAVIOR AND REPRODUCTION

Behavior and reproduction differs widely between rabbits and hares, and pikas, and within each group. Pikas are mainly diurnal, meaning they are mostly active during the day. Rabbits and hares are generally nocturnal, meaning they are mostly active at night. Some species are crepuscular (kri-PUS-kyuh-lur), meaning they are most active at dawn and twilight. Various environmental conditions and the effects of nearby humans may cause species to alternate between nocturnal, diurnal, and crepuscular activities.

Pikas have several types of social structures. Those that live in rocky areas of North America are unsocial, with males and females having separate territories and rarely interacting except to mate. Pikas in rocky areas of Asia live in pairs within a communal territory. Burrowing pikas, in contrast, are extremely social animals. Families of up to thirty individuals live within burrows and there are about ten family groups within a territory. There is a lot of interaction between family members, including grooming, playing, and sleeping together.

Rabbits and hares have similar differences in social organization. Most rabbits and hares in the wild live solitary lives, although they will often graze together, and are not territorial. The European rabbit is very social. They live in "warrens" or groups of six to twelve adults controlled by a dominant male. The warren consists of a maze of burrows and chambers.

Pikas breed in the spring, with peak breeding occurring in May and early June. Female pikas reach sexual maturity at about one year of age. The gestation period, the time the females carry their young in the womb, is about thirty days. Litters consist of two to six babies and are cared for exclusively by the mother. Females breed for a second time shortly after the first litter is born and usually produce a second litter before the end of summer. Babies are born blind and nearly hairless but grow quickly, reaching adult size in forty to fifty days.

Rabbits breed throughout the year, depending on climate. Generally the breeding season in the wild is spring and summer. Females have multiple litters per year with litter sizes of two to eight babies on average, although it can be as high as fifteen babies. The gestation period is twenty-five to fifty days, with the longer periods occurring in hares.

There is extremely limited parental care of babies in lagomorphs. Most mothers visit the young in their nest once a day, usually between midnight and 5:00 A.M. for a short period of nursing. In rabbits and hares, the young are weaned, stop feeding on their mother's milk, at about one or two months of age. They reach sexual maturity, able to reproduce, in four to six months.

LAGOMORPHS AND PEOPLE

Pikas have little economic importance to humans. They are too small to be used as food, although they are sometimes hunted for their fur, particularly in China. Pikas are sometimes considered agricultural pests and killed by farmers. Rabbits and hares are hunted worldwide for sport and for their meat and fur. They are also raised commercially for their fur and meat. Several species are used extensively by humans as experimental subjects in laboratories. Rabbits are also raised as pets, primarily in the United States, Canada, and Western Europe. They are sometimes considered agricultural and horticultural pests and killed by farmers and other humans.

CONSERVATION STATUS

Six species of lagomorphs are listed by the World Conservation Union (IUCN) as Critically Endangered, facing an extremely high risk of extinction. Twelve species are listed as Endangered, facing a very high risk of extinction; fourteen species are listed as Vulnerable, facing a high risk of extinction; and one species, the Sardinian pika is listed as Extinct, died out. Eight species are listed as Near Threatened, not currently threatened, but could become so.

The primary reason for declining populations of lagomorphs are loss of habitat, disease, especially the pox virus myxomatosis (mix-oh-mah-TOE-sus), and conversion of habitats to agricultural use by humans.

FOR MORE INFORMATION

Books:

Macdonald, David. *The New Encyclopedia of Mammals.* Oxford, U.K.: Oxford University Press, 2001.

Miller, Sara Swan. *Rabbits, Pikas, and Hares.* New York: Franklin Watts, Inc., 2002.

Morris, Ting. *Rabbit (Animal Families.)* Mankato, MN: Smart Apple Media, 2004.

National Research Council. "Rabbits." In *Microlivestock: Little-Known Small Animals with a Promising Economic Future.* Washington, DC: National Academies Press, 1991. Online at http://books.nap.edu/books/030904295X/html/179.html (accessed on July 12, 2004).

National Research Council. "Domestic Rabbit." In *Microlivestock: Little-Known Small Animals with a Promising Economic Future.* Washington, DC: National Academies Press, 1991. Online at http://books.nap.edu/books/030904295X/html/183.html (accessed on July 12, 2004).

Nowak, Ronald M. *Walker's Mammals of the World,* 6th ed. Baltimore: Johns Hopkins University Press, 1999.

Swanson, Diane. *Welcome to the World of Rabbits and Hares.* Portland, OR: Graphic Arts Center Publishing Co., 2000.

Swanson, Diane. *Rabbits and Hares (Welcome to the World of Animals).* Milwaukee: Gareth Stevens, 2002.

Periodicals:

Chapman, Joseph A., et al. "*Sylvilagus floridanus.*" *Mammalian Species* (April 15, 1980): 1–8.

Cohen, Philip. "Rabbit-Human Stem Cell Claims Provoke Controversy and Doubt: Scientists in China Say Stem Cell Capable of Forming Muscle or Nerve Tissue can be Derived by Interspecies Cloning, Overcoming the Shortage of Human Eggs." *New Scientist* (August 23, 2003): 14.

Graur, Dan, et al. "Phylogenetic Position of the Order Lagomorpha (Rabbits, Hares, and Allies.)" *Nature* January 25, 1996): 333–335.

Hacklander, Klaus, et al. "The Effect of Dietary Fat Content on Lactation Energetics in the European Hare (*Lepus europaeus*)." *Physiological and Biochemical Zoology* (January 2002): 19–28.

Krebs, Charles J., et al. "What Drives the 10-Year Cycle of Snowshoe Hares?" *BioScience* (January 2001): 25.

Roach, John. "Rabbit Woes: Easter Icons Face Survival Struggles." *National Geographic News* (April 17, 2003). Online at http://news.nationalgeographic.com/news/2003/04/0417_030417_rabbits.html (accessed on July 12, 2004).

Smith, Andrew T., and Marla L. Weston. "*Ochotona princeps.*" *Mammalian Species* (April 26, 1990): 1–8.

Sohn, Emily. "Now Mammals are Feeling the Heat." *New Scientist* (October 5, 2002): 9.

Web sites:

House Rabbit Society. http://www.rabbit.org (accessed on July 12, 2004).

Myers, Phil. "Order Lagomorpha." Animal Diversity Web. http://animaldiversity.ummz.umich.edu/site/accounts/information/Lagomorpha.html (accessed on July 12, 2004).

IUCN/SSC Lagomorph Specialist Group. http://www.ualberta.ca/dhik/lsg (accessed on July 12, 2004).

PIKAS

Ochotonidae

Class: Mammalia
Order: Lagomorpha
Family: Ochotonidae
Number of species: 30 species

family
CHAPTER

PHYSICAL CHARACTERISTICS

All pikas (PEE-kuhz) are similar in appearance, being small, compact mammals with large, round ears and short front and rear legs. They resemble guinea pigs in size and appearance, ranging in length from 5 to 12 inches (12.5 to 30.0 centimeters) and weighing 3.5 to 7 ounces (100 to 200 grams). Pikas lack a noticeable tail. They have long, soft fur that is usually gray or brown, often with red accents.

GEOGRAPHIC RANGE

Pikas are found in the mountains of western North America, including Alaska and the Yukon, and the mountains and plains of central Asia, including the Himalayan and Ural mountain ranges. The countries they live in include Iran, Afghanistan, Pakistan, Nepal, Tibet, Bhutan, Russia, Japan, Mongolia, North Korea, and China.

HABITAT

Pikas are found in two distinct habitats. Some live among rocks and rocky areas. Others live in meadows, steppes (semi-arid, grass-covered plains), shrubs and desert.

DIET

Pikas are herbivores, meaning they eat primarily plants.

BEHAVIOR AND REPRODUCTION

Pikas are mainly diurnal, active during the day. An exception is the steppe pika, which is nocturnal, meaning it is most active

phylum

class

subclass

order

monotypic order

suborder

▲ **family**

VICTIM OF GLOBAL WARMING

Many scientists believe the American pika will become the first mammal to become extinct due to the effects of global warming. The American pika lives in the high mountains of the western United States and Canada but as the climate gets warmer, the mammals are forced to move to higher elevations to find suitable habitats. A study between 1994 and 1999 in the Great Basin, eastern Sierra Nevada, and western Rocky Mountains found a 30 percent drop in the population of American pikas. Scientists believe the decline of the American pika should be a wake-up call about the consequences of global warming, which many blame on human pollution of the atmosphere.

at night. They have several types of social structure. Those that live in rocky areas of North America are unsocial, with males and females having separate territories and rarely interacting except to mate. Pikas in rocky areas of Asia live in pairs within a communal territory. Burrowing pikas, in contrast, are extremely social animals. Families of up to thirty individuals live within burrows and there are about ten family groups within a territory. There is much interaction between family members, including grooming, playing, and sleeping together.

Pikas breed in the spring, with peak breeding occurring in May and early June. Female pikas reach sexual maturity as early as twenty-one days of age. The gestation, or pregnancy, period is about thirty days. Litters consist of one to thirteen babies and are cared for exclusively by the mother. Females breed for a second time shortly after the first litter is born and usually produce a second litter before the end of summer. Some pika species can have as many as five litters per years, including the Afghan pika, with each litter having up to eleven babies. Pikas are born blind and nearly hairless but grow quickly, reaching adult size in forty to fifty days.

Pikas have a keen sense of sight and hearing, which helps them detect predators, such as weasels, hawks, eagles, and owls. When a pika feels threatened, it issues a loud, shrill, alarm bark and nearby pikas immediately hide in their burrows or in rock crevices. The one exception is when a weasel is detected, the pika remains silent, since the small weasel can follow pikas into their hiding places. Pikas live an average of one to two years and more rarely, four to six years in the wild.

PIKAS AND PEOPLE

Pikas have little economic importance to humans. They are too small to be used as food, although they are sometimes hunted for their fur, particularly in China. Pikas are sometimes considered agricultural pests and killed by farmers.

CONSERVATION STATUS

Four species of pika are listed by the World Conservation Union (IUCN) as Critically Endangered, facing an extremely high risk of extinction, dying out, in the wild; four species are listed as Endangered, facing a very high risk of extinction; and ten species are listed as Vulnerable, facing a high risk of extinction. One species, the Sardinian pika is considered Extinct.

American pika (*Ochotona princeps*)

AMERICAN PIKA
Ochotona princeps

Physical characteristics: The American pika is a medium-sized pika with short ears, an oval body shape, and no apparent tail. American pikas have a body length of 6 to 8.5 inches (16.2 to 21.6 centimeters) and weigh about 6 ounces (168 grams). Their hind feet are relatively large compared to their body, 1 to 1.4 inches (2.5 to 3.5 centimeters).

Geographic range: The American pika is found in the western United States in Oregon, Washington, Idaho, Montana, Wyoming, Colorado, Nevada, California, and New Mexico, and in British Columbia in western Canada.

Habitat: American pikas are found in rocky mountain areas, grassland, coniferous forest, deciduous forest, and the border between meadows and rocky terrain.

Diet: American pikas are herbivores, meaning they eat mainly plants. Their diet includes grasses, thistles, sedges (a wetland plant that resembles grass), and fireweed. Because pikas live in climates with harsh winters, most species build large hay piles during the summer to provide food during the winter. They cut off grass stems at the root and bring them to selected places on the surface, piling them into conical-shaped mounds. Once dry, each hay pile can weigh from 2 to 5 pounds (0.9 to 2.25 kilograms). Some pikas store their hay in tree hollows, under tree stumps, and in rock cavities. Each of these stashes can weigh from 15 to 40 pounds (6.75 to 18 kilograms).

The American pika lives in the western United States and Canada. (John Shaw/Bruce Coleman Inc. Reproduced by permission.)

Behavior and reproduction: American pikas are diurnal, meaning they are most active during the day. They are territorial, meaning they defend an area they consider their home from intruders. Males and females have separate territories. They spend most of their day looking for food, guarding their territory, and sunning themselves on rocks.

American pikas usually breed from late April to early July. The female gives birth to two to four babies in the spring or summer. The gestation period is about thirty days.

American pikas and people: American pikas play an important role in maintaining the diversity and abundance of alpine meadow plants through their storage of grasses for food during the winter.

Conservation status: The American pika is not listed as threatened by the IUCN. However, populations have drastically declined between 1994 and 1999 and continued to decline into 2004. Seven subspecies (populations of a species living in specific areas) are listed by the IUCN as Vulnerable and several subspecies are considered threatened or endangered by other conservation groups. ■

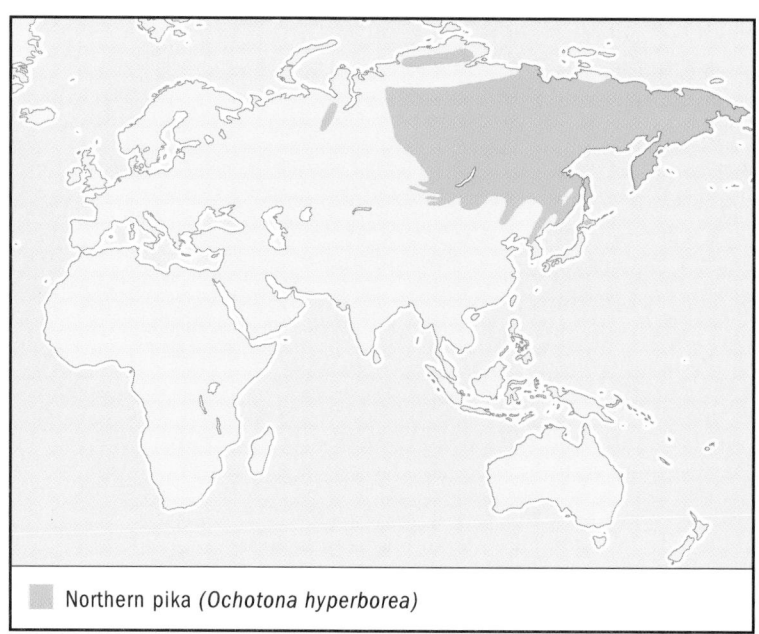

Northern pika (*Ochotona hyperborea*)

NORTHERN PIKA
Ochotona hyperborea

Physical characteristics: The northern pika, also known as the Siberian pika, is slightly larger than the American pika. It has a body length of 7 to 12 inches (17.5 to 30.0 centimeters) and weighs about 7 ounces (200 grams). Northern pikas have medium brown fur on their upper bodies and orange to cream fur on their undersides.

Geographic range: The northern pika has the largest distribution range of any pika species. It ranges from eastern Siberia to Sakhalin Island in the Sea of Okhotsk and the northernmost Japanese island of Hokkaido. It is found in eastern Russia, Japan, Mongolia, North Korea, and Manchuria in northern China.

Habitat: Northern pikas live in high grassy plains, coniferous forest, tundra, among rocky outcroppings and crevices, and in burrows under large stones on the land surface.

Diet: Northern pikas are herbivores, meaning they eat mainly plants. Their diet consists mostly of grasses and herbs. Like other pikas, they build hay piles of grasses that they feed on during the harsh winters.

Behavior and reproduction: Northern pikas are generally very social and curious. They are believed to be monogamous (muh-NAH-guh-mus), meaning a male and female pair for life. The pairs usually live in small colonies. Most females have two litters of babies during the summer, with each litter consisting of one to five babies.

Northern pikas do not survive in captivity. The subspecies Manehurian (Manchurian) pika dies within an hour after being caught by humans.

Northern pikas and people: Northern pikas have little economic importance to humans.

Conservation status: Northern pikas are not listed as threatened by the IUCN. However, the subspecies *Ochotona hyperborea yesoensis* found on Hokkaido Island is considered endangered by the Japanese government.   ■

Male and female pairs of northern pikas usually live in colonies with other pikas. (© D. Robert & Lorri Franz/Corbis. Reproduced by permission.)

FOR MORE INFORMATION

Books:

Macdonald, David. *The New Encyclopedia of Mammals.* Oxford, U.K.: Oxford University Press, 2001.

Miller, Sara Swan. *Rabbits, Pikas, and Hares.* New York: Franklin Watts, Inc., 2002.

Nowak, Ronald M. *Walker's Mammals of the World,* 6th ed. Baltimore: Johns Hopkins University Press, 1999.

Periodicals:

Brown, Paul. "American Pika Doomed as First Mammal Victim of Climate Change."*The Guardian* (August 21, 2003).

Buck, Kelly L., and Brandon Sheafor. "Selection of Phenolics in Alpine Plans by *Ochotona princepes* (North American Pikas)." *The Ohio Journal of Science* (March 2003): A-11.

Smith, Andrew T., and Marla L. Weston. "*Ochotona princeps.*" *Mammalian Species* (April 26, 1990): 1–8.

Sohn, Emily. "Now Mammals are Feeling the Heat." *New Scientist* (October 5, 2002): 9.

Web sites:

Myers, Phil, and Anna Bess Sorin. "Family Ochotonidae (Pikas)." Animal Diversity Web. http://animaldiversity.ummz.umich.edu/site/accounts/information/Ochotonidae.html (accessed on July 7, 2004).

Jansa, Sharon. "*Ochotona princeps* (American Pika)." Animal Diversity Web. http://animaldiversity.ummz.umich.edu/site/accounts/information/Ochotona_princeps.html (accessed on July 7, 2004).

HARES AND RABBITS
Leporidae

Class: Mammalia
Order: Lagomorpha
Family: Leporidae
Number of species: 62 species

PHYSICAL CHARACTERISTICS

Adult rabbits and hares have a body length of 10 to 28 inches (25.4 to 71.1 centimeters) and weigh 14 ounces to 15.3 pounds (400 grams to 7 kilograms). They have short, furry tails and ear sizes vary greatly and generally are shorter in rabbits and longer in hares. The main exceptions are the rabbit breeds known as lops, which have long, floppy ears. Females are generally larger than males. Hares generally are larger than rabbits and have black-tipped ears.

Rabbits and hares usually have thick, soft fur that comes in a wide spectrum of colors, shades, and combinations, including black, white, brown, beige, tan, blue, orange, red, pink, cream, lilac, silver, and lavender.

Hares and rabbits have eyes set high on their head, looking sideways, giving them a wide field of vision. They have weak but flexible necks, allowing them to turn their heads with a wide range of motion. They have a single opening to pass both urine and feces. They also have a specialized part of their large intestine, called the cecum (SEE-kum), which acts as a fermentation chamber that aids in digestion of grasses.

GEOGRAPHIC RANGE

Hares and rabbits are found on every continent except Antarctica. They are native to every continent they are found on, except Australia where they were introduced.

TEN-YEAR CYCLE

A unusual and striking feature of the snowshoe hare is its ten-year cycle of population increase and decline. The number of litters per year and the number of young per litter is higher for about three years, declines in the next three or four years, and then drops significantly in the last three or four years of the cycle. Why this happens is not completely understood by scientists but they believe it is caused by one or more factors, such as food availability, predation, and social interactions.

HABITAT

Hares live in arctic tundra, steppes, wetlands, forests, and deserts. Rabbits live in pine and deciduous forests, desert, mountainous areas, scrubland, tropical rainforest, near rivers and streams, rocky outcroppings, grasslands, and areas of dense brush or other low-lying vegetation.

DIET

Hares and rabbits are herbivores, meaning they are plant-eaters. With a primary diet of grasses and herbs but also will feed on fruit, seeds, leaves, shoots, and bark.

BEHAVIOR AND REPRODUCTION

Rabbits and hares have several types of social structure. Most rabbits and hares in the wild live solitary lives, although they will often graze together, and are not territorial. The European rabbit is very social. It lives in "warrens," groups of six to twelve adults controlled by a dominant male. The warren consists of a maze of burrows and chambers.

Rabbits breed throughout the year depending upon the climate, with spring and summer being the general breeding seasons in the wild. Females have multiple litters per year with litter sizes of two to eight babies on average, although it can be as high as 15 babies. The gestation period, the length of time the mother carries her babies in the womb, is twenty-five to fifty days, with the longer periods occurring in hares.

HARES AND RABBITS AND PEOPLE

Rabbits and hares are hunted worldwide for sport. They are both hunted and raised commercially for their meat and fur. Several species are used extensively in laboratories. Rabbits are also raised as pets.

CONSERVATION STATUS

Two species are listed by the World Conservation Union (IUCN) as Critically Endangered, facing an extremely high risk of extinction; eight species are listed as Endangered, facing a very high risk of extinction; four species are listed as Vulnerable, facing a high risk of extinction; and six species are listed as Near Threatened, not currently threatened, but could become so.

The primary reasons for declining populations of hares and rabbits are loss of habitat, disease, especially the pox virus myxomatosis (mix-oh-mah-TOE-sus), and conversion of habitats to agricultural use by humans.

In the United States, the pygmy rabbit has experienced a sudden decline that has caught even conservation groups off-guard. Although it is listed by IUCN as Near Threatened, it is listed as an endangered species by the state of Washington. Wildlife officials estimate that as of 2003, only thirty pygmy rabbits existed in the wild in the state's Columbia Basin. The decline is blamed on loss of sagebrush, its primary habitat. Mexico's volcano rabbit is found only on the slopes of four volcanoes near Mexico City. Its population is estimated at about 1,000 and declining due to encroachment on its habitat by human development. The Davis Mountains cottontail is not listed by the IUCN but Portland (Oregon) State University biologist Luis Ruedas has tried unsuccessfully to get the state of Texas to list it as endangered. It is found only in a small mountain range in Texas.

Snowshoe hare (*Lepus americanus*)

SNOWSHOE HARE
Lepus americanus

Physical characteristics: Snowshoe hares range in length from 16.5 to 20.7 inches (41.3 to 51.8 centimeters). They weigh from 3.12 to 3.4 pounds (1.4 to 1.56 kilograms). Females are slightly larger than males.

In the summer, their fur is rust or gray-brown with a black line running down their mid-back, cream colored on the sides of their lower body, and a white underside. Their face and legs are cinnamon colored. Their ears are brown with black tips and white or cream edges. During the winter, they turn white except for their black eyelids and black ear tips. The bottom of their paws are covered with dense fur, hence the name snowshoe hare.

Geographic range: Snowshoe hares are found throughout Canada and the northern United States, including Alaska, and the Rocky Mountains as far south as northern New Mexico.

Habitat: Snowshoe hares live in open fields, swampy areas, riverside thickets, coniferous forests, including subarctic coniferous forests located south of tundra, and tundra.

Diet: Snowshoe hares have a varied diet. In the summer, it includes grasses, flowers, wild strawberry plants and fruit, dandelion, clover, horsetails, and new growth of aspen, birch, and willow trees. In the winter, they forage, search, for buds, twigs, bark, and evergreens.

Behavior and reproduction: Snowshoe hares are generally solitary but large populations often live within a small geographic area. They are nocturnal, meaning they are most active at night, and crepuscular (kri-PUS-kyuh-lur), meaning they are also active during dawn and twilight.

This snowshoe hare's color is changing from a winter white coat to a summer brown. (Leonard Lee Rue/Bruce Coleman Inc. Reproduced by permission.)

When snowshoe hares sense a predator is near, they often stand completely still, blending in with their surroundings. They are also fast runners, and have been clocked at speeds of up to 27 miles (43 kilometers) per hour. They can cover 10 feet (3 meters) in a single leap. They have acute hearing and are capable swimmers, able to swim across small lakes and rivers, usually to escape predators.

Snowshoe hares breed from mid-March through August. Females can have up to four litters per season, with litter sizes ranging from one to eight babies. The average litter size is two to four babies. The gestation period, the time the females carry the young in their womb, is thirty-six days. The young reach sexual maturity, ability to reproduce, at one year of age.

Snowshoe hares and people: The snowshoe hare is widely hunted by humans for its meat and fur.

Conservation status: The snowshoe hare is not listed as threatened by the IUCN. They are common throughout their range and populations seem to be remaining steady. ∎

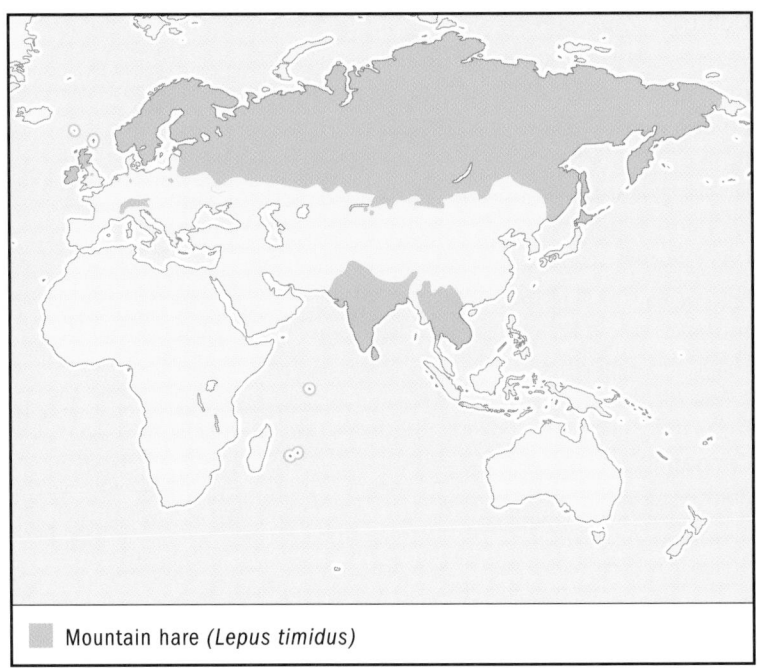

Mountain hare (*Lepus timidus*)

MOUNTAIN HARE
Lepus timidus

Physical characteristics: The mountain hare is medium-sized with short ears and hind legs. It has a body length of 18 to 24 inches (46 to 61 centimeters) and weighs 2.2 to 8.8 pounds (1 to 4 kilograms.) Their fur changes from brown in the summer to white in the winter.

Geographic range: Mountain hares are found in Arctic and adjacent temperate areas of northern Europe and Asia, from Ireland to eastern Siberia.

Habitat: Mountain hares live in tundra, subarctic coniferous forests, mixed coniferous and deciduous forests, and transitional zones with open clearings, swamps, and river valleys.

Diet: Mountain hares are herbivores, meaning they are plant-eaters. Their diet varies by habitat and season. In the summer, forest dwellers eat mostly grasses, leaves, and twigs. Tundra inhabitants eat primarily alpine plants along with grasses, lichen, and bark. In the winter, heather is the main food source.

Behavior and reproduction: The mountain hare is primarily solitary and is seen in groups only when breeding. The breeding season is from January to September. Females have one or two litters per year, with a litter size of one to four babies. If there is an early spring, females can have up to three litters. The gestation period, the time the female carries the young in her womb, is forty-seven to fifty-four days.

Mountain hares and people: Hunted by humans for its meat and fur.

Conservation status: The mountain hare is not considered threatened by the IUCN. ■

The mountain hare is usually solitary, only coming together into groups to breed. (Illustration by Amanda Smith. Reproduced by permission.)

Desert cottontail *(Sylvilagus audubonii)*

DESERT COTTONTAIL
Sylvilagus audubonii

Physical characteristics: A larger cottontail with large ears. Head and body length of 14 to 15 inches (37 to 40 centimeters) and its weight is 26.5 to 44 ounces (750 to 1,250 grams).

Geographic range: Desert cottontails are found in North America, from Montana south to central Mexico and west through California.

Habitat: Desert and forest, from coastal areas to higher altitudes.

Diet: Desert cottontails are herbivores, eating mainly grasses but some wood and bark.

Behavior and reproduction: The breeding season for the desert cottontail is from January to August, with multiple litters per year, and an average litter size of two to four babies. They reach sexual maturity at eighty days.

Desert cottontails and people: Hunted by humans mainly for sport.

Conservation status: The desert cottontail is not listed as threatened by the IUCN. ∎

FOR MORE INFORMATION

Books:

Morris, Ting. *Rabbit (Animal Families).* Mankato, MN: Smart Apple Media, 2004.

National Research Council. "Rabbits." In *Microlivestock: Little-Known Small Animals with a Promising Economic Future.* Washington, DC: National Academies Press, 1991. Online at http://books. nap. edu/books/030904295X/html/179.html (accessed on July 12, 2004).

National Research Council. "Domestic Rabbit." In *Microlivestock: Little-Known Small Animals with a Promising Economic Future.*Washington, DC: National Academies Press, 1991. Onlin at http://books.nap.edu/books/030904295X/html/183.html (accessed on July 12, 2004).

Nowak, Ronald M. *Walker's Mammals of the World,* 6th ed. Baltimore: Johns Hopkins University Press, 1999.

Swanson, Diane. *Welcome to the World of Rabbits and Hares.* Portland, OR: Graphic Arts Center Publishing Co., 2000.

Swanson, Diane. *Rabbits and Hares (Welcome to the World of Animals).* Milwaukee: Gareth Stevens, 2002.

Periodicals:

Angerbjörn, Anders, and John E. C. Flux. *"Lepus timidus." Mammalian Species* (June 23, 1995): 1–11.

Chapman, Joseph A., and Gale R. Willner. *"Sylvilagus audubonii." Mammalian Species* (September 21, 1978): 1–4.

Chapman, Joseph A., et al. *"Sylvilagus floridanus." Mammalian Species* (April 15, 1980): 1–8.

Hacklander, Klaus, et al. "The Effect of Dietary Fat Content on Lactation Energetics in the European Hare (*Lepus europaeus*)." *Physiological and Biochemical Zoology* (January 2002): 19–28.

Krebs, Charles J., et al. "What Drives the 10-Year Cycle of Snowshoe Hares?" *BioScience* (January 2001): 25.

Desert cottontails live in desert and forest areas. (John Shaw/Bruce Coleman Inc. Reproduced by permission.)

Roach, John. "Rabbit Woes: Easter Icons Face Survival Struggles." *National Geographic News* (April 17, 2003). Online at http://news.nationalgeographic.com/news/2003/04/0417_030417_rabbits.html (accessed on July 12, 2004).

Web sites:

House Rabbit Society. http://www.rabbit.org (accessed on July 12, 2004).

Myers, Phil, and Anna Bess Sorin. "Family Leporidae." Animal Diversity Web. http://animaldiversity.ummz.umich.edu/site/accounts/information/Leporidae.html (accessed on July 12, 2004).

Class: Mammalia

Order: Macroscelidea

One family: Macroscelididae

Number of species: 15 species

monotypic order
C H A P T E R

PHYSICAL CHARACTERISTICS

Sengis (SEN-jeez) are commonly known as elephant shrews, although they are not related to the shrew. Sengis range in size from that of a mouse to a rabbit.

They have a head and body length of 3.5 to 12.5 inches (9.0 to 31.5 centimeters), a tail length of 3 to 11 inches (8.0 to 26.3 centimeters) and weigh from 1 ounce to 10 pounds (28 grams to 4.5 kilograms). They have long, spindly legs and a nose that is turned down. They have large heads and ears and large, dark eyes. Their hind legs are larger then their front legs. Sengis walk on their toe tips rather than the feet bottoms.

The larger species of sengis have brightly colored fur ranging in color from olive, brown, black, and red, while the smaller species are various shades of brown and gray. Some are multi-colored, such as the golden-rumped sengi, which has upper body fur of a deep reddish brown and black, lighter fur on its undersides, and black feet, ears, and legs. Its tail is black except for the lower third, which is white with a black tip. There is a large patch of fur on its rump that is bright yellow. In the rufous sengi, the long, soft fur ion the upper body is light brown, light gray, or light orange. The underside fur is white or gray. The fur on its face is a patchwork of white spots and black streaks.

GEOGRAPHIC RANGE

Sengis are found throughout Africa except western Africa and the Sahara Desert region. They are most common and diverse in southern and eastern Africa.

IDENTITY CRISIS

Sengis or elephant shrews have been one of the most often misclassified species of animals. Scientists who first classified the mammal in the mid 1800s placed it in the order Insectivora along with true shrews (family Soricidae). It got its name because its long down-turned nosed resembled an elephant's trunk and physically looked like a shrew. It was reclassified in the order Scandentia (tree shrews) and then reclassified again as an ungulate, a group of mammals with hooves that include horses and giraffes. Later, it was classified as a lagomorph, along with rabbits and hares. More recently, examination of the elephant shrew's molecular structure indicates it is a distinct order and the order Macroscelidea was established. Based on genetic evidence, the elephant shrew, now called the sengi, is related to the proposed superorder Afrotheria composed of six orders, whose members include elephants, manatees, and aardvarks.

HABITAT

Sengis live in deciduous forest, rainforest, grassland, and desert areas of Africa, especially where there is an abundance of water. They are found in the thick ground cover of coastal bush forests, rocky outcroppings, and highland and lowland forests.

DIET

Sengis are insectivores, meaning they eat primarily insects. Their diet of insects includes ants, termites, beetles, spiders, caterpillars, and worms. However, several species are omnivores, meaning they eat insects, flesh, and plants. Their diet includes toads, frogs, lizards, fruits, seeds, and plants. One species, the golden-rumped sengi, is an omnivore, meaning it eats only flesh, mainly insects and small animals.

BEHAVIOR AND REPRODUCTION

Sengis are mainly diurnal, meaning they are most active during the day, but during hot weather, they can be nocturnal, meaning they are most active at night. Several species are crepuscular, meaning they are most active during early morning and twilight. They have well developed senses of sight, hearing, and smell. Most species are territorial, meaning they are protective of an area they consider home and claim exclusively for themselves. Pairs of males and females usually have separate but overlapping and sometimes identical territories.

Most species of sengis are believed to be monogamous (muh-NAH-guh-mus), meaning they have only one sexual partner during a breeding season or lifetime. Several species are solitary and males and females get together for only several days to mate. Females usually produce several litters a year, each with usually one or two babies, but more rarely with three or four. The gestation period, the time the female carries the young in her womb, is about sixty days.

SENGIS AND PEOPLE

Sengis are sometimes hunted in areas of Africa for their meat. Since they eat mostly insects, they help control insects such as termites, ants, and grasshoppers, that are problems for farmers because of the damage the insects cause to crops.

CONSERVATION STATUS

Three species of sengi are listed by IUCN as Endangered, facing a very high risk of extinction: Somali sengi, the golden-rumped sengi, and the black and rufous sengi. One species is listed as Vulnerable, facing a high risk of extinction: the checkered sengi. The reasons for the listings are severely fragmented populations and declining habitats. No other species are listed as currently threatened.

Checkered sengi *(Rhynchocyon cirnei)*

CHECKERED SENGI
Rhynchocyon cirnei

Physical characteristics: The checkered sengi adult has a head and body length of 9 to 12.5 inches (23.5 to 31.5 centimeters) and a tail length of 7 to 10 inches (19.0 to 26.3 centimeters).

Geographic range: The checkered sengi is found in northern and eastern Democratic Republic of the Congo, Uganda, southern Tanzania, northeastern Zambia, Malawi, and northern Mozambique.

Habitat: Checkered sengis live in dense, lowland and mountain regions of tropical rainforest.

Diet: Checkered sengis are mainly insectivores, meaning they eat primarily insects. Their diet includes ants, termites, and beetles.

However, they have also been known to eat small mammals, birds, bird eggs, and snails.

Behavior and reproduction: Checkered sengis are primarily diurnal, meaning they are most active during the day, They can on occasion become nocturnal, meaning they are most active at night, especially during hot weather. They can live alone, in mated pairs, or in small groups. They are monogamous, meaning they have only one sexual partner for life. They are extremely nervous animals and are always on the lookout for predators, such as pythons and other snakes, and birds of prey such as eagles, hawks, owls, and kestrels. Checkered sengis have an average lifespan in the wild of three to five years.

A checkered sengi searches for food. Checkered sengis eat mainly insects, but they also may eat small mammals, birds, bird eggs, and snails. (© Tom McHugh/Photo Researchers, Inc. Reproduced by permission.)

Checkered sengis are territorial, meaning they are protective of an area they consider home and claim exclusively for themselves. Pairs of males and females usually have separate but overlapping territories. Individuals` sleep in nests made of small pits covered with leaves. Checkered sengis build new nests every few days, digging a shallow depression in the ground and lining and covering it with leaves. Once constructed, it is difficult for humans to detect. A pair may build up to ten shelters in their territories.

The checkered sengi breed year-round and have several litters per year. The gestation period, the time the female carries the young in her womb, is about forty-two days. The litter size is one baby, which stays in the nest for about ten days before going out with its mother to forage for food. It goes its own way after five to ten weeks.

Checkered sengis and people: Checkered sengis are of no known significance to humans.

Conservation status: The checkered sengi is listed by the IUCN as Vulnerable, due primarily to severely fragmented populations and declining habitats. ■

FOR MORE INFORMATION

Books:

Macdonald, David. *The New Encyclopedia of Mammals.* Oxford, U.K.: Oxford University Press, 2001.

Nicoll, Martin E., and Galen B. Rathbun. *African Insectivora and Elephant Shrews: An Action Plan for Their Conservation.* Gland, Switzerland: IUCN, 1990.

Nowak, Ronald M. *Walker's Mammals of the World,* 6th ed. Baltimore: Johns Hopkins University Press, 1999.

Periodicals:

Downs, Calleen T., and M. R. Perrin. "The Thermal Biology of Three Southern African Elephant Shrews." *Journal of Thermal Biology* (December 1995): 445–450.

Fredericks, Ilse. "Elephant Shrews May Help Astronauts." *Africa News Service* (September 21, 2003).

Koontz, Fred W., and Nancy J. Roeper. "*Elephantulus rufescens.*" *Mammalian Species* (December 15, 1983): 1–5.

Rathbun, Galen B. "*Rhynchocyon chrysopygus.*" *Mammalian Species* (June 8, 1979): 1–4.

Tabuce, Rodolphe, et al. "A New Genus of Mavroscelidea (Mammalia) From the Eocene of Algeria: A Possible Origin for Elephant Shrews." *Journal of Vertebrate Paleontology* (August 2001): 535–546.

Web sites:

Myers, Phil. "Order Macroscelidea." Animal Diversity Web. http://animaldiversity.ummz.umich.edu/site/accounts/information/Macroscelidea.html (accessed on July 12, 2004).

Species List by Biome

CONIFEROUS FOREST
American black bear
American pika
American water shrew
Asian elephant
Bobcat
Brown-throated three-toed
  sloth
Chimpanzee
Common bentwing bat
Coypu
Desert cottontail
Eastern mole
Edible dormouse
Ermine
Gambian rat
Geoffroy's spider monkey
Giant panda
Gray squirrel
Gray wolf
Greater sac-winged bat
Hairy-footed jerboa
Human
Indian crested porcupine
Kirk's dikdik
Lar gibbon
Little brown bat
Malayan moonrat
Mandrill
Moose

Mountain beaver
Mountain hare
Nine-banded armadillo
North American beaver
North American porcupine
Northern pika
Pacarana
Pallas's long-tongued bat
Pallid bat
Pileated gibbon
Puma
Red deer
Red panda
Red-shanked douc langur
Reindeer
Rhesus macaque
Serow
Siamang
Siberian musk deer
Snow leopard
Snowshoe hare
South African porcupine
Southern tree hyrax
Star-nosed mole
Striped skunk
Tasmanian devil
Three-striped night monkey
Tiger
Valley pocket gopher
Venezuelan red howler monkey

Virginia opossum
Weeper capuchin
Western barbastelle
White-tailed deer
White-throated capuchin

DECIDUOUS FOREST
Aardvark
African civet
American bison
American black bear
American least shrew
American pika
American water shrew
Ashy chinchilla rat
Asian elephant
Aye-aye
Bobcat
Bornean orangutan
Bridled nail-tailed wallaby
Brush-tailed phascogale
Brush-tailed rock wallaby
Capybara
Central American agouti
Chimpanzee
Collared peccary
Common bentwing bat
Common brush-tailed possum
Common genet

Common ringtail
Common tenrec
Common wombat
Cotton-top tamarin
Coypu
Crowned lemur
Degu
Desert cottontail
Eastern chipmunk
Eastern gray kangaroo
Eastern mole
Eastern pygmy possum
Edible dormouse
Ermine
Eurasian wild pig
European badger
Forest elephant
Forest hog
Funnel-eared bat
Gambian rat
Geoffroy's spider monkey
Giant panda
Goeldi's monkey
Gray squirrel
Gray wolf
Greater dog-faced bat
Greater glider
Greater horseshoe bat
Greater sac-winged bat
Ground pangolin
Human
Indian crested porcupine
Indian muntjac
Indian rhinoceros
Koala
Lar gibbon
Lesser Malay mouse deer
Lesser New Zealand short-
   tailed bat
Lion
Little brown bat
Lord Derby's anomalure
Lowland tapir
Malayan moonrat
Mara
Mountain beaver
Mountain hare

North American beaver
North American porcupine
Northern raccoon
Numbat
Paca
Pacarana
Pallas's long-tongued bat
Parnell's moustached bat
Pileated gibbon
Puma
Pygmy glider
Red deer
Red fox
Red kangaroo
Red panda
Red-tailed sportive lemur
Rhesus macaque
Ringtailed lemur
Rock cavy
Senegal bushbaby
Serow
Siamang
Silky anteater
South African porcupine
Southern flying squirrel
Spotted hyena
Star-nosed mole
Striped skunk
Sugar glider
Three-striped night monkey
Tiger
Valley pocket gopher
Venezuelan red howler
   monkey
Virginia opossum
Water buffalo
Weeper capuchin
Western barbastelle
Western European hedgehog
White rhinoceros
White-tailed deer
White-throated capuchin

DESERT
Australian jumping mouse
Bighorn sheep

Bobcat
Brazilian free-tailed bat
California leaf-nosed bat
Collared peccary
Damaraland mole-rat
Dassie rat
Desert cottontail
Dromedary camel
Egyptian slit-faced bat
Egyptian spiny mouse
Grant's desert golden mole
Gray wolf
Hairy-footed jerboa
Hardwicke's lesser mouse-
   tailed bat
Human
Kirk's dikdik
Lion
Mzab gundi
Naked mole-rat
North American porcupine
Pallid bat
Parnell's moustached bat
Pink fairy armadillo
Pronghorn
Puma
Red fox
Rhesus macaque
San Joaquin pocket mouse
Savanna elephant
Short-beaked echidna
Southern marsupial mole
Spotted hyena
Striped skunk
Trident leaf-nosed bat
Valley pocket gopher
Virginia opossum
White-footed sportive lemur

GRASSLAND
Aardvark
Aardwolf
African civet
Alpaca
Alpine marmot
American bison

American black bear
American least shrew
American pika
Ashy chinchilla rat
Asian elephant
Australian false vampire bat
Australian jumping mouse
Black wildebeest
Black-bellied hamster
Black-tailed prairie dog
Brazilian free-tailed bat
Bridled nail-tailed wallaby
California leaf-nosed bat
Capybara
Central American agouti
Chimpanzee
Common bentwing bat
Common genet
Common tenrec
Coypu
Degu
Dwarf epauletted fruit bat
Eastern barred bandicoot
Eastern chipmunk
Eastern gray kangaroo
Eastern mole
Egyptian rousette
Egyptian slit-faced bat
Egyptian spiny mouse
Ermine
Eurasian wild pig
Forest elephant
Gambian rat
Giant anteater
Giant kangaroo rat
Giraffe
Grant's desert golden mole
Gray wolf
Greater bilby
Greater dog-faced bat
Greater horseshoe bat
Grevy's zebra
Ground pangolin
Hardwicke's lesser mouse-
  tailed bat
Hispaniolan solenodon
Hispid cotton rat

Human
Indian crested porcupine
Indian muntjac
Indian rhinoceros
Kiang
Lesser New Zealand short-
  tailed bat
Lion
Llama
Long-tailed chinchilla
Lowland tapir
Maned wolf
Mara
Naked bat
Nine-banded armadillo
Northern pika
Numbat
Paca
Pallas's long-tongued bat
Pallid bat
Parnell's moustached bat
Pearson's tuco-tuco
Pink fairy armadillo
Pronghorn
Przewalski's horse
Puma
Red deer
Red fox
Red kangaroo
Rock cavy
Rock hyrax
San Joaquin pocket mouse
Savanna elephant
Senegal bushbaby
Short-beaked echidna
Smoky bat
Snow leopard
South African porcupine
Spix's disk-winged bat
Spotted hyena
Springhare
Star-nosed mole
Striped skunk
Tasmanian wolf
Thomson's gazelle
Tiger
Valley pocket gopher

Vampire bat
Virginia opossum
Water buffalo
Western European hedgehog
Western red colobus
White rhinoceros
Yellow-streaked tenrec

LAKE AND POND
American water shrew
Babirusa
Capybara
Central American agouti
Common hippopotamus
Coypu
Duck-billed platypus
European otter
Greater bulldog bat
Malayan tapir
Muskrat
North American beaver
North American porcupine
Prehensile-tailed porcupine
Tiger

OCEAN
Antarctic fur seal
Beluga
Blue whale
Burmeister's porpoise
California sea lion
Common bottlenosed dolphin
Dugong
Franciscana dolphin
Galápagos sea lion
Gray whale
Harbor porpoise
Harp seal
Hawaiian monk seal
Humpback whale
Killer whale
Narwhal
North Atlantic right whale
Northern bottlenosed whale
Northern elephant seal
Northern minke whale

Pygmy right whale
Pygmy sperm whale
Shepherd's beaked whale
Sperm whale
Spinner dolphin
Steller's sea cow
Walrus
West Indian manatee

RAINFOREST
Australian false vampire bat
Aye-aye
Babirusa
Bald uakari
Bennett's tree kangaroo
Bornean orangutan
Brazilian free-tailed bat
Brown-throated three-toed sloth
Brush-tailed rock wallaby
Central American agouti
Checkered sengi
Chevrotains
Chimpanzee
Collared peccary
Colombian woolly monkey
Common brush-tailed possum
Common ringtail
Common squirrel monkey
Common tenrec
Common tree shrew
Cotton-top tamarin
Coypu
Crowned lemur
Cuban hutia
Eastern pygmy possum
Eurasian wild pig
Forest elephant
Fossa
Funnel-eared bat
Geoffroy's spider monkey
Giant anteater
Goeldi's monkey
Greater sac-winged bat
Ground cuscus
Hispaniolan solenodon

Hoffman's two-toed sloth
Human
Indian crested porcupine
Indian flying fox
Indian muntjac
Indri
Kitti's hog-nosed bat
Lar gibbon
Lesser New Zealand short-tailed bat
Lord Derby's anomalure
Lowland tapir
Malayan colugo
Malayan tapir
Mandrill
Masked titi
Milne-Edwards's sifaka
Monito del monte
Mountain beaver
Musky rat-kangaroo
Naked bat
North American beaver
Northern bettong
Northern greater bushbaby
Okapi
Old World sucker-footed bat
Paca
Pacarana
Philippine tarsier
Pileated gibbon
Potto
Prehensile-tailed porcupine
Proboscis monkey
Pygmy hippopotamus
Pygmy marmoset
Pygmy slow loris
Queensland tube-nosed bat
Red mouse lemur
Red-shanked douc langur
Rhesus macaque
Ring-tailed mongoose
Rock hyrax
Rufous spiny bandicoot
Short-beaked echidna
Siamang
Siberian musk deer
Silky anteater

Silky shrew opossum
Smoky bat
Southern pudu
Spiny rat
Spix's disk-winged bat
Sugar glider
Sumatran rhinoceros
Three-striped night monkey
Valley pocket gopher
Vampire bat
Venezuelan red howler monkey
Virginia opossum
Water opossum
Weeper capuchin
Western gorilla
Western red colobus
Western tarsier
White bat
White-faced saki
White-tailed deer
White-throated capuchin
Yellow-streaked tenrec

RIVER AND STREAM
American water shrew
Aye-aye
Babirusa
Baiji
Black-bellied hamster
Boto
Capybara
Central American agouti
Common hippopotamus
Common squirrel monkey
Coypu
Duck-billed platypus
European otter
Ganges and Indus dolphin
Greater bulldog bat
Greater cane rat
Lowland tapir
Malayan tapir
Mountain beaver
Muskrat
North American beaver

North American porcupine
Northern raccoon
Old World sucker-footed bat
Paca
Prehensile-tailed porcupine
Pygmy hippopotamus
Smoky bat
Tiger
Virginia opossum
Water opossum
West Indian manatee
White-footed sportive lemur

SEASHORE

Antarctic fur seal
California sea lion
Cape horseshoe bat
European otter
Galápagos sea lion
Grant's desert golden mole
Greater bulldog bat
Harp seal
Hawaiian monk seal
Honey possum
Lesser New Zealand short-
  tailed bat

Marianas fruit bat
Northern elephant seal
Pearson's tuco-tuco
Walrus

TUNDRA

American black bear
Ermine
Gray wolf
Hairy-footed jerboa
Human
Long-tailed chinchilla
Moose
Mountain hare
North American porcupine
Northern pika
Norway lemming
Polar bear
Red fox
Reindeer
Snowshoe hare
Striped skunk

WETLAND

American black bear

Bobcat
Bornean orangutan
Brazilian free-tailed bat
Capybara
Common squirrel monkey
Coypu
European otter
Giant anteater
Greater bulldog bat
Greater cane rat
Greater dog-faced bat
Indian flying fox
Malayan moonrat
Marianas fruit bat
North American beaver
Northern raccoon
Old World sucker-footed bat
Pacarana
Parnell's moustached bat
Proboscis monkey
Puma
Rhesus macaque
Spix's disk-winged bat
Star-nosed mole
Tiger
Valley pocket gopher

Species List by Geographic Range

AFGHANISTAN
Common bentwing bat
Dromedary camel
Eurasian wild pig
Gray wolf
Greater horseshoe bat
Hardwicke's lesser mouse-
  tailed bat
Red deer
Red fox
Rhesus macaque
Snow leopard
Trident leaf-nosed bat

ALBANIA
Blue whale
Common bentwing bat
Common bottlenosed dolphin
Edible dormouse
Eurasian wild pig
European badger
European otter
Gray wolf
Greater horseshoe bat
Humpback whale
Northern minke whale
Pygmy sperm whale
Red deer
Red fox
Sperm whale

ALGERIA
Blue whale
Common bentwing bat
Common bottlenosed dolphin
Common genet
Dromedary camel
Eurasian wild pig
European otter
Greater horseshoe bat
Humpback whale
Killer whale
Mzab gundi
Northern bottlenosed whale
Northern minke whale
Pygmy sperm whale
Red deer
Red fox
Sperm whale
Trident leaf-nosed bat

ANDORRA
European badger
Red fox

ANGOLA
Aardvark
African civet
Blue whale
Common bentwing bat

Common bottlenosed dolphin
Common genet
Dassie rat
Egyptian slit-faced bat
Gambian rat
Giraffe
Ground pangolin
Humpback whale
Kirk's dikdik
Lion
Northern minke whale
Pygmy sperm whale
South African porcupine
Sperm whale
Spinner dolphin
Spotted hyena
Springhare
Western gorilla
White rhinoceros

ANTARCTICA
Antarctic fur seal
Blue whale
Northern minke whale

ARGENTINA
Blue whale
Brazilian free-tailed bat
Brown-throated three-toed sloth

Burmeister's porpoise
Capybara
Central American agouti
Collared peccary
Common bottlenosed dolphin
Coypu
Franciscana dolphin
Giant anteater
Greater bulldog bat
Humpback whale
Killer whale
Llama
Lowland tapir
Maned wolf
Mara
Monito del monte
Northern minke whale
Pallas's long-tongued bat
Pearson's tuco-tuco
Pink fairy armadillo
Prehensile-tailed porcupine
Puma
Pygmy right whale
Red deer
Shepherd's beaked whale
Southern pudu
Sperm whale
Three-toed tree sloths
Vampire bat
Water opossum

ARMENIA
Common bentwing bat
Edible dormouse
Eurasian wild pig
European badger
Gray wolf
Red deer
Red fox

AUSTRALIA
Australian false vampire bat
Australian jumping mouse
Bennett's tree kangaroo
Blue whale
Bridled nail-tailed wallaby

Brush-tailed phascogale
Brush-tailed rock wallaby
Common bentwing bat
Common bottlenosed dolphin
Common brush-tailed possum
Common ringtail
Common wombat
Duck-billed platypus
Dugong
Eastern barred bandicoot
Eastern gray kangaroo
Eastern pygmy possum
Greater bilby
Greater glider
Honey possum
Humpback whale
Killer whale
Koala
Musky rat-kangaroo
Northern bettong
Northern minke whale
Numbat
Pygmy glider
Pygmy right whale
Pygmy sperm whale
Queensland tube-nosed bat
Red fox
Red kangaroo
Rufous spiny bandicoot
Short-beaked echidna
Southern marsupial mole
Sperm whale
Spinner dolphin
Sugar glider
Tasmanian devil
Tasmanian wolf

AUSTRIA
Alpine marmot
Common bentwing bat
Edible dormouse
Ermine
Eurasian wild pig
European badger
Greater horseshoe bat
Mountain hare

Red deer
Red fox
Western European hedgehog

AZERBAIJAN
Common bentwing bat
Edible dormouse
Eurasian wild pig
European badger
Gray wolf
Red deer
Red fox

BANGLADESH
Asian elephant
Blue whale
Common bentwing bat
Common bottlenosed dolphin
Eurasian wild pig
Ganges and Indus dolphin
Gray wolf
Greater horseshoe bat
Humpback whale
Indian crested porcupine
Indian flying fox
Indian muntjac
Indian rhinoceros
Northern minke whale
Pygmy sperm whale
Red fox
Rhesus macaque
Serow
Sperm whale
Spinner dolphin
Tiger

BELARUS
Black-bellied hamster
Edible dormouse
Ermine
Eurasian wild pig
European badger
Gray wolf
Moose
Mountain hare

Red deer
Red fox

BELGIUM
Black-bellied hamster
Blue whale
Common bottlenosed dolphin
Edible dormouse
Ermine
Eurasian wild pig
European badger
Greater horseshoe bat
Harbor porpoise
Humpback whale
Killer whale
North Atlantic right whale
Northern minke whale
Pygmy sperm whale
Sperm whale
Western European hedgehog

BELIZE
Blue whale
Brazilian free-tailed bat
Central American agouti
Collared peccary
Common bottlenosed dolphin
Funnel-eared bat
Geoffroy's spider monkey
Giant anteater
Greater bulldog bat
Greater dog-faced bat
Greater sac-winged bat
Hispid cotton rat
Humpback whale
Nine-banded armadillo
Northern minke whale
Paca
Pallas's long-tongued bat
Parnell's moustached bat
Pygmy sperm whale
Silky anteater
Sperm whale
Spinner dolphin
Spix's disk-winged bat
Vampire bat

Virginia opossum
Water opossum
White-tailed deer

BENIN
Aardvark
African civet
Blue whale
Common bottlenosed dolphin
Common genet
Gambian rat
Humpback whale
Lord Derby's anomalure
Northern minke whale
Pygmy sperm whale
Rock hyrax
Senegal bushbaby
South African porcupine
Sperm whale
Spinner dolphin

BHUTAN
Asian elephant
Common bentwing bat
Gray wolf
Greater horseshoe bat
Indian crested porcupine
Red fox
Red panda
Rhesus macaque
Serow
Snow leopard
Water buffalo

BOLIVIA
Alpaca
Ashy chinchilla rat
Boto
Brazilian free-tailed bat
Brown-throated three-toed
  sloth
Capybara
Central American agouti
Collared peccary
Coypu
Giant anteater
Goeldi's monkey

Greater bulldog bat
Greater dog-faced bat
Greater sac-winged bat
Hoffman's two-toed sloth
Llama
Lowland tapir
Maned wolf
Nine-banded armadillo
Pacarana
Pallas's long-tongued bat
Puma
Pygmy marmoset
Silky anteater
Spix's disk-winged bat
Three-toed tree sloths
Vampire bat
White-faced saki
White-tailed deer

BOSNIA AND HERZEGOVINA
Common bentwing bat
Edible dormouse
Eurasian wild pig
European badger
Greater horseshoe bat
Red deer
Red fox

BOTSWANA
Aardvark
Aardwolf
African civet
Common genet
Common hippopotamus
Damaraland mole-rat
Egyptian slit-faced bat
Giraffe
Ground pangolin
Lion
Savanna elephant
Springhare

BRAZIL
Bald uakari
Blue whale

Boto
Brazilian free-tailed bat
Brown-throated three-toed
  sloth
Burmeister's porpoise
Capybara
Central American agouti
Collared peccary
Common bottlenosed dolphin
Common squirrel monkey
Coypu
Franciscana dolphin
Funnel-eared bat
Giant anteater
Goeldi's monkey
Greater bulldog bat
Greater dog-faced bat
Greater sac-winged bat
Hoffman's two-toed sloth
Humpback whale
Killer whale
Lowland tapir
Maned wolf
Masked titi
Nine-banded armadillo
Northern minke whale
Paca
Pacarana
Pallas's long-tongued bat
Parnell's moustached bat
Prehensile-tailed porcupine
Pygmy marmoset
Pygmy right whale
Pygmy sperm whale
Red deer
Rock cavy
Silky anteater
Smoky bat
Sperm whale
Spinner dolphin
Spix's disk-winged bat
Three-striped night monkey
Three-toed tree sloths
Vampire bat
Venezuelan red howler
  monkey
Water opossum

Weeper capuchin
White-faced saki
White-tailed deer

BULGARIA
Common bentwing bat
Edible dormouse
Eurasian wild pig
European badger
Gray wolf
Greater horseshoe bat
Harbor porpoise
Red deer
Red fox

BURKINA FASO
Aardvark
African civet
Common genet
Egyptian slit-faced bat
Rock hyrax
Senegal bushbaby

BURUNDI
Aardvark
African civet
Common bentwing bat
Common genet
Egyptian slit-faced bat
Gambian rat
Lord Derby's anomalure
Senegal bushbaby
South African porcupine

CAMBODIA
Asian elephant
Blue whale
Common bentwing bat
Common bottlenosed dolphin
Dugong
Eurasian wild pig
Greater horseshoe bat
Humpback whale
Indian muntjac
Lesser Malay mouse deer

Malayan tapir
Northern minke whale
Pileated gibbon
Pygmy sperm whale
Serow
Sperm whale
Spinner dolphin

CAMEROON
Aardvark
African civet
Blue whale
Chimpanzee
Common bottlenosed dolphin
Common genet
Dwarf epauletted fruit bat
Egyptian rousette
Forest elephant
Forest hog
Gambian rat
Greater cane rat
Humpback whale
Lord Derby's anomalure
Mandrill
Northern minke whale
Potto
Pygmy sperm whale
Rock hyrax
Senegal bushbaby
South African porcupine
Sperm whale
Spinner dolphin
Western gorilla
Western red colobus

CANADA
American bison
American black bear
American least shrew
American pika
American water shrew
Beluga
Bighorn sheep
Black-tailed prairie dog
Bobcat
California sea lion

Eastern chipmunk
Eastern mole
Ermine
Gray squirrel
Gray wolf
Harbor porpoise
Harp seal
Killer whale
Little brown bat
Moose
Mountain beaver
Muskrat
Narwhal
North American beaver
North American porcupine
North Atlantic right whale
Northern bottlenosed whale
Northern raccoon
Pallid bat
Polar bear
Pronghorn
Puma
Red deer
Red fox
Reindeer
Snowshoe hare
Southern flying squirrel
Star-nosed mole
Striped skunk
Virginia opossum
Walrus
White-tailed deer

CENTRAL AFRICAN REPUBLIC
Aardvark
African civet
Chimpanzee
Common genet
Dwarf epauletted fruit bat
Egyptian rousette
Forest elephant
Gambian rat
Giraffe
Greater cane rat
Lord Derby's anomalure

Rock hyrax
Senegal bushbaby
South African porcupine
Western gorilla
White rhinoceros

CHAD
Aardvark
African civet
Common genet
Dromedary camel
Egyptian slit-faced bat
Gambian rat
Ground pangolin
Mzab gundi
Rock hyrax
Senegal bushbaby
Spotted hyena
Trident leaf-nosed bat
White rhinoceros

CHILE
Alpaca
Ashy chinchilla rat
Blue whale
Brazilian free-tailed bat
Burmeister's porpoise
Common bottlenosed dolphin
Coypu
Degu
Humpback whale
Killer whale
Llama
Long-tailed chinchilla
Monito del monte
Northern minke whale
Pallas's long-tongued bat
Pearson's tuco-tuco
Pygmy right whale
Pygmy sperm whale
Red deer
Shepherd's beaked whale
Southern pudu
Sperm whale
Vampire bat

CHINA
Asian elephant
Baiji
Blue whale
Common bentwing bat
Common bottlenosed dolphin
Dugong
Edible dormouse
Ermine
European badger
Giant panda
Gray wolf
Greater horseshoe bat
Hairy-footed jerboa
Humpback whale
Indian muntjac
Kiang
Killer whale
Lar gibbon
Lesser Malay mouse deer
Moose
Mountain hare
Northern minke whale
Northern pika
Pygmy slow loris
Pygmy sperm whale
Red deer
Red fox
Red panda
Reindeer
Rhesus macaque
Serow
Siberian musk deer
Snow leopard
Sperm whale
Spinner dolphin
Tiger

COLOMBIA
Bald uakari
Blue whale
Boto
Brazilian free-tailed bat
Brown-throated three-toed sloth
Capybara

Central American agouti
Collared peccary
Colombian woolly monkey
Common bottlenosed dolphin
Common squirrel monkey
Cotton-top tamarin
Funnel-eared bat
Giant anteater
Goeldi's monkey
Greater bulldog bat
Greater sac-winged bat
Hispid cotton rat
Hoffman's two-toed sloth
Humpback whale
Killer whale
Llama
Lowland tapir
Nine-banded armadillo
Northern minke whale
Paca
Pacarana
Pallas's long-tongued bat
Parnell's moustached bat
Prehensile-tailed porcupine
Pygmy marmoset
Pygmy sperm whale
Silky anteater
Silky shrew opossum
Smoky bat
Sperm whale
Spinner dolphin
Spiny rat
Spix's disk-winged bat
Three-striped night monkey
Three-toed tree sloths
Vampire bat
Water opossum
White-faced saki
White-tailed deer
White-throated capuchin

CONGO
African civet
Blue whale
Common bottlenosed dolphin
Common genet

Dwarf epauletted fruit bat
Egyptian rousette
Egyptian slit-faced bat
Forest elephant
Forest hog
Humpback whale
Lord Derby's anomalure
Northern minke whale
Potto
Pygmy sperm whale
South African porcupine
Sperm whale
Spinner dolphin
Springhare
Western gorilla

COSTA RICA
American least shrew
Blue whale
Brazilian free-tailed bat
Brown-throated three-toed
  sloth
Central American agouti
Collared peccary
Common bottlenosed dolphin
Funnel-eared bat
Geoffroy's spider monkey
Giant anteater
Greater bulldog bat
Greater dog-faced bat
Greater sac-winged bat
Hispid cotton rat
Hoffman's two-toed sloth
Humpback whale
Killer whale
Nine-banded armadillo
Northern minke whale
Paca
Pallas's long-tongued bat
Parnell's moustached bat
Puma
Pygmy sperm whale
Silky anteater
Smoky bat
Sperm whale
Spinner dolphin

Spiny rat
Spix's disk-winged bat
Three-toed tree sloths
Vampire bat
Virginia opossum
Water opossum
White bat
White-tailed deer
White-throated capuchin

CROATIA
Blue whale
Common bentwing bat
Common bottlenosed dolphin
Edible dormouse
Eurasian wild pig
European badger
Greater horseshoe bat
Humpback whale
Northern minke whale
Pygmy sperm whale
Red deer
Red fox
Sperm whale

CUBA
Blue whale
Brazilian free-tailed bat
Central American agouti
Collared peccary
Common bottlenosed dolphin
Cuban hutia
Funnel-eared bat
Greater bulldog bat
Humpback whale
Killer whale
Northern minke whale
Pallid bat
Parnell's moustached bat
Pygmy sperm whale
Sperm whale
Spinner dolphin

CYPRUS
Blue whale

Common bottlenosed dolphin
Humpback whale
Northern minke whale
Pygmy sperm whale
Sperm whale

CZECH REPUBLIC
Black-bellied hamster
Common bentwing bat
Edible dormouse
Ermine
European badger
Greater horseshoe bat
Red deer
Red fox

DEMOCRATIC REPUBLIC OF THE CONGO
Aardvark
African civet
Blue whale
Checkered sengi
Chimpanzee
Common bentwing bat
Common bottlenosed dolphin
Common genet
Common hippopotamus
Dwarf epauletted fruit bat
Egyptian rousette
Egyptian slit-faced bat
Forest elephant
Forest hog
Gambian rat
Giraffe
Humpback whale
Lord Derby's anomalure
Mandrill
Northern minke whale
Okapi
Potto
Pygmy sperm whale
Rock hyrax
South African porcupine
Sperm whale

Spinner dolphin
Western gorilla
Western red colobus
White rhinoceros

DENMARK
Blue whale
Common bottlenosed dolphin
Ermine
Eurasian wild pig
European badger
Harbor porpoise
Humpback whale
Killer whale
North Atlantic right whale
Northern minke whale
Norway lemming
Pygmy sperm whale
Red deer
Red fox
Sperm whale
Western European hedgehog

DJIBOUTI
Aardvark
Blue whale
Common bottlenosed dolphin
Common genet
Dromedary camel
Dugong
Humpback whale
Northern minke whale
Rock hyrax
Senegal bushbaby
Sperm whale
Spinner dolphin

DOMINICAN REPUBLIC
Blue whale
Brazilian free-tailed bat
Common bottlenosed dolphin
Funnel-eared bat
Greater bulldog bat
Hispaniolan solenodon

Humpback whale
Killer whale
Northern minke whale
Parnell's moustached bat
Pygmy sperm whale
Sperm whale
Spinner dolphin

ECUADOR
Blue whale
Boto
Brazilian free-tailed bat
Brown-throated three-toed sloth
Capybara
Central American agouti
Collared peccary
Common bottlenosed dolphin
Galápagos sea lion
Giant anteater
Goeldi's monkey
Greater bulldog bat
Greater dog-faced bat
Greater sac-winged bat
Hoffman's two-toed sloth
Humpback whale
Killer whale
Llama
Lowland tapir
Nine-banded armadillo
Northern minke whale
Pacarana
Pallas's long-tongued bat
Pygmy marmoset
Pygmy sperm whale
Silky anteater
Silky shrew opossum
Sperm whale
Spinner dolphin
Spiny rat
Spix's disk-winged bat
Three-toed tree sloths
Vampire bat
Water opossum
White-faced saki
White-tailed deer

EGYPT

Blue whale
Common bottlenosed dolphin
Common genet
Dromedary camel
Egyptian rousette
Egyptian slit-faced bat
Egyptian spiny mouse
Eurasian wild pig
Greater horseshoe bat
Hardwicke's lesser mouse-
  tailed bat
Humpback whale
Northern minke whale
Pygmy sperm whale
Red fox
Rock hyrax
Sperm whale
Trident leaf-nosed bat

EL SALVADOR

Blue whale
Brazilian free-tailed bat
Brown-throated three-toed
  sloth
Collared peccary
Common bottlenosed dolphin
Funnel-eared bat
Geoffroy's spider monkey
Giant anteater
Greater bulldog bat
Greater sac-winged bat
Hispid cotton rat
Humpback whale
Killer whale
Nine-banded armadillo
Northern minke whale
Paca
Pallas's long-tongued bat
Parnell's moustached bat
Pygmy sperm whale
Silky anteater
Sperm whale
Spinner dolphin
Spix's disk-winged bat
Three-toed tree sloths

Vampire bat
Virginia opossum
Water opossum
White-tailed deer

EQUATORIAL GUINEA

African civet
Blue whale
Common bottlenosed dolphin
Common genet
Forest elephant
Humpback whale
Lord Derby's anomalure
Mandrill
Northern minke whale
Potto
Pygmy sperm whale
South African porcupine
Sperm whale
Spinner dolphin
Western gorilla

ERITREA

Aardvark
Blue whale
Common bottlenosed dolphin
Common genet
Dromedary camel
Dugong
Egyptian slit-faced bat
Humpback whale
Northern minke whale
Rock hyrax
Sperm whale
Spinner dolphin

ESTONIA

Blue whale
Common bottlenosed dolphin
Ermine
Eurasian wild pig
European badger
Gray wolf
Harbor porpoise
Humpback whale

Moose
Mountain hare
Northern minke whale
Red deer
Red fox
Sperm whale

ETHIOPIA

Aardvark
Common genet
Dromedary camel
Egyptian slit-faced bat
Forest hog
Grevy's zebra
Lion
Naked mole-rat
Rock hyrax
Senegal bushbaby
Thomson's gazelle

FINLAND

Blue whale
Common bottlenosed dolphin
Ermine
Eurasian wild pig
European badger
European otter
Gray wolf
Humpback whale
Moose
Mountain hare
Northern minke whale
Norway lemming
Red fox
Reindeer
Sperm whale
Western European hedgehog

FRANCE

Alpine marmot
Blue whale
Common bentwing bat
Common bottlenosed dolphin
Common genet
Edible dormouse

Ermine
Eurasian wild pig
European badger
European otter
Greater horseshoe bat
Harbor porpoise
Humpback whale
Killer whale
North Atlantic right whale
Northern bottlenosed whale
Northern minke whale
Pygmy sperm whale
Red deer
Red fox
Sperm whale
Western European hedgehog

FRENCH GUIANA
Blue whale
Capybara
Collared peccary
Common bottlenosed dolphin
Common squirrel monkey
Funnel-eared bat
Giant anteater
Greater bulldog bat
Greater dog-faced bat
Greater sac-winged bat
Humpback whale
Lowland tapir
Nine-banded armadillo
Northern minke whale
Paca
Pallas's long-tongued bat
Parnell's moustached bat
Prehensile-tailed porcupine
Pygmy sperm whale
Silky anteater
Smoky bat
Sperm whale
Spinner dolphin
Spix's disk-winged bat
Three-toed tree sloths
Vampire bat
Water opossum
Weeper capuchin

White-faced saki
White-tailed deer

GABON
African civet
Blue whale
Common bottlenosed dolphin
Common genet
Common hippopotamus
Dwarf epauletted fruit bat
Egyptian rousette
Forest elephant
Forest hog
Humpback whale
Lord Derby's anomalure
Mandrill
Northern minke whale
Potto
Pygmy sperm whale
South African porcupine
Sperm whale
Spinner dolphin
Western gorilla

GAMBIA
Aardvark
African civet
Blue whale
Common bottlenosed dolphin
Common genet
Gambian rat
Greater cane rat
Humpback whale
Killer whale
Northern minke whale
Pygmy sperm whale
Senegal bushbaby
South African porcupine
Sperm whale
Spinner dolphin
Western red colobus

GEORGIA
Common bentwing bat
Edible dormouse

Eurasian wild pig
European badger
Gray wolf
Harbor porpoise
Red deer
Red fox

GERMANY
Alpine marmot
Black-bellied hamster
Blue whale
Common bentwing bat
Common bottlenosed dolphin
Edible dormouse
Ermine
Eurasian wild pig
European badger
Greater horseshoe bat
Harbor porpoise
Humpback whale
Killer whale
North Atlantic right whale
Northern minke whale
Northern raccoon
Pygmy sperm whale
Red deer
Red fox
Sperm whale
Western European hedgehog

GHANA
Aardvark
African civet
Blue whale
Chimpanzee
Common bottlenosed dolphin
Common genet
Dwarf epauletted fruit bat
Egyptian rousette
Forest elephant
Forest hog
Gambian rat
Humpback whale
Lord Derby's anomalure
Northern minke whale
Potto

Pygmy sperm whale
Rock hyrax
Senegal bushbaby
South African porcupine
Sperm whale
Spinner dolphin
Western red colobus

GREECE
Blue whale
Common bentwing bat
Common bottlenosed dolphin
Edible dormouse
European badger
European otter
Gray wolf
Greater horseshoe bat
Harbor porpoise
Humpback whale
Northern minke whale
Pygmy sperm whale
Red deer
Red fox
Sperm whale

GREENLAND
Blue whale
Ermine
Harbor porpoise
Harp seal
Humpback whale
Killer whale
North Atlantic right whale
Northern bottlenosed whale
Northern minke whale
Polar bear
Reindeer
Walrus

GRENADA
Nine-banded armadillo
Pallas's long-tongued bat

GUAM
Marianas fruit bat

GUATEMALA
American least shrew
Blue whale
Brazilian free-tailed bat
Central American agouti
Collared peccary
Common bottlenosed dolphin
Funnel-eared bat
Geoffroy's spider monkey
Giant anteater
Greater bulldog bat
Greater dog-faced bat
Greater sac-winged bat
Hispid cotton rat
Humpback whale
Killer whale
Nine-banded armadillo
Northern minke whale
Paca
Pallas's long-tongued bat
Parnell's moustached bat
Puma
Pygmy sperm whale
Silky anteater
Sperm whale
Spinner dolphin
Spix's disk-winged bat
Vampire bat
Virginia opossum
Water opossum
White-tailed deer

GUINEA
Aardvark
African civet
Blue whale
Chimpanzee
Common bottlenosed dolphin
Common genet
Egyptian slit-faced bat
Forest hog
Gambian rat
Humpback whale
Killer whale
Northern minke whale
Pygmy hippopotamus

Pygmy sperm whale
Rock hyrax
Senegal bushbaby
South African porcupine
Sperm whale
Spinner dolphin

GUINEA-BISSAU
Aardvark
African civet
Blue whale
Common bottlenosed dolphin
Common genet
Forest hog
Gambian rat
Humpback whale
Killer whale
Northern minke whale
Pygmy sperm whale
Rock hyrax
Senegal bushbaby
South African porcupine
Sperm whale
Spinner dolphin
Western red colobus

GUYANA
Blue whale
Boto
Capybara
Collared peccary
Common bottlenosed dolphin
Common squirrel monkey
Funnel-eared bat
Giant anteater
Greater bulldog bat
Greater dog-faced bat
Greater sac-winged bat
Humpback whale
Lowland tapir
Nine-banded armadillo
Northern minke whale
Paca
Pallas's long-tongued bat
Parnell's moustached bat
Prehensile-tailed porcupine

Pygmy sperm whale
Silky anteater
Smoky bat
Sperm whale
Spinner dolphin
Spix's disk-winged bat
Three-toed tree sloths
Vampire bat
Water opossum
Weeper capuchin
White-faced saki
White-tailed deer

HAITI
Blue whale
Brazilian free-tailed bat
Common bottlenosed dolphin
Funnel-eared bat
Greater bulldog bat
Hispaniolan solenodon
Humpback whale
Killer whale
Northern minke whale
Parnell's moustached bat
Pygmy sperm whale
Sperm whale
Spinner dolphin

HONDURAS
American least shrew
Blue whale
Brazilian free-tailed bat
Brown-throated three-toed
  sloth
Central American agouti
Collared peccary
Common bottlenosed dolphin
Funnel-eared bat
Geoffroy's spider monkey
Giant anteater
Greater bulldog bat
Greater dog-faced bat
Greater sac-winged bat
Hispid cotton rat
Hoffman's two-toed sloth
Humpback whale

Killer whale
Nine-banded armadillo
Northern minke whale
Paca
Pallas's long-tongued bat
Parnell's moustached bat
Pygmy sperm whale
Silky anteater
Sperm whale
Spinner dolphin
Spiny rat
Spix's disk-winged bat
Three-toed tree sloths
Vampire bat
Virginia opossum
Water opossum
White bat
White-tailed deer
White-throated capuchin

HUNGARY
Black-bellied hamster
Common bentwing bat
Edible dormouse
Ermine
Eurasian wild pig
European badger
Greater horseshoe bat
Red deer
Red fox

ICELAND
Blue whale
Harbor porpoise
Humpback whale
Killer whale
North Atlantic right whale
Northern bottlenosed whale
Northern minke whale
Norway lemming

INDIA
Asian elephant
Blue whale
Common bentwing bat

Common bottlenosed dolphin
Dromedary camel
Dugong
Ermine
Eurasian wild pig
Ganges and Indus dolphin
Gray wolf
Greater horseshoe bat
Hardwicke's lesser mouse-
  tailed bat
Humpback whale
Indian crested porcupine
Indian flying fox
Indian muntjac
Indian rhinoceros
Kiang
Killer whale
Lion
Northern minke whale
Pygmy sperm whale
Red fox
Red panda
Rhesus macaque
Serow
Snow leopard
Sperm whale
Spinner dolphin
Tiger
Water buffalo

INDONESIA
Asian elephant
Babirusa
Blue whale
Bornean orangutan
Common bentwing bat
Common bottlenosed dolphin
Common tree shrew
Dugong
Eurasian wild pig
European otter
Humpback whale
Indian muntjac
Killer whale
Lar gibbon
Lesser Malay mouse deer

Malayan colugo
Malayan moonrat
Malayan tapir
Naked bat
Northern minke whale
Proboscis monkey
Pygmy sperm whale
Serow
Siamang
Sperm whale
Spinner dolphin
Sumatran rhinoceros
Tiger
Western tarsier

IRAN
Blue whale
Common bentwing bat
Common bottlenosed dolphin
Dromedary camel
Dugong
Edible dormouse
Egyptian rousette
Egyptian spiny mouse
Eurasian wild pig
European badger
Gray wolf
Greater horseshoe bat
Hairy-footed jerboa
Humpback whale
Indian crested porcupine
Killer whale
Northern minke whale
Pygmy sperm whale
Red deer
Red fox
Sperm whale
Spinner dolphin
Trident leaf-nosed bat

IRAQ
Dromedary camel
Egyptian spiny mouse
Eurasian wild pig
Gray wolf
Greater horseshoe bat

Red fox
Trident leaf-nosed bat

IRELAND
Blue whale
Common bottlenosed dolphin
Ermine
Eurasian wild pig
European badger
European otter
Harbor porpoise
Humpback whale
Killer whale
Mountain hare
North Atlantic right whale
Northern bottlenosed whale
Northern minke whale
Red deer
Red fox
Sperm whale
Western European hedgehog

ISRAEL
Blue whale
Common bottlenosed dolphin
Dromedary camel
Egyptian rousette
Egyptian slit-faced bat
Egyptian spiny mouse
Eurasian wild pig
Gray wolf
Hardwicke's lesser mouse-
   tailed bat
Humpback whale
Indian crested porcupine
Northern minke whale
Pygmy sperm whale
Red fox
Rock hyrax
Sperm whale
Trident leaf-nosed bat

ITALY
Alpine marmot
Blue whale

Common bentwing bat
Common bottlenosed dolphin
Edible dormouse
Ermine
Eurasian wild pig
European badger
Gray wolf
Greater horseshoe bat
Humpback whale
Killer whale
Mountain hare
Northern minke whale
Pygmy sperm whale
Red deer
Red fox
Sperm whale
Western European hedgehog

IVORY COAST
Aardvark
African civet
Blue whale
Chimpanzee
Common bottlenosed dolphin
Common genet
Dwarf epauletted fruit bat
Egyptian rousette
Forest elephant
Forest hog
Gambian rat
Humpback whale
Lord Derby's anomalure
Northern minke whale
Pygmy hippopotamus
Pygmy sperm whale
Rock hyrax
Senegal bushbaby
South African porcupine
Sperm whale
Spinner dolphin
Western red colobus

JAMAICA
Blue whale
Brazilian free-tailed bat
Common bottlenosed dolphin

Funnel-eared bat
Greater bulldog bat
Humpback whale
Killer whale
Northern minke whale
Pallas's long-tongued bat
Parnell's moustached bat
Pygmy sperm whale
Sperm whale
Spinner dolphin

JAPAN
Blue whale
Common bentwing bat
Common bottlenosed dolphin
Dugong
Ermine
Eurasian wild pig
European badger
European otter
Gray whale
Greater horseshoe bat
Harbor porpoise
Humpback whale
Killer whale
Marianas fruit bat
Mountain hare
Northern minke whale
Northern pika
Pygmy sperm whale
Reindeer
Siberian musk deer
Sperm whale
Spinner dolphin

JORDAN
Dromedary camel
Egyptian slit-faced bat
Egyptian spiny mouse
Eurasian wild pig
Gray wolf
Hardwicke's lesser mouse-
    tailed bat
Red fox
Rock hyrax
Trident leaf-nosed bat

KAZAKHSTAN
Black-bellied hamster
Common bentwing bat
Edible dormouse
Ermine
Eurasian wild pig
European badger
Gray wolf
Hairy-footed jerboa
Moose
Mountain hare
Red deer
Red fox
Snow leopard

KENYA
Aardvark
Aardwolf
African civet
Blue whale
Common bentwing bat
Common bottlenosed dolphin
Common genet
Dugong
Egyptian rousette
Egyptian slit-faced bat
Forest hog
Gambian rat
Giraffe
Greater cane rat
Grevy's zebra
Ground pangolin
Humpback whale
Kirk's dikdik
Lion
Lord Derby's anomalure
Naked mole-rat
Northern greater bushbaby
Northern minke whale
Potto
Pygmy sperm whale
Rock hyrax
Senegal bushbaby
South African porcupine
Sperm whale
Spinner dolphin

Springhare
Thomson's gazelle

KUWAIT
Egyptian spiny mouse
Gray wolf
Trident leaf-nosed bat

KYRGYZSTAN
Common bentwing bat
Edible dormouse
Ermine
Eurasian wild pig
European badger
Gray wolf
Red deer
Red fox
Snow leopard

LAOS
Asian elephant
Common bentwing bat
Eurasian wild pig
Greater horseshoe bat
Indian muntjac
Lesser Malay mouse deer
Malayan tapir
Pileated gibbon
Pygmy slow loris
Red fox
Red-shanked douc langur
Rhesus macaque
Serow

LATVIA
Blue whale
Common bottlenosed dolphin
Ermine
Eurasian wild pig
European badger
Gray wolf
Harbor porpoise
Humpback whale
Moose
Mountain hare

Northern minke whale
Red deer
Red fox
Sperm whale

LEBANON
Blue whale
Common bottlenosed dolphin
Dromedary camel
Egyptian spiny mouse
Hardwicke's lesser mouse-
  tailed bat
Humpback whale
Northern minke whale
Pygmy sperm whale
Sperm whale
Trident leaf-nosed bat

LESOTHO
Aardvark
African civet
Common bentwing bat
Common genet
Egyptian slit-faced bat
South African porcupine

LESSER ANTILLES
Blue whale
Brazilian free-tailed bat
Common bottlenosed dolphin
Funnel-eared bat
Greater bulldog bat
Humpback whale
Killer whale
Northern minke whale
Pygmy sperm whale
Sperm whale
Spinner dolphin

LIBERIA
Aardvark
African civet
Blue whale
Common bottlenosed dolphin

Common genet
Forest elephant
Forest hog
Humpback whale
Killer whale
Lord Derby's anomalure
Northern minke whale
Pygmy hippopotamus
Pygmy sperm whale
Rock hyrax
South African porcupine
Sperm whale
Spinner dolphin
Western red colobus

LIBYA
Blue whale
Common bottlenosed dolphin
Dromedary camel
Egyptian spiny mouse
Eurasian wild pig
Greater horseshoe bat
Humpback whale
Mzab gundi
Northern minke whale
Pygmy sperm whale
Red fox
Sperm whale
Trident leaf-nosed bat

LIECHTENSTEIN
Ermine
Eurasian wild pig
Greater horseshoe bat
Red deer
Red fox

LITHUANIA
Blue whale
Common bottlenosed dolphin
Edible dormouse
Ermine
Eurasian wild pig
European badger
Harbor porpoise

Humpback whale
Moose
Mountain hare
Northern minke whale
Red deer
Red fox
Sperm whale

LUXEMBOURG
Edible dormouse
Ermine
Eurasian wild pig
European badger
Greater horseshoe bat
Red deer
Red fox

MACEDONIA
Common bentwing bat
Edible dormouse
Eurasian wild pig
European badger
Gray wolf
Greater horseshoe bat
Red deer
Red fox

MADAGASCAR
Aye-aye
Blue whale
Common bentwing bat
Common bottlenosed dolphin
Common tenrec
Crowned lemur
Dugong
Fossa
Humpback whale
Indri
Killer whale
Milne-Edwards's sifaka
Northern minke whale
Old World sucker-footed bat
Pygmy sperm whale
Red mouse lemur

Red-tailed sportive lemur
Ringtailed lemur
Ring-tailed mongoose
Sperm whale
Spinner dolphin
White-footed sportive lemur
Yellow-streaked tenrec

MALAWI
Aardvark
African civet
Checkered sengi
Common bentwing bat
Common genet
Egyptian slit-faced bat
Gambian rat
Ground pangolin
South African porcupine

MALAYSIA
Asian elephant
Blue whale
Bornean orangutan
Common bentwing bat
Common bottlenosed dolphin
Common tree shrew
Dugong
Eurasian wild pig
Humpback whale
Indian muntjac
Killer whale
Lar gibbon
Lesser Malay mouse deer
Malayan colugo
Malayan moonrat
Malayan tapir
Naked bat
Northern minke whale
Proboscis monkey
Pygmy sperm whale
Serow
Siamang
Sperm whale
Spinner dolphin
Sumatran rhinoceros

MALI
Aardvark
African civet
Common genet
Dromedary camel
Egyptian rousette
Egyptian slit-faced bat
Gambian rat
Mzab gundi
Rock hyrax
Savanna elephant
Senegal bushbaby

MARIANA ISLANDS
Marianas fruit bat

MAURITANIA
Aardvark
Blue whale
Common bottlenosed dolphin
Dromedary camel
Humpback whale
Killer whale
Northern minke whale
Pygmy sperm whale
Sperm whale
Spinner dolphin

MEXICO
American black bear
American least shrew
Bighorn sheep
Black-tailed prairie dog
Blue whale
Bobcat
Brazilian free-tailed bat
Brown-throated three-toed
 sloth
California leaf-nosed bat
California sea lion
Central American agouti
Collared peccary
Common bottlenosed dolphin
Desert cottontail
Eastern mole

Funnel-eared bat
Geoffroy's spider monkey
Gray whale
Greater bulldog bat
Greater dog-faced bat
Greater sac-winged bat
Hispid cotton rat
Humpback whale
Killer whale
Little brown bat
Muskrat
Nine-banded armadillo
North American beaver
North American porcupine
Northern elephant seal
Northern minke whale
Northern raccoon
Paca
Pallas's long-tongued bat
Pallid bat
Parnell's moustached bat
Pronghorn
Puma
Pygmy sperm whale
Silky anteater
Sperm whale
Spinner dolphin
Spix's disk-winged bat
Striped skunk
Three-toed tree sloths
Valley pocket gopher
Vampire bat
Virginia opossum
Water opossum
White-tailed deer

MOLDOVA
Black-bellied hamster
Common bentwing bat
Edible dormouse
Eurasian wild pig
European badger
Gray wolf
Greater horseshoe bat
Red deer
Red fox

MONACO
European badger
Red fox

MONGOLIA
Ermine
Eurasian wild pig
Gray wolf
Hairy-footed jerboa
Moose
Mountain hare
Northern pika
Przewalski's horse
Red deer
Red fox
Reindeer
Siberian musk deer
Snow leopard

MOROCCO
Blue whale
Common bentwing bat
Common bottlenosed dolphin
Dromedary camel
Eurasian wild pig
European otter
Greater horseshoe bat
Harbor porpoise
Hardwicke's lesser mouse-
  tailed bat
Humpback whale
Killer whale
North Atlantic right whale
Northern bottlenosed whale
Northern minke whale
Pygmy sperm whale
Red deer
Red fox
Sperm whale
Spinner dolphin
Trident leaf-nosed bat

MOZAMBIQUE
Aardvark

African civet
Blue whale
Checkered sengi
Common bentwing bat
Common bottlenosed dolphin
Common genet
Common hippopotamus
Dugong
Egyptian rousette
Egyptian slit-faced bat
Gambian rat
Ground pangolin
Humpback whale
Killer whale
Lord Derby's anomalure
Northern minke whale
Pygmy sperm whale
Rock hyrax
South African porcupine
Sperm whale
Spinner dolphin
Springhare
White rhinoceros

MYANMAR
Asian elephant
Blue whale
Common bentwing bat
Common bottlenosed dolphin
Eurasian wild pig
Gray wolf
Greater horseshoe bat
Humpback whale
Indian flying fox
Indian muntjac
Kitti's hog-nosed bat
Lar gibbon
Lesser Malay mouse deer
Malayan moonrat
Malayan tapir
Northern minke whale
Pygmy sperm whale
Red fox
Red panda
Rhesus macaque
Serow

Sperm whale
Spinner dolphin
Tiger

NAMIBIA
Aardvark
African civet
Blue whale
Common bentwing bat
Common bottlenosed dolphin
Common genet
Common hippopotamus
Damaraland mole-rat
Dassie rat
Egyptian slit-faced bat
Giraffe
Grant's desert golden mole
Ground pangolin
Humpback whale
Killer whale
Kirk's dikdik
Northern minke whale
Pygmy sperm whale
Rock hyrax
Savanna elephant
Sperm whale
Springhare

NEPAL
Asian elephant
Common bentwing bat
Eurasian wild pig
Ganges and Indus dolphin
Gray wolf
Greater horseshoe bat
Indian crested porcupine
Indian muntjac
Indian rhinoceros
Kiang
Red fox
Red panda
Rhesus macaque
Serow
Snow leopard
Water buffalo

NETHERLANDS
Black-bellied hamster
Blue whale
Common bottlenosed dolphin
Ermine
Eurasian wild pig
European badger
Harbor porpoise
Humpback whale
Killer whale
Northern minke whale
Northern raccoon
Pygmy sperm whale
Red deer
Red fox
Sperm whale
Western European hedgehog

NEW ZEALAND
Blue whale
Brush-tailed rock wallaby
Common bottlenosed dolphin
Common brush-tailed possum
Dugong
Humpback whale
Killer whale
Lesser New Zealand short-
  tailed bat
Northern minke whale
Pygmy right whale
Pygmy sperm whale
Shepherd's beaked whale
Sperm whale

NICARAGUA
American least shrew
Blue whale
Brazilian free-tailed bat
Brown-throated three-toed
  sloth
Central American agouti
Collared peccary
Common bottlenosed dolphin
Funnel-eared bat
Geoffroy's spider monkey

Giant anteater
Greater bulldog bat
Greater dog-faced bat
Greater sac-winged bat
Hispid cotton rat
Hoffman's two-toed sloth
Humpback whale
Killer whale
Nine-banded armadillo
Northern minke whale
Paca
Pallas's long-tongued bat
Parnell's moustached bat
Pygmy sperm whale
Silky anteater
Sperm whale
Spinner dolphin
Spiny rat
Spix's disk-winged bat
Three-toed tree sloths
Vampire bat
Virginia opossum
Water opossum
White bat
White-tailed deer
White-throated capuchin

NIGER
Aardvark
Dromedary camel
Egyptian slit-faced bat
Gambian rat
Mzab gundi
Rock hyrax
Senegal bushbaby
Trident leaf-nosed bat

NIGERIA
Aardvark
African civet
Blue whale
Chimpanzee
Common bottlenosed dolphin
Common genet
Dwarf epauletted fruit bat

Egyptian rousette
Egyptian slit-faced bat
Gambian rat
Humpback whale
Lord Derby's anomalure
Northern minke whale
Potto
Pygmy sperm whale
Rock hyrax
Senegal bushbaby
South African porcupine
Sperm whale
Spinner dolphin
Western gorilla
Western red colobus

NORTH KOREA
Blue whale
Common bentwing bat
Common bottlenosed dolphin
Eurasian wild pig
Humpback whale
Killer whale
Northern minke whale
Northern pika
Pygmy sperm whale
Red deer
Siberian musk deer
Sperm whale
Spinner dolphin

NORWAY
Blue whale
Common bottlenosed dolphin
Ermine
Eurasian wild pig
European badger
European otter
Harbor porpoise
Humpback whale
Killer whale
Moose
Mountain hare
North Atlantic right whale
Northern bottlenosed whale

Northern minke whale
Norway lemming
Polar bear
Red deer
Red fox
Reindeer
Sperm whale
Western European hedgehog

OMAN
Blue whale
Common bottlenosed dolphin
Dromedary camel
Dugong
Egyptian rousette
Egyptian spiny mouse
Gray wolf
Humpback whale
Killer whale
Northern minke whale
Pygmy sperm whale
Rock hyrax
Sperm whale
Spinner dolphin
Trident leaf-nosed bat

PAKISTAN
Blue whale
Common bentwing bat
Common bottlenosed dolphin
Dromedary camel
Dugong
Eurasian wild pig
Ganges and Indus dolphin
Gray wolf
Greater horseshoe bat
Hardwicke's lesser mouse-
  tailed bat
Humpback whale
Indian flying fox
Indian muntjac
Indian rhinoceros
Kiang
Killer whale
Northern minke whale

Pygmy sperm whale
Red fox
Rhesus macaque
Snow leopard
Sperm whale
Spinner dolphin
Trident leaf-nosed bat

PANAMA
American least shrew
Blue whale
Brazilian free-tailed bat
Brown-throated three-toed
  sloth
Capybara
Central American agouti
Collared peccary
Common bottlenosed dolphin
Funnel-eared bat
Geoffroy's spider monkey
Giant anteater
Greater bulldog bat
Greater dog-faced bat
Greater sac-winged bat
Hispid cotton rat
Hoffman's two-toed sloth
Humpback whale
Killer whale
Nine-banded armadillo
Northern minke whale
Northern raccoon
Paca
Pallas's long-tongued bat
Parnell's moustached bat
Puma
Pygmy sperm whale
Silky anteater
Smoky bat
Sperm whale
Spinner dolphin
Spiny rat
Spix's disk-winged bat
Three-toed tree sloths
Vampire bat
Water opossum
White bat

White-tailed deer
White-throated capuchin

PAPUA NEW GUINEA
Blue whale
Common bentwing bat
Common bottlenosed dolphin
Dugong
Ground cuscus
Humpback whale
Killer whale
Northern minke whale
Pygmy sperm whale
Rufous spiny bandicoot
Short-beaked echidna
Sperm whale
Spinner dolphin
Sugar glider

PARAGUAY
Brazilian free-tailed bat
Brown-throated three-toed
  sloth
Capybara
Collared peccary
Coypu
Giant anteater
Greater bulldog bat
Maned wolf
Nine-banded armadillo
Paca
Pallas's long-tongued bat
Prehensile-tailed porcupine
Three-toed tree sloths
Vampire bat
Water opossum

PERU
Alpaca
Ashy chinchilla rat
Bald uakari
Blue whale
Boto
Brazilian free-tailed bat
Burmeister's porpoise

Capybara
Central American agouti
Collared peccary
Common bottlenosed
  dolphin
Giant anteater
Goeldi's monkey
Greater bulldog bat
Greater dog-faced bat
Greater sac-winged bat
Hoffman's two-toed sloth
Humpback whale
Killer whale
Llama
Lowland tapir
Maned wolf
Nine-banded armadillo
Northern minke whale
Pacarana
Pallas's long-tongued bat
Parnell's moustached bat
Pearson's tuco-tuco
Pygmy marmoset
Pygmy sperm whale
Silky anteater
Sperm whale
Spinner dolphin
Spix's disk-winged bat
Vampire bat
Water opossum
White-faced saki
White-tailed deer

PHILIPPINES
Blue whale
Common bentwing bat
Common bottlenosed
  dolphin
Dugong
Humpback whale
Naked bat
Northern minke whale
Philippine tarsier
Pygmy sperm whale
Sperm whale
Spinner dolphin

POLAND
Black-bellied hamster
Blue whale
Common bentwing bat
Common bottlenosed
  dolphin
Edible dormouse
Ermine
Eurasian wild pig
European badger
Greater horseshoe bat
Harbor porpoise
Humpback whale
Moose
Northern minke whale
Red deer
Red fox
Sperm whale

PORTUGAL
Blue whale
Common bentwing bat
Common bottlenosed
  dolphin
Common genet
Eurasian wild pig
European badger
European otter
Greater horseshoe bat
Harbor porpoise
Humpback whale
Killer whale
North Atlantic right whale
Northern bottlenosed whale
Northern minke whale
Pygmy sperm whale
Red deer
Red fox
Sperm whale
Western barbastelle
Western European hedgehog

PUERTO RICO
Blue whale
Brazilian free-tailed bat

Common bottlenosed
  dolphin
Funnel-eared bat
Greater bulldog bat
Humpback whale
Killer whale
Northern minke whale
Pygmy sperm whale
Sperm whale
Spinner dolphin

QATAR
Egyptian spiny mouse

ROMANIA
Black-bellied hamster
Common bentwing bat
Edible dormouse
Eurasian wild pig
European badger
Gray wolf
Greater horseshoe bat
Harbor porpoise
Red deer
Red fox

RUSSIA
Beluga
Black-bellied hamster
Blue whale
Common bentwing bat
Common bottlenosed
  dolphin
Edible dormouse
Ermine
Eurasian wild pig
European otter
Gray whale
Gray wolf
Harbor porpoise
Harp seal
Humpback whale
Killer whale
Moose
Mountain hare
Narwhal

Northern minke whale
Northern pika
Northern raccoon
Polar bear
Red deer
Red fox
Reindeer
Siberian musk deer
Snow leopard
Sperm whale
Tiger
Walrus
Western European hedgehog

RWANDA
Aardvark
African civet
Chimpanzee
Common bentwing bat
Common genet
Egyptian slit-faced bat
Gambian rat
Lord Derby's anomalure
Rock hyrax
Senegal bushbaby
South African porcupine

SAUDI ARABIA
Blue whale
Common bottlenosed dolphin
Dromedary camel
Dugong
Egyptian slit-faced bat
Egyptian spiny mouse
Gray wolf
Hardwicke's lesser mouse-
   tailed bat
Humpback whale
Indian crested porcupine
Northern minke whale
Pygmy sperm whale
Rock hyrax
Sperm whale
Spinner dolphin
Trident leaf-nosed bat

SENEGAL
Aardvark
African civet
Blue whale
Chimpanzee
Common bottlenosed dolphin
Common genet
Egyptian slit-faced bat
Gambian rat
Hardwicke's lesser mouse-
   tailed bat
Humpback whale
Killer whale
Northern minke whale
Pygmy sperm whale
Rock hyrax
Senegal bushbaby
South African porcupine
Sperm whale
Spinner dolphin
Western red colobus

SIERRA LEONE
Aardvark
African civet
Blue whale
Chimpanzee
Common bottlenosed dolphin
Common genet
Egyptian slit-faced bat
Forest hog
Gambian rat
Humpback whale
Killer whale
Lord Derby's anomalure
Northern minke whale
Potto
Pygmy hippopotamus
Pygmy sperm whale
Rock hyrax
Senegal bushbaby
South African porcupine
Sperm whale
Spinner dolphin
Western red colobus

SINGAPORE
Lesser Malay mouse deer

SLOVAKIA
Black-bellied hamster
Edible dormouse
Ermine
European badger
Greater horseshoe bat
Red deer
Red fox

SLOVENIA
Blue whale
Common bentwing bat
Common bottlenosed dolphin
Edible dormouse
Ermine
Eurasian wild pig
European badger
Greater horseshoe bat
Humpback whale
Northern minke whale
Pygmy sperm whale
Red deer
Red fox
Sperm whale

SOMALIA
Aardwolf
African civet
Blue whale
Common bentwing bat
Common bottlenosed dolphin
Common genet
Dromedary camel
Dugong
Egyptian slit-faced bat
Humpback whale
Kirk's dikdik
Naked mole-rat
Northern greater bushbaby
Northern minke whale
Pygmy sperm whale

Rock hyrax
Senegal bushbaby
South African porcupine
Sperm whale
Spinner dolphin

SOUTH AFRICA
Aardvark
Aardwolf
African civet
Black wildebeest
Blue whale
Cape horseshoe bat
Common bentwing bat
Common bottlenosed dolphin
Common genet
Damaraland mole-rat
Dassie rat
Egyptian rousette
Egyptian slit-faced bat
Gambian rat
Giraffe
Grant's desert golden mole
Ground pangolin
Humpback whale
Killer whale
Northern minke whale
Pygmy right whale
Pygmy sperm whale
Rock hyrax
Savanna elephant
Shepherd's beaked whale
South African porcupine
Southern tree hyrax
Sperm whale
Spinner dolphin
Springhare

SOUTH KOREA
Blue whale
Common bentwing bat
Common bottlenosed dolphin
Eurasian wild pig
Humpback whale
Killer whale

Northern minke whale
Pygmy sperm whale
Sperm whale
Spinner dolphin

SPAIN
Alpine marmot
Blue whale
Common bentwing bat
Common bottlenosed dolphin
Common genet
Edible dormouse
Eurasian wild pig
European badger
European otter
Gray wolf
Greater horseshoe bat
Harbor porpoise
Humpback whale
Killer whale
North Atlantic right whale
Northern bottlenosed whale
Northern minke whale
Pygmy sperm whale
Red deer
Red fox
Sperm whale
Western barbastelle
Western European hedgehog

SRI LANKA
Asian elephant
European otter
Indian crested porcupine
Indian flying fox
Indian muntjac

SUDAN
Aardvark
African civet
Blue whale
Chimpanzee
Common bottlenosed dolphin
Common genet

Common hippopotamus
Dromedary camel
Dugong
Dwarf epauletted fruit bat
Egyptian slit-faced bat
Gambian rat
Giraffe
Greater cane rat
Ground pangolin
Humpback whale
Northern minke whale
Pygmy sperm whale
Rock hyrax
Senegal bushbaby
South African porcupine
Sperm whale
Spinner dolphin
Spotted hyena
Thomson's gazelle
Trident leaf-nosed bat
White rhinoceros

SURINAME
Blue whale
Collared peccary
Common bottlenosed dolphin
Common squirrel monkey
Funnel-eared bat
Giant anteater
Greater bulldog bat
Greater dog-faced bat
Greater sac-winged bat
Humpback whale
Lowland tapir
Northern minke whale
Paca
Pallas's long-tongued bat
Parnell's moustached bat
Prehensile-tailed porcupine
Pygmy sperm whale
Silky anteater
Smoky bat
Sperm whale
Spinner dolphin
Spix's disk-winged bat
Three-toed tree sloths

Vampire bat
Water opossum
Weeper capuchin
White-faced saki
White-tailed deer

SWAZILAND
Aardvark
African civet
Common bentwing bat
Common genet
Egyptian slit-faced bat
Gambian rat
Giraffe
Ground pangolin
South African porcupine

SWEDEN
Blue whale
Common bottlenosed dolphin
Ermine
Eurasian wild pig
European badger
Gray wolf
Harbor porpoise
Humpback whale
Moose
Mountain hare
Northern minke whale
Norway lemming
Red deer
Red fox
Sperm whale
Western European hedgehog

SWITZERLAND
Alpine marmot
Common bentwing bat
Edible dormouse
Ermine
Eurasian wild pig
European badger
Greater horseshoe bat
Mountain hare
Red deer

Red fox
Western European hedgehog

SYRIA
Blue whale
Common bottlenosed dolphin
Dromedary camel
Egyptian spiny mouse
Eurasian wild pig
Gray wolf
Greater horseshoe bat
Hardwicke's lesser mouse-
  tailed bat
Humpback whale
Northern minke whale
Pygmy sperm whale
Red deer
Red fox
Sperm whale
Trident leaf-nosed bat

TAJIKISTAN
Common bentwing bat
Edible dormouse
Ermine
Eurasian wild pig
European badger
Gray wolf
Greater horseshoe bat
Red deer
Red fox
Snow leopard

TANZANIA
Aardvark
African civet
Blue whale
Checkered sengi
Chimpanzee
Common bentwing bat
Common bottlenosed dolphin
Common genet
Common hippopotamus
Dugong
Egyptian rousette

Egyptian slit-faced bat
Gambian rat
Giraffe
Greater cane rat
Ground pangolin
Humpback whale
Killer whale
Kirk's dikdik
Lion
Lord Derby's anomalure
Northern greater bushbaby
Northern minke whale
Pygmy sperm whale
Rock hyrax
Senegal bushbaby
South African porcupine
Sperm whale
Spinner dolphin
Springhare
Thomson's gazelle

THAILAND
Asian elephant
Blue whale
Common bentwing bat
Common bottlenosed dolphin
Common tree shrew
Dugong
Eurasian wild pig
Greater horseshoe bat
Humpback whale
Indian muntjac
Kitti's hog-nosed bat
Lar gibbon
Lesser Malay mouse deer
Malayan colugo
Malayan moonrat
Malayan tapir
Northern minke whale
Pileated gibbon
Pygmy sperm whale
Red fox
Rhesus macaque
Serow
Sperm whale

Spinner dolphin
Water buffalo

TOGO
Aardvark
African civet
Blue whale
Common bottlenosed dolphin
Common genet
Forest hog
Gambian rat
Humpback whale
Lord Derby's anomalure
Northern minke whale
Pygmy sperm whale
Rock hyrax
Senegal bushbaby
South African porcupine
Sperm whale
Spinner dolphin

TRINIDAD AND TOBAGO
Pallas's long-tongued bat
Prehensile-tailed porcupine
Silky anteater
Smoky bat
Vampire bat

TUNISIA
Blue whale
Common bentwing bat
Common bottlenosed dolphin
Common genet
Dromedary camel
Eurasian wild pig
European otter
Greater horseshoe bat
Humpback whale
Killer whale
Northern minke whale
Pygmy sperm whale
Red deer
Red fox
Sperm whale
Trident leaf-nosed bat

TURKEY
Blue whale
Common bentwing bat
Common bottlenosed dolphin
Edible dormouse
Egyptian rousette
Eurasian wild pig
European badger
Gray wolf
Greater horseshoe bat
Harbor porpoise
Humpback whale
Northern minke whale
Pygmy sperm whale
Red deer
Sperm whale

TURKMENISTAN
Common bentwing bat
Edible dormouse
Eurasian wild pig
European badger
Gray wolf
Greater horseshoe bat
Hairy-footed jerboa
Red deer
Red fox

UGANDA
Aardvark
African civet
Checkered sengi
Chimpanzee
Common bentwing bat
Common genet
Dwarf epauletted fruit bat
Egyptian rousette
Egyptian slit-faced bat
Forest hog
Gambian rat
Giraffe
Greater cane rat
Ground pangolin
Lord Derby's anomalure
Potto

Senegal bushbaby
South African porcupine
White rhinoceros

UKRAINE
Alpine marmot
Black-bellied hamster
Common bentwing bat
Edible dormouse
Ermine
Eurasian wild pig
European badger
Gray wolf
Greater horseshoe bat
Harbor porpoise
Moose
Red deer
Red fox

UNITED ARAB EMIRATES
Dromedary camel
Egyptian spiny mouse
Gray wolf
Trident leaf-nosed bat

UNITED KINGDOM
Blue whale
Common bottlenosed dolphin
Ermine
Eurasian wild pig
European badger
European otter
Greater horseshoe bat
Harbor porpoise
Humpback whale
Killer whale
Mountain hare
North Atlantic right whale
Northern bottlenosed whale
Northern minke whale
Pygmy sperm whale
Red deer
Red fox
Sperm whale

Western barbastelle
Western European hedgehog

UNITED STATES
American bison
American black bear
American least shrew
American pika
American water shrew
Beluga
Bighorn sheep
Black-tailed prairie dog
Blue whale
Bobcat
Brazilian free-tailed bat
California leaf-nosed bat
California sea lion
Collared peccary
Common bottlenosed dolphin
Desert cottontail
Eastern chipmunk
Eastern mole
Ermine
Giant kangaroo rat
Gray squirrel
Gray whale
Gray wolf
Harbor porpoise
Hawaiian monk seal
Hispid cotton rat
Humpback whale
Killer whale
Little brown bat
Moose
Mountain beaver
Muskrat
Narwhal
Nine-banded armadillo
North American beaver
North American porcupine
North Atlantic right whale
Northern bottlenosed whale
Northern elephant seal
Northern minke whale
Northern raccoon
Pallid bat

Polar bear
Pronghorn
Puma
Pygmy sperm whale
Red deer
Red fox
Reindeer
San Joaquin pocket mouse
Snowshoe hare
Southern flying squirrel
Sperm whale
Spinner dolphin
Star-nosed mole
Steller's sea cow
Striped skunk
Valley pocket gopher
Virginia opossum
Walrus
West Indian manatee
White-tailed deer

URUGUAY
Blue whale
Brazilian free-tailed bat
Burmeister's porpoise
Capybara
Collared peccary
Common bottlenosed dolphin
Coypu
Franciscana dolphin
Giant anteater
Humpback whale
Killer whale
Maned wolf
Northern minke whale
Pearson's tuco-tuco
Prehensile-tailed porcupine
Pygmy right whale
Red deer
Sperm whale
Vampire bat

UZBEKISTAN
Common bentwing bat
Edible dormouse

Eurasian wild pig
European badger
Gray wolf
Hairy-footed jerboa
Red deer
Red fox
Snow leopard

VENEZUELA
Blue whale
Boto
Brazilian free-tailed bat
Capybara
Collared peccary
Colombian woolly monkey
Common bottlenosed dolphin
Common squirrel monkey
Funnel-eared bat
Giant anteater
Greater bulldog bat
Greater dog-faced bat
Greater sac-winged bat
Hispid cotton rat
Hoffman's two-toed sloth
Humpback whale
Lowland tapir
Northern minke whale
Paca
Pacarana
Pallas's long-tongued bat
Parnell's moustached bat
Prehensile-tailed porcupine
Puma
Pygmy sperm whale
Silky anteater
Silky shrew opossum
Smoky bat
Sperm whale
Spinner dolphin
Spix's disk-winged bat
Three-striped night monkey
Three-toed tree sloths
Vampire bat
Venezuelan red howler
  monkey
Water opossum

Weeper capuchin
White-tailed deer

VIETNAM
Asian elephant
Blue whale
Common bentwing bat
Common bottlenosed dolphin
Dugong
Eurasian wild pig
Greater horseshoe bat
Humpback whale
Indian muntjac
Malayan tapir
Northern minke whale
Pygmy slow loris
Pygmy sperm whale
Red fox
Red-shanked douc langur
Rhesus macaque
Serow
Sperm whale
Spinner dolphin

YEMEN
Blue whale
Common bottlenosed dolphin
Dromedary camel
Dugong
Egyptian rousette

Egyptian slit-faced bat
Egyptian spiny mouse
Gray wolf
Hardwicke's lesser mouse-
  tailed bat
Humpback whale
Northern minke whale
Pygmy sperm whale
Rock hyrax
Sperm whale
Spinner dolphin
Trident leaf-nosed bat

YUGOSLAVIA
Alpine marmot
Blue whale
Common bentwing bat
Common bottlenosed dolphin
Edible dormouse
Ermine
Gray wolf
Greater horseshoe bat
Humpback whale
Northern minke whale
Pygmy sperm whale
Red deer
Sperm whale

ZAMBIA
Aardvark

Aardwolf
African civet
Checkered sengi
Common bentwing bat
Common genet
Common hippopotamus
Egyptian rousette
Egyptian slit-faced bat
Gambian rat
Giraffe
Ground pangolin
Lord Derby's anomalure
South African porcupine
Spotted hyena
Springhare

ZIMBABWE
Aardvark
African civet
Common bentwing bat
Common genet
Damaraland mole-rat
Egyptian rousette
Egyptian slit-faced bat
Gambian rat
Ground pangolin
Savanna elephant
South African porcupine
Spotted hyena
Springhare

Index

Italic type indicates volume number; **boldface** type indicates entries and their pages; (ill.) indicates illustrations.

Cougars. *See* Pumas

Cows, mountain. *See* Tapirs

Cows, sea, 4: 828–32, **833–40**

Coyotes, 1: 72, 3: **583–92**

Coypus, 5: **1194–99,** 1195 (ill.), 1196 (ill.)

Crab-eater seals, 3: 580

Craseonycteridae. See Kitti's hog-nosed bats

Craseonycteris thonglongyai. See Kitti's hog-nosed bats

Crested capuchins, 3: 488

Crested genets, 3: 629

Crested porcupines
    Indian, 5: 1115–16, 1115 (ill.), 1116 (ill.)
    North African, 5: 1114

Cricetomys gambianus. See Gambian rats

Cricetus cricetus. See Black-bellied hamsters

Crocuta crocuta. See Spotted hyenas

Crowned lemurs, 3: 455–57, 455 (ill.), 456 (ill.)

Cryptomys damarensis. See Damaraland mole-rats

Cryptoprocta ferox. See Fossa

Cryptoprocta spelea, 3: 646

Cryptotis parva. See American least shrews

Ctenodactylidae. See Gundis

Ctenomyidae. See Tuco-tucos

Ctenomys pearsoni. See Pearson's tuco-tucos

Cuban hutias, 5: 1188, 1189, 1191–93, 1191 (ill.), 1192 (ill.)

Cuban solenodons, 2: 240, 242

Cuniculus brisson. See Pacas

Cuscomys ashaninki, 5: 1178

Cuscomys oblativa, 5: 1178

Cuscuses, 1: 99, **116–23**

Cuvier's whales, 4: 751

Cyclopes didactylus. See Silky anteaters

Cynocephalidae. See Colugos

Cynocephalus variegatus. See Malayan colugos

Cynomys ludovicianus. See Black-tailed prairie dogs

D

Dactylopsilinae. See Striped possums

d'Albertis's ringtail possums, 1: 156

Dall's porpoises, 4: 729–30

Damaraland mole-rats, 5: 1106–7, 1106 (ill.), 1107 (ill.)

Dance of death, 3: 615

Dassie rats, 5: **1093–96,** 1094 (ill.), 1095 (ill.)

Dasypodidae. See Armadillos

Dasyprocta punctata. See Central American agoutis

Dasyprocta species, 5: 1153

Dasyproctidae. See Agoutis

Dasypus novemcinctus. See Nine-banded armadillos

Dasyuridae. See Marsupial cats; Marsupial mice; Tasmanian devils

Dasyuromorphia. See Australasian carnivorous marsupials

Daubentonia madagascariensis. See Aye-ayes

Daubentoniidae. See Aye-ayes

Davis Mountains cottontails, 5: 1215

De-stressing behavior, 3: 517

De Winton's golden moles, 2: 227

Death, dance of, 3: 615

Decompression sickness, 3: 691

Deer, 4: 889–90, **933–53**
    See also Mouse deer

Degus, 5: 1172, 1173, 1174–75, 1174 (ill.), 1175 (ill.)

Delacour langurs, 3: 537

Delphinapterus leucas. See Belugas

Delphinidae. See Dolphins

Demidoff's bushbabies, 3: 436

Dendrohyrax arboreus. See Southern tree hyraxes

Dendrolagus bennettianus. See Bennett's tree kangaroos

Dermoptera. See Colugos

Desert bandicoots, 1: 77, 82

Desert cottontails, 5: 1220–21, 1220 (ill.), 1221 (ill.)

Desert golden moles, Grant's, 2: 226, 229–31, 229 (ill.), 230 (ill.)

Desert rat-kangaroos, 1: 131–32

Desmans, 2: **255–62**

Desmarest's hutias. *See* Cuban hutias

Desmodus rotundus. See Vampire bats

Devil fish. *See* Gray whales

Dian's tarsiers, 3: 481

Dibblers, southern, 1: 54

Dicerorhinus sumatrensis. See Sumatran rhinoceroses

Diclidurus species, 2: 304

Didelphidae. See New World opossums

Didelphimorphia. See New World opossums

Didelphis virginiana. See Virginia opossums

Digestive recycling, 1: 156
    See also specific species

Dikdiks, Kirk's, 4: 981–82, 981 (ill.), 982 (ill.)

Dingoes, 1: 63

Dinomyidae. See Pacaranas

Dinomys branickii. See Pacaranas

Dipodidae. See Birch mice; Jerboas; Jumping mice

Dipodomys ingens. See Giant kangaroo rats

Diprotodontia, 1: **99–104**

Dipus sagitta. See Hairy-footed jerboas

Disk-winged bats, 2: 384, **388–94,** 396

Pteropodidae. *See* Old World fruit bats

Pteropus giganteus. See Indian flying foxes

Pteropus mariannus. See Marianas fruit bats

Pudu pudu. See Southern pudus

Pudus, southern, *4:* 946–47, 946 (ill.), 947 (ill.)

Puma concolor. See Pumas

Pumas, *3:* 658, 665–67, 665 (ill.), 666 (ill.)

Punarés, *5:* 1182

Pygathrix nemaeus. See Red-shanked douc langurs

Pygmy anteaters. *See* Silky anteaters

Pygmy fruit bats, *2:* 282

Pygmy gliders, *1:* 172–74, 175–77, 175 (ill.), 176 (ill.)

Pygmy hippopotamuses, *4:* 908, 909, 913–14, 913 (ill.), 914 (ill.)

Pygmy hogs, *4:* 892, 894

Pygmy marmosets, *3:* 423, 496, 505–7, 505 (ill.), 506 (ill.)

Pygmy mice, *5:* 996

Pygmy mouse lemurs, *3:* 423, 444

Pygmy possums, *1:* 101, 102, **149–53**

Pygmy rabbits, *5:* 1215

Pygmy right whales, *4:* **783–86,** 785 (ill.), 786 (ill.)

Pygmy shrews, Savi's, *2:* 246

Pygmy sloths. *See* Monk sloths

Pygmy slow lorises, *3:* 428, 431–32, 431 (ill.), 432 (ill.)

Pygmy sperm whales, *4:* 765–66, 765 (ill.), 766 (ill.)

Pygmy squirrels, *5:* 1008

Q

Queensland tube-nosed bats, *2:* 295–97, 295 (ill.), 296 (ill.)

Querétaro pocket gophers, *5:* 1032

Quill pigs. *See* Old World porcupines

Quills, throwing, *5:* 1113

Quolls, spotted-tailed, *1:* 52

R

Rabbit-eared bandicoots. *See* Greater bilbies

Rabbits, *1:* 82, *5:* 1200–1204, **1213–22**

Raccoon dogs, *3:* 583, 629

Raccoons, *3:* 578, 579–80, 581, **605–13**

Rainforest bandicoots. *See* Spiny bandicoots

Rangifer tarandus. See Reindeer

Rat-kangaroos, *1:* **129–34**
   See also Musky rat-kangaroos

Rat opossums. *See* Shrew opossums

Rato de Taquara, *5:* 1183

Rats, *5:* 996–1000, **1051–68**
   cane, *5:* **1097–1102**
   chinchilla, *5:* **1177–81**
   dassie, *5:* **1093–96,** 1094 (ill.), 1095 (ill.)
   kangaroo, *5:* 997, 998, **1036–43**
   plains viscacha, *5:* 1173
   Polynesian, *2:* 373
   rock, *5:* 1173
   spiny, *5:* **1182–87,** 1185 (ill.), 1186 (ill.)
   water, *5:* 998
   See also Mole-rats; Moonrats

Red-backed squirrel monkeys, *3:* 488

Red-billed hornbills, *3:* 638

Red colobus
   eastern, *3:* 537
   western, *3:* 537, 538–40, 538 (ill.), 539 (ill.)

Red deer, *4:* 940–42, 940 (ill.), 941 (ill.)

Red foxes, *1:* 54, 65, 68, 134, *3:* 584, 588–89, 588 (ill.), 589 (ill.)

Red howler monkeys, Venezuelan, *3:* 528–30, 528 (ill.), 529 (ill.)

Red kangaroos, *1:* 101, 140–41, 140 (ill.), 141 (ill.)

Red List of Threatened Species. *See* World Conservation Union (IUCN) Red List of Threatened Species

Red mouse lemurs, *3:* 446, 447–48, 447 (ill.), 448 (ill.)

Red pandas, *3:* 579–80, 605, 606, 610–12, 610 (ill.), 611 (ill.)

Red ruffed lemurs, *3:* 450

Red-shanked douc langurs, *3:* 537, 544–45, 544 (ill.), 545 (ill.)

Red-tailed sportive lemurs, *3:* 469–71, 469 (ill.), 470 (ill.)

Red-toothed shrews, *2:* 248

Red wolves, *3:* 581, 584

Reindeer, *4:* 951–52, 951 (ill.), 952 (ill.)

Rhesus macaques, *3:* 426, 546–47, 546 (ill.), 547 (ill.)

Rhesus monkeys. *See* Rhesus macaques

Rhinoceros unicornis. See Indian rhinoceroses

Rhinoceroses, *4:* 821, 848–50, 852, 853, **874–86**

Rhinocerotidae. *See* Rhinoceroses

Rhinolophidae. *See* Horseshoe bats

Rhinolophus capensis. See Cape horseshoe bats

Rhinolophus ferrumequinum. See Greater horseshoe bats

Rhinopoma hardwickei. See Hardwicke's lesser mouse-tailed bats

Rhinopomatidae. *See* Mouse-tailed bats

on western barbastelles,
2: 416
on western gorillas, 3: 570
on white bats, 2: 356
on woolly monkeys,
3: 534
on Xenarthra, 1: 181
World Wildlife Fund, 4: 797
Wroughton free-tailed bats,
2: 402

X

Xenarthra, *1*: 178–82

Y

Yapoks. *See* Water opossums
Yellow-bellied gliders, *1*: 163
Yellow-breasted capuchins,
3: 488
Yellow-footed rock wallabies,
1: 101
Yellow golden moles, 2: 226
Yellow-streaked tenrecs,
2: 237–38, 237 (ill.), 238 (ill.)
Yellow-tailed woolly monkeys,
3: 527
Yellow-winged bats, 2: 324,
325

Yellowstone National Park,
3: 587
Yerbua capensis. See Springhares

Z

Zalophus californianus. See
California sea lions
Zalophus wollebaeki. See
Galápagos sea lions
Zebras, *4*: 848–50, 852,
854–64
Zenkerella species, *5*: 1069
Ziphiidae. See Beaked whales